Tales from

My voyages on some of Britain's last traditional cargo ships

Austin Guest

Published by New Generation Publishing in 2023, Copyright ©
Austin Guest

First edition 2021

Second edition 2023

The author asserts the moral right under the Copyright, Designs and Patents Act 1988 to be identified as the author of this work.

All Rights reserved. No part of this publication may be reproduced, stored in a retrieval system or transmitted, in any form or by any means without the prior consent of the author, nor be otherwise circulated in any form of binding or cover other than that which it is published and without a similar condition being imposed on the subsequent purchaser.

ISBN
        Paperback: 978-1-80369-788-8
        eBook: 978-1-80369-7-895

www.newgeneration-publishing.com

New Generation Publishing

In memory of Albert, Irene and Alison

A ship in harbour is safe, but that is not what ships are built for.

John Augustus Shedd

Fill your life with experiences, not things. Have stories to tell, not stuff to show.

Unknown

Contents

	Author's Note	1
1	Tuning In	4
2	Some Radio History	12
3	College	24
4	Radar	48
5	P & O	56
6	Coastal Tekoa	62
7	Watch-keeping	74
8	Deep-Sea Tekoa	86
9	Somerset	114
10	Dwarka – New Lands	134
11	Dwarka – Bus Route	157
12	Strathdirk	183
13	Gulf Runs	211
14	Vendee	236
15	Triangles	247
16	Falklands	266
17	Sequels and Endings	287

Author's Note

This is a personal history; everyone has their own and even my fellow travellers on the same ships will have had some differing experiences as well as all the shared ones. After all, mine was usually a one-person role, an aspect of the ship that few others saw or understood. What was with all the dots and dashes? Was it really all codes and made-up words? Sitting in a room with headphones and a Morse key was seen as the road to insanity, or a stop along the way to somewhere beyond. But for me, the listening and messaging were just the routine while in transit; what elevated my role was being able to step out of it at times. Once in port I was usually able to see more of the places the ship visited while others were committed to handling cargo or maintaining engines.

With hindsight, it was a poignant time for sailors and ship lovers. They were the final days of docks hosting ships of different shapes and sizes, framed by smoke, dust and oil and surrounded by people, ropes and the clutter and clatter of cranes and cargo. Ships could spend days, even weeks, in port, sometimes becoming well-known within their host towns and cities. I also saw some of the decline of the British merchant fleet, particularly affecting these traditional cargo ships. Much larger container ships were about to dominate the seas, however anonymous they might remain during their short visits to clean and spacious quaysides. The decline of traditional ship-to-shore radio and its use of Morse code began around the same time, suddenly appearing inevitable in the face of new technology and procedures, yet so unforeseen just a few years earlier when prospective Radio Officers were still investing in their future.

Cargo ships were the bedrock of many shipping companies, and without them the companies themselves began to melt away. My entire seagoing career, just under eight years of it, was with a heavily-diversified and theoretically resilient conglomerate which nevertheless was to retreat in stages from being a ship owner and ultimately from being an independent company. At the time of selling one batch of tankers, a company spokesperson described the ships as 'a management distraction'. It was hardly the language of a company focused on making best use of what remained of its core business and heritage, or that of someone who might have joined a shipping company voluntarily. Traditional shipping may well have been impacted by wider evolution and economic factors but it was also eroded from within. I describe how some of this turned out later in the book.

Perhaps none of it should have been surprising. Decline was a widely-accepted theme, particularly in the 1970s and early 1980s, a time of austerity, social upheavals and concern over possible world war. While better economic times followed for many, much of the British shipping industry did not benefit. Perhaps its seagoing people were right to party while they could.

I have set out to describe my experiences at sea during this time. Some of it is quite specific to the role: a short history of radio, qualifying, work patterns, faults and distress calls. Other subjects would have been familiar to anyone at sea, in various forms: maritime history, joining and leaving ships, daily life, fads, food and drink, ports, routes, conflicts, mishaps, madness, discoveries, downtime and, of course, the great (and a few lesser) people who had found themselves drawn to this wondrous, even if sometimes complicated, way of life. All while trying not to repeat too much from one trip to the next, which will give a sense of time speeding up later in the book. But that happens elsewhere in life too. It is mostly chronological, as I usually like stories to have a beginning and an end. Some names have been changed and some not. This revised edition provides more details on a variety of subjects, from the early days of radio through to the end of the radio age and beyond. I feel grateful and honoured for the many positive comments and memories I received from readers, some of which added to my knowledge of existing subjects while others, and the passage of time, led to my recalling and writing even more. I have also added more pictures in response to requests for these. So here, with both author and text refreshed, is my nautical career. Once upon a time, going to sea was really like this.

1 Tuning In

Going to sea meant overcoming many contradictions. I lived in the middle of England, distant from the sea and its history, traditions and major ports. Horizons were short; seaside holidays, even in Britain, were big undertakings and not always affordable. I liked science but only connected with it on my own terms. I knew a bit about astronomy, geology and geography, while often zoning out of subjects taught in classrooms. Like many boys in school, paying attention was not always a strong point. I had no practical skills either, struggling with woodwork, metalwork, gardening or anything requiring care or attention to detail. When given something to do I would often race through it without understanding the instructions. Sometimes I just wanted to get outside and continue from where I had left off, usually either getting into trouble or playing football. I was a decent goalie, acrobatic with good hands, but I also wore glasses which often got broken in action. I was therefore often unable to see very far ahead, in any way.

None of this would have looked good for a career which called for the practical application of science and the careful following of procedures, with no support available. I made things harder for myself, failing plenty of exams from Eleven Plus through to college finals. I did however gradually begin to work harder and to learn from my many mistakes, even if avoiding some of them would have been even better.

As a secondary modern pupil in a Midlands mining area, my first introduction to a careers event was in a colliery building opposite the local pit heads. I soon found, to my surprise, that all the jobs on show were at the pit, something we had not been told but which we should probably have guessed. It was only then that I began to understand the level of expectation which existed between the community and its biggest employer. I shuffled from stand to stand, finally pausing to look more closely at the underground jobs as they paid the most, and trying with great difficulty to visualise myself working down there. Someone looked me in the eye. 'You're not going to work here, are you?' I was defiant, having no other options. 'Might do,' I replied.

I finished top of my first year class, and still treasure my end of year report, especially as I never received such a good one again! I still have the prize too. The school head recommended me to the grammar school in the nearby town, and after a short interview there I was accepted. I have since read that there was some formal provision for this within the system, in order to "catch" promising pupils who had missed out on their perhaps rightful place, but I never saw any other instances of it being applied. Perhaps in my area it enabled them to rectify the occasional iniquity in a notorious system whereby schools were awarded Eleven Plus "passes" on a quota basis, with my village school having only two pupils allocated to "grammar" each year while comparable schools in town sent up to half of their year there.

Moving schools presented me with the challenge of catching up on what was considered a missed year. I thought I had stepped up and learned a lot at secondary school but now I saw the range and depth of subjects which had been covered in the first year at my new school. As I struggled through some of the new lessons, being at grammar school also gave me delusions of future scientific careers which might just have been attainable had I started there earlier. Instead I enjoyed some good times when I seemed to be succeeding in one subject or another for a while, and bad times when I just drifted while going through what we call imposter syndrome today. This was exacerbated by some kids suggesting I had no right to be there; sometimes I pushed back but I got to a point where I no longer cared. Little did they know that their own places could also have been open to question. My time there helped me build some mental toughness, a beneficial thing in the adult world ahead.

My interest in astronomy spilled over into closely following the Apollo missions, and an article related to these captivated me. It transpired that people could actually listen to mission communications on their own radio sets, without the delay via NASA or any editing to fit within TV coverage. The same radio enthusiasts had apparently listened to much earlier Russian missions, including some which seemed to end in disaster and remain unknown to history. It was accepted as fact that the Soviet Union only announced its successes. Wherever any truth may be, and today there are many writings and conspiracy theories on lost cosmonauts, I was fascinated by the notion of gaining some inside track on what was happening, not only in space but wherever else radio was being broadcast from.

I acquired a short wave radio with multiple bands, and began to listen to worldwide broadcast stations. I bought *Practical Wireless* regularly and tried to learn from the circuit diagrams while also noting the lists people submitted of the stations they had heard. One day I sent in my own list, and a small part of it was published! I was surprised to find how many discussions this started at school, with kids being impressed by my name appearing in the magazine and keen to discuss their own listening. It was clearly not just a niche or obscure activity, at least not in my age range. There was also a little teenage subversiveness about it as for some it led to their contacting Russian or Chinese radio stations requesting propaganda material, an unusual and tradeable product.

The school had a well-stocked careers room and I spent many hours there, looking in vain for something I might actually enjoy and be able to do. I still liked science subjects but poor maths severely limited my options. My maths stream lost its teacher for part of a year and we were expected to slot into other classes and cope somehow; in practice this meant sitting together at the back of higher streams and wondering what was going on. I sifted through countless brochures from companies and Government bodies while trying to resist a sinking feeling. The careers mistress was one of the senior staff, Mrs Aston, who despite clearly being an excellent teacher and a good person was known to all as "Speedy Edie" for how swiftly she could appear onto a scene and take action. She burst in and threw me out on several occasions, telling me I should go and play instead. Then one day she actually gave me some good careers advice. The whole year went to a careers fair at the old Bingley Hall in Birmingham, and during the coach journey she saw me reading *Practical Wireless*. I thought I was in trouble at first, until she leaned closer and uttered some fateful words. 'Why don't you be a Radio Officer? On ships. It might be a good job for you.' I managed to mumble a reply consisting of little more than 'Yes miss,' but that moment gave me some much-needed focus for the day.

The idea may have struck a chord with me, and indeed with Mrs Aston, as I was in the Sea Cadets and, separately, had actually been to sea already. While still at my old school I had signed up for what then seemed a pioneering educational cruise on *SS Uganda*. By the time of the cruise I had moved to the grammar school, which was a few years away from joining in with such things, and on my return I found I had gained some notoriety. One teacher took great offence, initially at my having untidily copied up the work covered in my absence, but his real issue lay deeper. What began as increasingly loud complaints over my not underlining some headings with a ruler developed into a full-blown and lengthy onslaught against my having missed school to go on a *cruise*, of all things. I don't think I saw another outburst like it until watching Adolf's much-parodied meltdown in the movie *Downfall*! The whole class sat in shocked, shuddering silence as they waited for the eruption to pass. And this was in a Religious Education lesson!

Having some official blessing this time, I went around the stands looking for shipping companies, and actually found some, even in Birmingham. Through collecting company folders I viewed world maps and artistic representations of tramp steamers, and began to sense exotic possibilities. I also learned what qualifications were involved, and the options for gaining them.

There was going to college and there was being paid for going to college, and I investigated the paid option first. Most shipping companies I had approached still used Radio Officers (R/Os) engaged on a temporary basis via the Marconi company, but the oil companies at the exhibition spoke of a more direct route they were at least considering. When I contacted Shell afterwards they invited me to a cadet selection day at their centre on the South Bank in London. They organised hotel rooms in Kensington for my Dad and I, and I duly presented myself at Shell Centre one morning along with many other hopeful faces. After a short introduction we were each presented with application forms, and I paused over an early question which asked whether I was applying to be a deck or engineering cadet. I added another box, wrote 'Radio' beside it and completed the form. We all moved on to another presentation before I was summoned from the room by someone from Personnel. They did not take radio cadets yet. 'I'm sorry, there seems to have been a misunderstanding. Stay in touch.' And with that I was returned to the foyer.

My dad collected me. His plan was to call Shell at times to check whether my selection day was still in progress, and on his first call he was told that I had been 'rejected'. His sympathy towards me soon turned towards annoyance with Shell, but he found a constructive way forward. We went to Leadenhall Street looking for shipping companies, and found many in that area. We went into John Swire, a long-established company who made us very welcome in their wood-panelled offices lined with ship models. Although they only recruited fully qualified people, they took the time to give me some good information about themselves and their routes, which made a positive impression on me at the time. When I eventually qualified they did not seem to be recruiting, although when I saw them advertising a few years into my career I was tempted, if only the circumstances had been just right. I used to pore over their far eastern routes, which seemed to follow in the footsteps of Somerset Maugham and Alfred Russel Wallace, and think how interesting sailing with them might be.

Much later, I read *Doctor at Sea* by Richard Gordon, and his narrator, when looking for seagoing work, was advised to walk along Leadenhall Street in his best suit, and it worked for him. I think my Dad was intuitively on to something.

Next I had to find a college, and unsurprisingly this involved studying somewhere near a coast. In practice any college anywhere could have offered the course as it was entirely classroom based, but maritime history must have been a factor in the options available. I applied to Bristol, and went for an interview at Brunel Technical College at Ashley Down, on the north side of the city. The college was in Muller House, a former Victorian orphanage building with wire aerials and a platform of radar scanners incongruously situated on the roof. It offered courses in both marine and aircraft electronics and was, geographically at least, a part of Bristol Polytechnic which occupied similar stone buildings on the other side of the road. I met the Head, Mr Barltrop, and his deputy Mr

Chapman, who were both friendly while asking the expected interview questions. After a short wait in the corridor and a chat with a couple of other interviewees I was offered a place from the start of the September term.

The college handed out a list of addresses offering accommodation. There were no halls of residence, just rooms being let within family homes. Across the road from the college was a long straight road full of parked cars, Sefton Park Road, and I was destined to live there throughout my studies. There was no actual Sefton Park; the nearby park was called St Andrews Park, which I mainly remember for one night some time later when several of us left the student bar and climbed over the park fences to play on the swings at midnight. I've no recollection of where that idea came from.

We called at the first house on the list and a lady chatted with us, told us she was fully booked but recommended another lady further along. Thus we met Mrs Beckhurst, who greeted us in a strong Belfast accent and led us into her immaculate "special occasions only" front parlour. She was a widow in her sixties and students were basically her "family". She provided us with tea and advised us that she would indeed have a vacant room. It was soon resolved that she would let it to me from September onwards, for a pound a day including weekday evening meals. She worked at weekends and her students were expected to fend for themselves more then.

I now had a plan, which was just as well as my O-Level results were disappointing, and mystifying. I failed exams for which I thought I had prepared and performed strongly, and got my best pass in an exam where I had written very little. Still, it hardly mattered, at least assuming the course went well. After a summer at home I left my Saturday job in Woolworth's, packed a case and was driven to Bristol. I had tried to read more about the syllabus but the details were too high-level to make much sense. I knew I would be studying electronics and had to learn how some complicated equipment worked. Despite knowing Morse code would be involved, I had no idea of exactly how, when or why communications took place, or how this could take two years to learn. A little historical background might have been a big help.

2 Some Radio History

Radio, like any success story, has many fathers. There are some complications because the term "wireless" has always had a variety of meanings. Basically the study of electromagnetism through the 1800s by such pioneers as Faraday, Maxwell, Hertz and Tesla, led to Guglielmo Marconi becoming interested in the possibilities of what came to be known as radio.

He read Heinrich Hertz's 1887 account of his experiments involving producing an electrical spark across a gap and using an aerial to receive the electromagnetic waves caused by the spark. At the time no-one, Hertz included, saw the potential within electromagnetism. In a way this was a strange oversight as it showed a way forward which many scientists were actively looking for. Patents had already been filed for "wireless telegraphy" communication systems. However these were not matched to any of the competing strands of research, and seemed to depend upon notions of "atmospheric electricity" or "convection currents" with no scientific basis.

Hertz's waves took up a very wide bandwidth, akin to interference from nearby equipment or strong signals affecting everything on a modern set. This made the use of "Hertzian waves" impractical as any separately-generated waves caused interference to each other and it was not possible to select, or "tune into" just one. Nikola Tesla solved this problem by following new ideas on the use of resonance and devising a coil circuit, one effect of which was the exclusion of any frequencies beyond a certain range. This preserved a relatively narrow frequency band which was adjustable, a result he demonstrated publicly in 1893. It is important in the history of radio although Tesla's main interest was in transmitting electrical power rather than electromagnetic waves; his dream was to run lighting tubes "wirelessly" and his most enduring practical contribution to the wider world was the use of alternating current in power supplies. Marconi's own great contribution was to develop the scientific research of Hertz and Tesla into a genuinely practical means of communication. He was far from alone in working towards this as Bose and Popov conducted parallel experiments, but Marconi took the concepts from the laboratory out into the field and onwards into widespread use.

After a series of new experiments in Bologna, Italy, Marconi demonstrated his innovations to the British Government in 1896 and filed a British patent the following year, while also founding the Wireless Telegraph and Signal Company which later bore his surname. He conducted experiments on the Isle of Wight from 1897 as well as providing demonstrations to Queen Victoria and the Royal family at Osborne House and on the Royal yacht. His work on the island led to an active shore station being established near its southern tip, at Niton.

A factory was established in 1898 in Chelmsford, and the company remained based in the town throughout its near-hundred year existence. Work at various experimental locations pushed the boundaries of the technology, including a 32 mile communication across Salisbury Plain and a 186 mile transmission from Niton to Housel Bay, on the Lizard peninsula, Cornwall, in early 1901. These experiments swept away the previous assumption that radio waves could only be transmitted along a line of sight.

The most famous demonstration was between Poldhu, also on the Lizard, and Newfoundland in December 1901, through which the first transatlantic communication was claimed. Accounts of this feat and its effectiveness vary. Marconi's station within an abandoned fever hospital at the aptly-named Signal Hill in Newfoundland depended upon long wire aerial systems lifted up to 500 feet in the air by kites blown around in the variable weather conditions. This would have made tuning very difficult given the limitations of the time, and Marconi is known to have experimented with three different signal detection devices known as coherers while seeking better results. He and his assistant, George Kemp, documented their travails with equipment and weather over several days, during which time they claimed the successful receipt of some of the prearranged transmissions from Poldhu, 2,200 miles away.

A number of concerns have been raised over this. One, expressed consistently once greater knowledge of signal propagation had developed, was that Marconi had used an unfeasibly low frequency, a medium wave one, believed to be c.850 kHz. The value of short wave transmission for long distance communications was yet to be recognised. A related concern is that the claimed communication took place entirely during daylight hours, when range is shorter as much of the signal is absorbed by charged particles in the lowest layer of the ionosphere. At night this layer disappears and signals can bounce from higher layers back to more distant points on the earth's surface. The phenomenon was not yet understood and Marconi's response to distance limitations had mainly been to build more powerful transmission equipment. Marconi himself gave different accounts of the frequency used, and also remained vague over exactly which combinations of equipment at Signal Hill had apparently proved successful.

Finally, the scheduled message itself consisted of a single letter "S" repeated over and over in Morse code. This was known in advance, and it has been suggested that Marconi and Kemp may have listened too hard for the three clicks, signifying the letter, within the background noise. Even the positive results claimed seem to have been highly sporadic and difficult to replicate. However there are no suggestions of devious intent. Furthermore, signals could conceivably have been received despite all the reservations;

it is possible that Marconi's equipment at Poldhu transmitted not only medium wave signals but also unintended harmonics at multiples of the intended frequency, which would have had a greater chance of travelling the required distance.

After returning to England and receiving numerous congratulations on his claimed success he planned further installations and experiments to substantiate it. Most significantly he sailed from Southampton to New York on SS *Philadelphia* in February 1902, and methodically used updated equipment to establish communications on a daily basis. He achieved ranges of up to 700 miles by day and over 1,500 miles by night and thus began to recognise the "daylight effect". After trying a different type of coherer the night-time range was extended to over 2,000 miles, even with lower aerials than at Signal Hill. Greater recognition followed swiftly, leading to agreements for Marconi to open transatlantic radio stations in Canada and the United States. Within a year these were exchanging two-way communications with Poldhu, and with the building of more stations on both sides of the Atlantic, reliable services evolved over time.

Marconi himself continued to travel on transatlantic ships for many years, conducting experiments and building knowledge of equipment and of how to choose the most appropriate frequencies at any given time. Meanwhile Karl Ferdinand Braun was developing more efficient methods of transmission and reception. In 1909 Marconi and Braun shared the Nobel Prize for Physics.

As commercial opportunities developed, the timeline of radio became contested. In 1912 Marconi settled a dispute with British physicist Oliver Lodge, purchasing his 1898 patent for a separate tuning system. Disputes over competing patents between Tesla and Marconi continued until after the original innovations had become obsolete.

Communication took place using Morse code, which had been devised by 1844, initially for communicating within an expanding system of Samuel Morse's own design using wires linked by telegraph poles. Morse's primary invention, receiving a US patent, was repeater circuitry, whereby a signal could pass through a series of stages without loss of quality. This enabled him to defeat rival methods and begin to construct networks of lines. In a separate project, the same Samuel Morse is considered the co-creator of his eponymous code, along with Alfred Vail, with whom he collaborated over several years. Applying the repeater and the code together established a sound-based "telegraph" system to supersede the older and slower semaphore-based visual signalling along railroads and, ultimately, in shipping. The original code was modified in 1851 into International Morse Code, when new code letters with diacritic marks were added to enable the accurate transmission of non-English words.

Marconi's business expanded quickly, with wireless communications competing with the existing fixed telegraph networks for business. This is analogous to the communications options available today, between physical lines and mobile communications. The word "radio" was coined, and its use for Morse transmissions became an accepted basis for the previously vague term "Wireless Telegraphy", often abbreviated to "W/T". In time, this term helped to differentiate this form of radio from the output of newly-formed broadcast stations such as the BBC. On land, telegraph poles gradually became more useful for telephone communications, but kept their original name. Ships began to carry Marconi equipment and to be able to communicate with each other as well as with coast stations. They hired specialist operators on assignment from Marconi's company; these were known as "Sparkies" or "Sparks", referring to their spark gap transmitters which were used until about 1930, a legacy of Hertz's experiments. Other names were fashioned within different cultures, paying homage to the role's origin; these included "Marconista" and "Marconi Sahib". A significant part of their work was to send and receive telegrams (also called radio-grams, before this term became adopted in a different way), both for company business and for communication to and from passengers. Initially this developed on an informal basis, with all kinds of message sent on the same frequencies and at the same times, and without fixed listening times or universal codes. Important information could be obliterated by less important but more powerful signals. This changed after the sinking of the *Titanic* in April 1912.

Titanic was not the first such ship in distress to use radio to request assistance. This dubious honour fell to White Star Line's *Republic* on 23rd January 1909 following a collision with Italian liner *Florida* in thick fog near Nantucket, Massachusetts. A "CQD" (All ships – distress) call was sent by operator John "Jack" Binns as his ship flooded and listed before beginning to sink. There were three deaths on each ship from the actual collision, and *Florida* rescued the remainder of *Republic*'s 742 passengers and crew. However this caused *Florida* to become dangerously overcrowded, and passengers had to be transferred to other ships responding to the distress message. This incident actually reinforced the belief that ships would not need a full complement of lifeboats, since it was seen that assistance would be available close by and that passengers could be ferried to safety in stages. A similarly successful rescue operation followed the first known distress call in British waters, after SS *Minnehaha* ran aground off the Scilly Isles on 18th April 1910.

Binns was offered an operator's position on *Titanic*, which he declined for personal reasons; he moved to New York, married his American fiancée and became a newspaper reporter. Within two days of starting work he was extensively covering the *Titanic* disaster.

Titanic was able to summon assistance, eventually in the form of *Carpathia,* through radio communication, although help tragically only arrived after the loss of some 1,500 lives out of over 2,200 on board. Without the use of radio there may have been no survivors at all, but there were tantalising glimpses of how more lives might have been saved. It was not possible to contact every ship within range as "wireless operators" tended to go off duty overnight leaving the receiver unmonitored. Even *Carpathia*'s operator, Harold Cottam, had not heard the initial distress messages; his shift ended at midnight when he checked in with the bridge before retiring. He had left his receiver on as he hoped to hear a response from earlier communications with another ship, and listened from his nearby sleeping quarters. As he unlaced his boots, he heard a coast station trying to contact *Titanic* with private messages and decided to return to his desk and let them know. He sent a message and received a call for assistance from *Titanic*'s Jack Phillips in return: 'Come at once. We have struck a berg.' Further communications followed while *Carpathia* turned around and steamed towards the stricken ship.

Evidence was presented at both the UK and US inquiries of at least one ship being nearer than *Carpathia*, but not receiving the distress messages and being unable to correctly interpret the distant lights through their binoculars. There may also have been confusion over the recognition of a distress message, with the archaic CQD signal not being immediately memorable and the newer "SOS" not being universally adopted, although the convention including the new signal had come into force in 1908. In practice it appears that the operators on *Titanic* tried both signals, but some circumstances were not in their favour that night even if the contact with *Carpathia* was a fortunate development. *Carpathia* was able to reach the scene five hours before any other responding ship.

The disaster led to the second International Telegraph Convention in late 1912 and the first Safety of Life at Sea (SOLAS) conventions (1914 and 1929), which introduced numerous safety measures to the shipping industry, including the provision of sufficient lifeboats. The new directives for communications included the following:

- Standard equipment levels, including a reserve transmitter and receiver with their own independent power source capable of operating for at least six hours.
- Continuous watch-keeping hours, either in person or with gaps covered by an auto alarm device capable of identifying a distress message and providing an alert.
- Standardised message priorities, with distress signals the highest priority.
- Standardised distress frequency of 500 kHz (600 metres).
- Silence periods, when only ships in distress could transmit. These were two breaks of three minutes each within the hour, marked on radio room clocks, when all non-distress radio traffic had to cease.
- The use of codes to shorten and sharpen radio communications. These were many three-letter codes beginning with the letter "Q", each having its own meaning.
- The keeping of a "wireless log" to maintain a record of communications and related actions.

This created the framework into which the modern Radio Officer's role developed. Communication took place between qualified personnel using Morse code. This included distress calls, usually sent by Morse on the international MF (Medium Frequency) distress and calling frequency of 500 kHz (600 metres). This came about as it lay within the spectrum of usable frequencies in radio technology's infancy. It also suited the specifications of early receivers and aerials, both on ships and at coast stations.

The term "wavelength" dominated at the time; this is the inverse of frequency. With radio waves, like those of light, travelling at a fixed speed, as frequency increases so the length of a single wave decreases, and vice versa. To provide an example recognisable to today's listeners, BBC Radio 2 once promoted itself, well within my lifetime, as being on 1500 metres. If we divide the speed of the waves (in kilometres per second) – 300,000 – by the wavelength (in metres) – 1,500 – we get 200, which is the frequency in kHz, the location on more modern radio dials. Actually it appears to be billed at 198 in these digital times, so perhaps the "1500 metres" was only ever approximate – or the signal so strong and the airwaves so uncluttered that the discrepancy did not matter.

The emphasis on wavelength diminished as communication on ever higher frequencies became widespread. Higher numbers can continue to be understood, while ever-reducing wavelengths become harder to visualise. However the phrase "on the same wavelength" continues to resonate with people.

Commercial traffic was no longer actually sent on 500 kHz, although this frequency remained the starting point. When within range of coast radio stations, typically up to 200 miles by day and double that at night, a ship would make contact on 500 kHz before both ship and coast station moved to "working frequencies" to exchange their messages, leaving 500 kHz clear. Coast stations had their own fixed working frequencies; ship's transmitters had set working frequencies, typically 454, 468, 480 and 512 kHz) and during the initial contact would suggest one nearest to that of the coast station. For example, Niton Radio (dating back to Marconi's experiments) "worked" on 464 kHz, so a ship would listen there while usually transmitting to it on 468 kHz, its nearest suitable frequency.

Longer and shorter-distance communications evolved over time. These included the introduction of radio telephony, with its own calling and distress range based on the initial use of 2182 kHz, and the use of higher frequencies (HF, also known by those accustomed to wavelength as "short wave") which enabled communication over much greater distances to take place.

HF communications took place on multiple bands; the most commonly-used were 4, 8, 12 and 16 MHz. Within these bands a station would follow the same principle of having calling and working frequencies. The selection of a communications band was determined by time of day, distance and conditions above the earth in the ionosphere; a transmitted signal would bounce back to earth from unseen and variable layers high above, and its "skip distance" varied from one band to the next. How an operator found the most appropriate band came from applying this knowledge, and also from experience, trial and error, with actual conditions not always matching expectations.

During World War II, new technology known as "TBS" (Talk Between Ships) enabled bridge officers to communicate by voice over short distances; this subsequently became the Marine VHF band. Deck officers learned some basic protocols to qualify them to use this equipment themselves. The calling and distress frequency was again kept as clear as possible; contact was made on VHF channel 16 (156.8 MHz) with both parties then moving to another channel to communicate further.

Radio Officers were understandably expected to understand both the technical and procedural aspects of communication at sea and the training time became longer as technology and procedures developed. It was important to be able to operate, maintain and repair a growing suite of equipment. UK certification was issued through successive, and very British, ministries for communications, from the

Postmaster General's PMG certificates (Class 1 and 2) to the Ministry of Posts and Telecommunications (MPT), or, as I used to call them, 'Million Painful Tribulations', issuing the Marine Radiocommunications General Certificate (MRGC). The latter, which I was to obtain eventually, was considered equivalent to PMG First Class, with the lower qualification now abolished. Separately the Department of Trade and Industry, in various incarnations, oversaw radar certification, in its own unique way, following on from one of its antecedents, the Board of Trade. In addition, City & Guilds certification progressively became more integral to technical training within the industry.

Following the growth in world trade after 1945, seafarers were in high demand and this included Radio Officers. Marconi remained the market leader, supplying R/Os to many shipping lines on a bureau basis; their personnel could find themselves on any type of ship and with any kind of company every time they went away. New competitors such as Redifon, another communications equipment manufacturer, provided a similar service. At the time of my leaving school, many shipping lines were opting to employ their own Radio Officers, and perhaps to incorporate them into their own company culture for the first time. The role itself had become a more mature one; there are numerous recollections of the R/O being a young man, a teenager or little more than that, assigned to a ship and spending most of his time either in the radio room or living in a small adjacent space. Over time this developed into his (and it was almost always a man until the 1970s when more ladies began to follow the pioneers) becoming a more integral part of the ship's company, with the accommodation, rank and a certain amount of status to match.

Changes like these were continuing to take effect as I first went to sea in 1975, and more would follow, accelerated by new technology until the final shipping

Morse was transmitted and the waves fell silent. The job would only exist in recognisable form through the 20th Century, if even that. The Marconi Company's own history would follow a similar timeline and outcome. Time was also running out for much of the centuries-old business of running cargo ships, replaced by a larger-scale and more cost-effective business model. Both an era, and a way of life, stood on the brink of ending. Although I had seen container ships I had not linked the rise of one type of ship with the fate of another. Nor did I know what kind of ships I might work on, just that there was a big, varied and interesting world out there and that I was going to try to experience some of it. But first I had to qualify, which was to prove a long and rocky road…

3 College

Arriving in Bristol was a culture shock for some unexpected reasons. Mrs Beckhurst, or "Mrs B" as everyone called her, had not mentioned that her seemingly-tranquil home was a major forum for heated political argument! We had Arabs with emphatic views on the Middle East, and Xenophon, a Greek Cypriot with numerous worldwide political views equally strongly expressed, including some on the situation on his home island. Mrs B's views on Northern Ireland frequently surfaced in response to the latest news from the troubles there. Everyone had opinions on Britain's politics and industrial disputes. Each evening news broadcast on TV sparked someone or other into vehement comment, with everyone else joining in, myself included. I sometimes knew little or nothing about the subjects in question, but that did not seem to be a drawback in a room full of instinctive reactions. Some evenings the arguments went on for hours, with occasional pauses for programmes that someone actually wanted to watch; for example Monty Python prompted a weekly thirty-minute ceasefire. At the end of the evening, people would just stop arguing and turn in. The opinions expressed, however controversial or strongly-expressed, never degenerated into anything personal and everyone was able to remain friends. Each morning saw us greet each other amiably, enjoy breakfast together and then go our separate ways. Most evenings saw the cycle begin again. I never felt the need to join the college's debating society!

I spent some time living in Bristol before my course started. My ears were ringing from the nightly shouting matches at the house and also from my getting to see Deep Purple performing at the city's main concert venue, fresh from their tour of Japan from which their famous live album would soon appear. It was an experience which cost me a princely fifty pence and left me wondering if my hearing would recover fully. Actually the support band was louder than the main act, their volume remaining unmatched through the many other performances I would witness at the city's music venues.

I received some early warning of how tough the course might be, as I was told of a neighbour's son who had attempted it unsuccessfully. This was not what I wanted to hear, but eventually I presented myself at Brunel College ready to find out for myself. About sixty students were enrolled onto the course, separated into three equal and parallel classes. I took my seat, aiming to be towards the back and against a wall. I had sat in too many classroom front rows at school and suddenly decided that had to change. I had a good view of my classmates; some had clearly left school at 16 as I had, and even among these I may have been the youngest. Yet I began to feel a little bit worldly among most of them as I had actually left home and made my way to a few places around town. In turn some of them seemed suspicious of me for having a strange accent and needing to wait for grants to arrive before buying books rather than having parental money to spend immediately. Some were reluctant to speak with someone so different, while others were more open to friendship. There was only one other student in the class whose situation matched mine; Stuart had left home at 16 to study, and also happened to be from the Midlands, so we tended to speak more to each other. Another group in the class were around 18 years old and spoke mainly among themselves, unless trying to ingratiate themselves with the third group, the impossibly-old people in their twenties.

We gradually formed small sub-groups and became familiar with our new environment, and with the neighbouring Poly buildings with their larger refectory and student bar. Reaching these was sometimes a hazardous move since it meant sprinting across a busy road with no proper crossing point. There was a long and unsuccessful campaign for one, and after a year or so people turned up for college to find a hand-painted zebra crossing had appeared overnight, with long streaks of white paint down the road in each direction from the cars which had driven over it. Most of the mess was cleaned away by council contractors but traces of it remained for a long time. Back on our side of the road we also discovered the alluring classrooms of Mary Carpenter House, where hairdressing students offered free, if sometimes chaotic, haircuts to brave souls willing to "model".

Another thing I had to get used to was the formality: it was always "Mr" followed by surname, between teacher and student and often between students too. The teachers addressed students in this manner throughout my time there, while first name terms crept in between students over time.

The first year was to be mainly dedicated to the "fundamentals" of electronics, which proved to be quite detailed with many new concepts. The first hurdle would be three City & Guilds exams at the end of the first term. Some careful and sympathetic teaching would be a big help. Instead our first teacher, Mr Barber, seemed to relish keeping his students as uncomfortable as possible, ridiculing their lack of knowledge, sneering over their written answers and picking out targets for sarcasm during lessons. He told students, myself included, that they had no chance of passing, right from the start and ongoing without any reference to progress made on the limited coursework covered so far. All this may sound like reverse psychology but for some occasional pointed and blunt remarks he directed at certain people when they questioned him. I kept quiet and told myself to ignore him. Others played along; Barry constantly relished suggestions that he knew nothing and his exchanges with Mr Barber became a running joke which somehow took the pressure off the rest of the class at times. The more serious side of this was that he clearly had learned almost nothing so far and that simply laughing off Mr Barber's comments would not help in the end.

The theory was a steep learning curve but I made lots of neat notes and felt I was more or less holding my own. Even the maths seemed much easier than it had done in school, as algebra and equations began to properly make sense at last. Going to a new place really could make a difference.

There were timetabled breaks from Mr Barber's classes, but these held more terrifying prospects. We were introduced to two new rooms, the arenas for more practical subjects. "The Cabin" held the contents of a ship's radio room and other communications-related equipment, including transmitters, receivers, VHF set and direction finder. In time we would learn to operate and then find faults on them, but the first sight of these units, especially the imposing-looking Commander main transmitter and the Apollo main receiver with its seemingly ground-breaking digital display, made us shuffle our feet and contemplate the floor. The other was "The Lab" where each desk space simply hosted a Morse key and a headphone socket; there would be nowhere to hide in such an environment.

We plugged in the Bakelite headphones we had been instructed to order from a nearby hardware shop, and were taught the first five letters of the alphabet in Morse code. We had to receive and transcribe them slowly, at four words per minute, while blanking out the knowledge that we would eventually be examined at five times that speed. We received the letters in sequence, and then in short groups. We also used a Morse key for the first time and became used to sending the same characters. After a couple of lessons we learned the next five letters, and the teaching method was becoming clear. I had expected this to be the most challenging aspect of the course and that it would need some special way of thinking, and was relieved to find I could just treat it as a practical game. By the end of the first term we had learned all the letters and could work in pairs, sending messages to each other and sometimes sniggering over their contents. We also started receiving longer batches of code in groups of five letters, which prevented any guessing of word endings. Similarly, groups of five figures, and eventually of punctuation marks, followed. For additional variation, without being able to predict words or their length, we were also sent passages in Serbo-Croat; their translations into English were never divulged, if even known. Gradually our operating speed increased, with receiving speeds always ahead of how quickly we could send, a more physical operation.

At this stage we all learned on the same standard, or "straight" type of Morse key. We would find that in practice they were manufactured in numerous shapes and sizes. Straight keys were operated by pressing a plastic or Bakelite knob downwards enabling a sprung lever to close a contact and send a dot or dash. A key could be adjusted for different gaps or levels of spring tension. Sometimes we would adjust them from one day to the next, seeking a combination which seemed to work best for us just then. Other variations were based on the self-explanatory "side swiper" type of key, moving one or two finger paddles from side to side. These could be entirely manual in operation or use different degrees of automation to enable a single finger twitch to generate multiple dots or dashes. Operators usually became experienced on straight keys first, adopting the alternatives either from later aesthetic preference or to aim for better rhythm or speed. I experimented with these but decided I preferred a more conventional key.

There was a break in the timetable on Wednesday afternoon, ostensibly for sport. After looking in vain for a sports hall I walked over two miles into the city centre with Stuart and two other classmates to find another college site at Unity Street, close to the old harbourside area where regeneration had yet to begin. There we found a better bar and also a large high-ceilinged upstairs room where all-comers could play badminton. This became a fixture of those afternoons, later extended to the Poly site at times. Later I would also visit that room when it hosted visiting bands. One of these bands which enjoyed some success later, once I was at sea, had an appropriate name: Sailor. Some of their songs even conveyed situations or stories which wayward mariners could easily identify with. Similarly their song *The Old Nickelodeon Sound* could easily be adopted one day as a sentimental anthem by former seafarers.

Striving to become more active, I also played badminton in a local church hall, and swam at the nearby North Bristol Baths. The latter, built in 1914, boasted fine architectural features inside and out, and changing cubicles right beside the actual pool. The place was so under-used that I often had the pool to myself.

Routines developed in other ways. I got a Saturday job at a city centre department store. Weekend staff turned up on Saturday mornings, checked in at a table in the entrance and were assigned their place for the day, which could be anywhere in the store. Over the next two years I sold just about everything, including books, records, cheese, TVs, lawn mowers and haberdashery. When living on minimal support in the form of parental help and a local authority grant of £10 per term, this was a lifeline. In addition to the £2 or so the job paid, when I occupied the book counter it was permissible to read the books, so I had no need to buy any. When selling cheese, which was where I worked most often, I did not need to buy food that day as it was essential to have tasted the different options and to be able to advise customers.

A class leader emerged, in the form of Mr James. Inevitably he was one of the older group and tall, plain speaking and seemingly competent in each subject. He had been in the army and people seemed to gravitate towards him, not only in class but also in the canteen and the student union bar where he often held court. Even Mr Barber appeared to treat him with respect. He was staying at the house next door so sometimes we found ourselves walking to or from college together. One day he told me he had forgotten his wallet and asked me if I could lend him a pound. I would have preferred not to as I lived on a shoestring and had little more than that myself, but he was too significant a figure to risk annoying so I handed it over. Even then I suspected I was never going to see the money again.

First, the December exams arrived. Shrugging off Mr Barber's "endorsements" I sat down to two exams in science and one in maths, and then went home for Christmas. My return to college presented a few surprises.

My exam results were good. Mr Barber glared and hardly addressed me at all that term. A few people disappeared, including my friend Stuart. I had thought he was doing well and could only assume that his exam results were not as expected.

Another surprise was that Mr James was no longer in class. It soon became apparent that he had borrowed money from many people, including large amounts from those classmates closer to his own age and presumably with adult grants and/or personal savings. My loss of a pound was not worth even mentioning to anyone. Those badly affected spent months finding ways to rebuild their finances while collectively going to court to win judgements in their favour for small fractions of their losses.

More rumours of criminality began to surface. At first these were faint whispers, and it was unclear exactly what had happened or just who knew everything. Then a student arrived in class one morning, loudly proclaiming that he had 'got off – insufficient evidence!' It was now clear *who* was involved. Shortly afterwards our Morse receiving practice consisted, courtesy of a mischievous lecturer, of a newspaper report of a shop burglary court case involving the theft of televisions and other items. Loud laughter arose as the substance and significance became clear and especially as the information had been received through our novel new signalling method. There was a final development as the student in question disappeared shortly afterwards, his claim of acquittal now assumed to be bogus.

Back at the house, the Arabs had left. Xenophon decided he needed more freedom and found a bedsit about a mile away. He tried to persuade me to move too and took me to see a room in his new home. It was a tiny space screened off from another fraction of the original room by a plywood partition, along with shared access to a small kitchen. The landlady appeared for a quick chat and said that students had to be out of the house throughout each day. I opted to stay put. Xenophon's new place soon lost its limited appeal and he returned to another house in Sefton Park Road, so our paths often crossed. Mrs B did not replace those who left but kept space available for a procession of her previous students who arrived to visit and stay from time to time. I was now her only tenant and she seemed pleased to occupy a quieter house for a while, although some things remained the same as we continued to discuss and argue politics.

My class size was diminishing and so were the others; we were all consolidated from three classes into two. This merged some groups of near strangers to get to know each other, and the course progressed, albeit with my class still under Mr Barber.

Practical work began to take a more prominent role. We learned additional foreign language Morse characters and gained speed at varying rates. We also spent more time in the cabin beginning to demystify the equipment there. We met new lecturers for the practical subjects, including "Lofty" Allen for Morse code, Phil Brouder for communications procedures and Dave Heald for hardware work; all initially known only by their surnames. Each occasionally told seafarers' anecdotes during classes, adding a more human and approachable side to our studies and providing insights into the world we aimed to join. They all, rather like how we saw our school teachers, seemed older than they really were; generally in their forties although Lofty was conspicuously older.

There was an increasing amount of theory, much of which seemed quite mathematical and seemingly intended for the design of circuits and devices rather than simply the course aims of operating and servicing them. Some class members, particularly the older contingent, recognised overlaps with their previous experience. Others could relate the work to amateur radio rigs they operated from home, sometimes using equipment they had built themselves. Some were sufficiently absorbed to rise to each new challenge. Personally much of it left me cold, especially as Mr Barber was always keen to enter long and obscure technical debates with the more advanced students while ignoring those who were beginning to struggle, other than continuing to ridicule Barry. I was not too concerned at first, as I continued to do well on the other aspects of the course; my Morse in particular became more advanced than most, and I found this motivating. Also the practical lecturers were more friendly and approachable than Mr Barber, and I looked forward more to their classes and paid more attention in them. But all these factors meant distraction from what was supposed to be the theoretical, and main, part of the early curriculum. Perhaps my flattering results from the first exams were not such a blessing after all; I was starting, slowly and imperceptibly, to fall behind. The pace of the course would make catching up extremely difficult.

During this time there were mixed reactions to a City & Guilds proposal for a "Full Technological Certificate". Much debate centred on whether this was a positive move with a view to modernising the Radio Officer's role and securing their future, or a "land grab". There was some reluctance due to the extra time at college and whether it would be worthwhile in relation to lost earnings. One conversation ran like this:

'It won't make any difference for at least ten years.'

'Well are you going to die within ten years? If not, you will need this!'

No-one imagined yet that they were studying for anything less than a lifetime of employment, although this was the first hint that things were likely to evolve. It certainly appeared that the "new" MRGC qualification we had signed up for might not remain the gold standard for long.

That summer brought another round of City & Guilds exams, and the first key milestone of the MRGC syllabus, the Fundamentals exam, a three hour paper with a sixty per cent pass mark. All these highlighted my shortcomings and misplaced focus in a painful way: only one City & Guilds pass out of three, and a fail in the crucial Fundamentals exam. This led to some pressure to drop down to the class following a term behind. I was reluctant to do this, seeing it as a greater sign of failure than the exam results themselves, and also knowing it would place a greater burden upon my parents. But staying on track now meant preparing to re-sit Fundamentals that Christmas while studying for the second key exam, Radio Communications, at the same time.

"Radio Comms" represented another technical step up, and within an accelerated syllabus leading to an exam after only two terms. Our second year lecturer was Mr Coates, one of the older lecturers with a more disciplinarian outlook, which prompted me to take the theory work more seriously. However my deficiencies were clear to see, and even though several other students were in the same position he could not ignore the fact that I was spreading myself too thinly. He vetoed my registration to re-sit the City & Guilds, forcing me to concentrate fully on the main syllabus. I was grumpy about this for a day or so but recognised that he was right. I began to push myself harder and to spend more spare time completing past papers, hoping that this would help me to understand the second year work better too.

I was far from the only one with issues. Barry returned after failing Fundamentals but soon dropped down a class. More students left and the classes were shuffled to balance them.

Female students arrived for the first time; two young ladies joined in the second year after transferring from other colleges. More would start the course in the following year. We gained Terry in Barry's place; he seemed to have as many issues with both theory and practical subjects but without the latter's good humour, bringing instead a despondent air to every conversation. Ben also joined our merged class; he was Nigerian and much older than everyone else, 40 when the youngest of us were barely 18. He was a very pleasant man and a willing student, but although his English was good he often struggled to understand the technical terms being conveyed to us in class. He was not alone in this and even though we had no language excuses we were often glad to hear his interventions of 'I don't follow that point', as the breaks and explanations which followed helped us too.

Despite more suggestions from above that I, and others, should really go back a class, those of us combining subjects tried to help each other revise and prepare for December. I made myself knuckle down, studying harder than ever before and no longer going out in the evenings. By now I had moved across the road to another house. Mrs B had to return to Belfast to help with some family commitments for a while, so all the political discussions ended with my being transferred to her near neighbours. My new hosts expected me to live in my room, with them delivering my breakfast and dinner on trays. It was not the most welcoming arrangement, and I made one attempt to leave which was vetoed by my parents. I then accepted that it was my own comfortable space and made the best of things. When I did have the run of the house while my hosts were on holiday, I saw how their faded downstairs rooms were overrun with mice and decided that living upstairs was just fine!

Exam day arrived, and I felt confident but apprehensive as the stakes were high. Every candidate resitting accepted that another fail would be the end. More students had left during the term and I was one of four survivors from my class who had stayed to attempt the exam again, joining others from the parallel class and the intake a term behind. Part A of the paper consisted of three half hour questions, of which two had to be attempted for up to one third of the overall marks available. The remaining two thirds of the marks were to come from twenty shorter questions with six minutes spent on each. I read through the questions in Part A and felt my stomach sink rapidly as I disliked each of them. For a minute I saw myself returning to my home town and looking for a job, perhaps at the warehouse where I had worked over the summer. I read the Part B questions and felt I could complete these respectably well, but I needed to pass each part. I read through Part A again and began to dig deep.

I would have failed each question a few months earlier. Now I began to reason through how to approach them. The first one was heavily mathematical but less daunting than at first glance; the second called for a circuit diagram with explanations, all of which I could now provide, and the third was on transmission lines, which I realised I could also answer. Suddenly I knew everything I needed to and began at the top, writing and drawing furiously for the next three hours. Afterwards, the lecturers commented that it was the toughest paper they had seen, and we braced ourselves for the outcome.

After Christmas the four of us from my class found ourselves outside Mr Chapman's office. The results were in, and we had promised ourselves that we were going to one of the nearby pubs regardless. We were each addressed, as ever, by our surnames, myself first. I had passed! Next was Tony, one of the class's more technically-focused students; he had also passed. The remaining two had failed, one narrowly and one with the lowest grade. The first of these, Andy, eventually decided to drop a class and fight on, successfully in the end. The other left the course, perhaps with fortunate timing as he had been running card games and word was just breaking that his pack contained only 43 cards!

Now I was back on track, but after prioritising passing the Fundamentals over some of the newer subjects. Some of my study issues from school were repeating themselves. The Radio Comms exam was already ominously near, and much more work was needed. I had taught myself how to study more intensively and made a determined effort to close the gap. My 18th birthday fell two days before the exam and I passed this milestone in riotous fashion, in my room completing and marking two three-hour past papers.

Sadly all this was not enough as I failed. It must have been close, but that was small consolation. I realised I had taken the bad news relatively well when more students left the course at this point, and the two classes became one. I never considered leaving or changing classes but again resolved to balance two workloads. I felt that despite failing

Radio Comms I could soon bridge that gap as I was confident in at least some of the upcoming subjects.

My next task was to telephone Shell's Personnel department. They and BP had by now decided that they would sponsor prospective Radio Officers after all, and each company sent representatives to the college to interview anyone interested. I was accepted by Shell and given a start date, which happened to coincide with the day of the exam results. When I called them it became clear that they had not anticipated anyone failing an exam, whether or not it affected the duration of their studies, and within a few minutes I had been terminated without pay or notice. 'It's all been a misunderstanding,' I was told. I knew I had heard that before.

In keeping with the accelerating nature of the course, the next term would be dedicated to finalising our skills in a range of practical subjects before the creatively-named "Part Two" exams. This included further intensive training and repetition in all aspects of communications. It enabled those proficient in Morse to enhance their speeds beyond exam level; the required standard was 20 words per minute for both sending and receiving; in practice I was sending at 25 and receiving good Morse, mainly from a punched tape machine, at 30. People reached their ceilings for various reasons, including the physical inability to operate a key or write legibly any faster. I found I could still write fairly clearly in capital letters at high speed, something I had been told early on would be impossible. I had persevered as I knew my normal scribbled handwriting would certainly not be readable after high speed receiving. Another new challenge was the receiving of Morse through interference. For some, it was just a matter of putting in the time and developing greater concentration. Whatever issues people had, the answer was always to practice more.

Sometimes we were kept focused by a novel aspect to Morse practice as we attempted to perform chart hits on our keys, tapping an outline of a tune while adjusting the oscillator to vary the tone and make it recognisable. The theme to a TV detective series, *Van der Valk*, a number one instrumental titled *Eye Level* by Simon Park, was most suitable for this, and competing performances punctuated each class for a while.

Another aspect of communications was how to exchange information easily and efficiently. This centred on the Handbook for Radio Operators, a Post Office production; over 200 pages of details on general regulations, handling radiotelegrams and radiotelephone calls, calling protocols and procedures, and distress communications for both telegraphy and telephony. Much communication involved the use of Q codes, three-letter groups all beginning with the letter Q and each conveying a different message. Some were useful for routine communications while others were essential knowledge against the possibility of handling distress signals. We worked in pairs exchanging messages over and over, polishing our use and understanding of the codes and procedures, and how we logged our exchanges in writing. Evidence emerged showing that we were being closely watched. Lofty left a page visible on his desk, accidentally or otherwise, grouping us according to our abilities. I was pleased to see myself in the top group! Below a few other categories, poor Terry was classified with one other student as having 'hardly a clue'.

Hands-on work in the cabin also became paramount, with more challenging lessons in operating and fault finding. There were faults in rotation, in which pairs of students stood at each item such as a main transmitter, main receiver and smaller emergency versions of same, and had to find a fault within a certain time. The faults would be things like disconnected wires (quite feasible on a vibrating ship), missing valves (less so, but we could pretend they were faulty) and components partly removed from circuit boards to simulate their being defective. Once the time was up and the faults either repaired or revealed to those who had not found them, we would all move around to the next item and begin again. This could go on for a whole afternoon, which would help to clear our heads from the Morse and Q codes, although it was tense and relentless in its own way.

The most impressive-looking item in the cabin was the Marconi Apollo receiver, which was distinctive through having red liquid crystal numbers displaying the frequency rather than the traditional method of moving a dial or needle in front of printed numbers. It was considered advanced in many ways, but with what seemed to be its own idiosyncrasies as we first worked on it. It became known that one of the practical lecturers, Mr Smith, had actually worked on the design of this in some way, and when failing to find a fault on it or being in trouble for any other reason, students would begin to upbraid him for his part in the existence of this device. Fortunately it was always taken in good part, and without him denying any involvement.

This kind of exchange went both ways. On one occasion I had to solder six joints on a board, practice for another aspect of the Part II exams; the demonstration of ability to solder and replace components on a circuit board after finding a fault. All my joints were all found to be dry, i.e. mechanically unsound and thus likely to break very easily. I must have been having a very bad day and Mr Smith remarked that by the law of averages at least one of them should have been good. When I next made a mistake he followed up with 'Can't you do anything right?' I took the serious point, and tended to respond positively to his Mr Coates-like tougher approach, but it became something of a humorous catch phrase, sometimes used by him and at other times against him.

We were under pressure and I tried to break the tension at times, for my own benefit and to attempt to entertain the class, or at least the younger element who still retained some sense of humour. I forged the Head of Department's signature on a letter announcing that on a given date he would streak eleven times around the radar scanner in aid of the class's Broken-down Students' Convalescent Scheme. There followed an Andersen-type fairy story in which Mr Brouder spoke only in Q codes. The Wombles were a cultural phenomenon at the time and I wrote of a college equivalent, The Brunles, with characters modelled on some of the staff, e.g. 'Great Uncle Barltrop', who found and recycled old radio equipment. This included a bossy "Brunle" named Smithington who arrived with 'Shut up' and upon finding some scrap equipment suggested that 'I bet Mr Guest built this. Can't he do anything right?' These things, tolerated by staff, were passed around on paper since memes and social media were decades away. It could be suggested that these took up valuable study time but each only took minutes and I was more focused after getting things off my chest!

Later and perhaps encouraged by the above, the hosts at a party I attended revealed and performed a song they had written featuring each class member present. My verse was:

A Staffordshire lad is good for a lark
We could call him our bright spark!

There was a one-day "defence" class, which taught us how to encode and decode secret messages in the event of war. Part of this involved signing the Official Secrets Act. The practical process involved establishing which code would be used and then processing the message through manipulating cards and sliders within metal frames. It seemed rather quaint and homespun even then, but was actually used at times while I was at sea. Occasionally the Ministry of Defence would send coded messages which ships were to decode and respond to. The ship's master was expected to decode the whole "secret" message but in practice the R/O did this, at least on my ships, with the Captain and occasionally another officer trying out a few words out of cursory interest.

In another diversion we were taken to Southampton to visit a container ship, *Dart Europe*. Dart was a consortium of shipowners and one of the earliest container operators, whose ships ran on a transatlantic route. It was an opportunity to see real radio installations and ship facilities, and we were also allowed to order anything from the steward at the bar, repeatedly and free of charge, ensuring we remembered little of the return journey.

Hidden in the Handbook like a submerged reef was a worrying regulation which had never been mentioned in class: the Part II exam could not be attempted until Part I had been passed. The Radio Comms results came out in the summer before we returned for the Part II exam, but the margin was small and seeing the statement in writing was a reminder of the high wire act I was attempting to pull off again.

At Brunel Technical College, 1974

I sat Radio Comms for the second time in June; I felt about as positive as the first time but knew that counted for very little. I had become very objective at marking my own completed past papers, and when I "marked" myself on how I recalled completing this one I found I had given myself 61 per cent; a pass, but with absolutely no room for error or differing interpretation. Fortunately whoever marked my paper must have concurred this time as I did manage to pass. Now I was up to date again, and looking forward to a new term and to exams in some of my stronger subjects. Surely nothing else could go wrong...

The Part II exams involved nine separate exams over four days, based on the following:

- Safety of Life at Sea (SOLAS)
- Regulations and Documents
- Technical and Practical Knowledge. Basically an understanding of relevant circuit diagrams
- Morse receiving
- Morse sending
- Commercial Working 1: Watch-keeping, log keeping and sending and receiving telegrams by radiotelegraphy
- Commercial Working 2: Sending and receiving telegrams by radiotelephony, again maintaining a log
- Operating marine radio equipment
- Fault finding on the same equipment, including making good through soldering

The exams were always presided over by a visiting examiner from the Ministry. We received plenty of advice on how the exams were conducted, based on the college hosting the same examiner over several previous years. This time someone new arrived, and instead of the genial presence we had been prepared for, Mr Tyson glowered at us from the front of the class.

Much preparation had gone into the SOLAS exam as this was not only first but the shortest and least forgiving. At ten minutes, with a 75 per cent pass mark, this four-question paper could end a student's hopes early on the first morning, whether or not they knew it straight away. The questions were unsurprising and probably varied little each time, and the exam raced by in a flurry of scribbling from well-drilled memory. So far, so good... This was followed by another exam in communications regulations, which had been laborious to learn in class but was easy to reproduce in an exam.

After lunch we progressed to the circuit diagram exam, and the atmosphere soon changed. We were to use our own diagrams, and it had long been accepted that students could write information on their diagrams on the grounds that it would all be available when using them at sea. Mine were the same as everyone else's, a pencilled jumble of component functions and purposes and a reflection of the term's work. Unfortunately I was sitting at an aisle seat and a few minutes into the exam Mr Tyson snatched the diagram I was using, shouting 'What's all this?' Everyone looked up from their work and clearly alarm bells had rung with Mr Heald, sitting in as an invigilator as he did not teach this subject. He quickly came over and led the examiner to the front of the room. There a barely-muffled argument took place and it was clear that Mr Tyson wanted to throw me out of the exam. Mr Heald tried to tell him about how things had always been done, but to little effect. Mr Tyson then asked for a clean circuit diagram and returned to my desk to slam it down in front of me, clearly seething with anger at even this compromise. Having made this gesture, he decided to go no further; the rest of the class continued with their annotated diagrams while I had to work with a clean one. I decided not to draw his attention to this. After the exam Mr Heald said he had smoothed things over with

Mr Tyson; despite having completed the exam in full and feeling I had more than passed, I was not so sure.

Morse receiving, with the whole class in the same room, passed immaculately. Morse sending involved stepping into a small room with Mr Tyson to send him some plain language, code and figures. I greeted him and he glared back at me. I duly sent him everything, in a well-practiced manner with, I was confident, no problems at all.

The remaining exams proceeded without incident, and by Thursday the unfortunate start to the exams seemed to have been forgotten. Mr Tyson departed, and the results arrived on Monday. He had failed me on SOLAS, which was not impossible even if hard to accept, and on Morse sending, which was absolutely inconceivable. This suggested had not moved on from my being the student he alighted upon during day one. It was generally believed that he had contrived my failure out of pique, especially given the subjects chosen: the most well-prepared-for and one of my most consistently-successful. Failing me in the contentious circuitry exam would have been too obvious, and these were alternatives where no-one else could witness his marking them, even if at least one of his choices made the motive look all too obvious.

I was far from alone; several other students were failed and the class now split into two; half moved on to Radar while the rest of us now definitely had to go back one term and join the next class in the production line. We joined some familiar faces who had either dropped a term earlier or looked up to us for advice on their way forward; now we were all in the same situation. It became known that Terry had left and become a postman. Ben disappeared around that time too, which was a shame given the extent of the challenge he had taken on and the investment he had made over two years.

Most students who had passed Part II moved on to the radar maintenance class, being expected to at least attempt it even if the qualification had not become mandatory. The exceptions were a small number who opted to sail as Radio Officers on Britain's still substantial fishing fleet, where radar training was not required. This option enabled them to take up paid employment immediately upon receiving their certificates, even if they found they were required to perform additional duties on board, such boiling cod livers to extract the oil! On the other hand they also received bonus payments based on the catch in the same way as the more hands-on fishermen on board. This lifestyle seemed to appeal to a few of the more mature students, while the younger students continued to aim for careers within the wider merchant fleet, leafing wistfully through numerous company brochures.

The next term was all practical work, repeating all the radio procedures and fault-finding; whatever we felt about how we had been examined, there was always room for improvement. There was also a genuine distress message as while practicing watch-keeping we received an SOS live from the Channel, a first for us all. It concerned *Morning Cloud*, the yacht belonging to the former Prime Minister, Edward Heath. It sank after overturning in a severe gale off the Sussex coast, with the loss of two of its crew.

I also joined a class studying for the radio amateur's licence. Some of the more technical class members who were already "hams" seemed to find it all-consuming and spoke with each other from their home radio rigs in the evenings, almost entirely in codes and acronyms and often following up in person during the day afterwards. I was not about to give up too many of my evenings out, or even my nights in, for this hobby but thought it helpful to understand more of what was being said, and to practice communications even more. I passed the theory exam and was exempted from the relatively slow Morse test, at 12 words per minute. I gained a licence which I used occasionally from a friend's home station but I never established my own. This may have happened in the end but time was becoming short.

January soon came around and we were delighted to find that the examiner was not the despised Mr Tyson! The notion of encountering him again and finding he still bore some kind of grudge was too appalling to dwell upon. Instead Mr Hopwood appeared, who seemed much more friendly. The college took no chances with the circuitry exam this time and we all worked from clean papers. I think we could already have written something on every component in the circuits anyway. Although this was yet another exam retake and thus another fight for survival, it never really felt like one. On a sunny Thursday afternoon with snow underfoot outside I completed the final exam, fault finding in the cabin. Marks for this were assigned on the spot as we finished on each piece of equipment, and mine were added up to a total of 96 out of 120. Mr Hopwood laughed at the passport photos I had submitted to be hopefully added to my "ticket" and then said 'I don't want to see your face again!' I took this as a good sign and went away to celebrate, and on Monday it was confirmed that I had passed. I was going to sea! At least I now knew this for certain. My friends who were also retaking the Part II exam also passed, so now we could all look our un-demoted former classmates in the eye, as well as learning from their continued studies and job searches.

Only two students failed the exam this time, and we all soon became aware of one of them. I was sitting in class with a friend soon after learning of our own successes. Suddenly a pair of glasses flew past, crashing onto the hard floor with a worrying sound. Then a wail erupted from behind us, first high-pitched before becoming a deepening roar of anguish. Finally he leapt forward through the classroom, crying out in anguish time and again and stamping on the floor near where the glasses had landed. Eventually someone collected the remains of his spectacles and led him, red-faced and crying, from the room. He returned next day and persevered with his studies.

The student bracketed with the now-departed Terry as having 'hardly a clue' had also failed the Part II exams first time around but passed this time. He went to sea and enjoyed a long career, once the company had sent him back to college to improve his Morse. I could definitely empathise with someone overcoming adversity in order to succeed. Overall, two thirds of the original intake had dropped out at various times; the rest of us must have done at least something right.

4 Radar

Our original class had moved on to the radar course three months ahead of us, and they had plenty of negative things to report. We found them hard to believe but soon found out for ourselves. If we thought the Ministry had a perverse approach with its requirements going far beyond those needed for going to sea, the DTI (as it continued to be called despite being split into three separate entities for several years from 1974) operated on yet another level. If ever there was a requirement for the R/O to design a complete self-build radar set and specify all the components to be loaded into a wheelbarrow at Radio Shack, then this was the course. One test question after another involved drawing, from memory, a circuit diagram of a module within a radar set and then describing in detail how a signal might pass through it. While this sounds like a reasonable thing to ask, the marking was extremely unforgiving. One small mistake in the diagram spelled zero marks since the circuit would not operate. A fully correct description also counted for nothing since it did not match the incorrect circuit. Papers came back with a soon-notorious comment: 'Circuit – you know the penalty.'

Linked to the classroom was another "cabin", containing the three large radar sets sitting beneath the landmark scanners on the roof. These were called Hermes, Radiolocator and Raymarc, all Marconi models, and we would be examined on two of them. Each seemed to be very temperamental, hardly needing faults added by the lecturer as they quickly and regularly developed new ones of their own. Fault finding became a Kafkaesque nightmare of random failures and disjointed documents which seemed specially designed to obscure how each set's various modules actually functioned together. Even when all faults had been resolved they were awkward to set up for optimum use, requiring the repeated tuning of strange and powerful microwave components: klystrons and magnetrons. All this was a slow and tedious process with two separate methods, until a smudge of pale green light near the outer rings indicated the reflection from a distant Somerset hill. Seeing this was an all-too-rare highlight as we usually ran out of time first. In my later time at sea I became quite adept at working on Sperry radar sets, helped, I felt, by their providing a single schematic, reminiscent of the Bayeux Tapestry and showing the complete radar set in one long diagram which could be extended along the deck (we were not supposed to say "floor" on ships) or, when in port, the chart table. Perhaps the Sperry sets seemed so good to work on because of how well their documentation compared to Marconi's.

Learning the whole subject in one term was another big challenge, especially for students who were no longer fully focused. The qualification was an optional one, desirable but not essential for work at sea. A string of celebratory meetups around Bristol followed our passing Part II, every night for about a week. Despite some attempts to make good we were soon behind schedule in a course even more compressed than those we had already completed.

While a few rose to the technical challenge, most of us were soon shamed as 'unskilled labour' in a more damning and public version of what we had previously seen on Lofty's list. Our new lecturer, Mr Masters, had clearly soon given up on most of us, arguably with good reason and based on past experience. We had other priorities, such as finding a job.

The recruitment situation seemed to be good, and in particular several of us had decided we liked what we had seen of P & O, who became our preferred employer. One of our fellow students from the class ahead was even about to leave for his first trip with them, which prompted yet another party. He was one of two to join the company that winter and the other, Martin, had already joined a P & O cargo ship without even time for a send-off. Another of our erstwhile classmates had joined a tanker company and promptly flown out from Heathrow to join a ship, sending a postcard bearing a scribbled 'First stop Tokyo'. Spurred on by all this, my friend Roger and I called P & O and were sent application forms. I completed and sent mine on a Monday which also featured an abysmally-failed radar test, and received a reply on the Thursday inviting me to an interview in London the following week. Roger received the same response and we travelled by train and tube to the company's office at Beaufort House, near Aldgate. We had interviews with a friendly man from Personnel and were taken immediately for medicals on another floor, then offered jobs on the spot.

We returned to Bristol triumphant, being first in the class to get jobs, and as we basked in our success our "tickets" arrived. Rather than being a conventional certificate these took the form of a small crimson leather-bound booklet including our personal details and a list of all the subjects we had been examined in. There were small forms to be completed by radio surveyors at key milestone dates in our service, and a perforated *Authority to Operate* page which could be easily removed in the event of unspecified misconduct. The only adverse thing about them was that they were signed by Mr Tyson, which prompted some disappointment at his still being employed by the Ministry and so just possibly being able to visit us on ships. A group of us were led into a new intake class to hold up our documents and show them how worthwhile their studies would be.

This was only the beginning of all the documentation. We also needed a Discharge Book and a Seaman's Card. The first of these, bound in blue cloth, was a record of ships served on, with joining and leaving dates. The latter item, in red leatherette, served as a visa-free pass into ports and even countries around the world and could, in theory, be shown instead of a passport when taking flights; I actually did this once, but doing so appears to be unlikely now, the benefit being limited to port arrivals by sea. Applying for these involved going to the marine office in Avonmouth and returning two weeks later. After completing a further two and a half hours of paperwork in the office they were finally issued upon payment of fees of 97 pence. Applying for both in person at a Marine Office costs a total of £160 today (GOV.UK, 2021). We immediately showed them at the dock gates, gained entry and visited a P & O cargo ship called *Taupo* which had just returned from New Zealand. We met the R/O, were shown around and invited back for a longer visit, primarily to enjoy the bar, at the weekend. Experiencing the ship and the camaraderie helped us to understand more of what lay ahead of us. It was more useful than we could have imagined, as when that ship returned after its next voyage Roger would join it; by then I was already sailing on its sister ship.

Meanwhile we needed multiple vaccinations before being able to go to sea, and we collected a sheaf of certificates for these: Yellow Fever, Smallpox and Cholera (two of) and TAB (Typhoid). As if I were not missing enough study time already, I suffered with the side effects of some of these.

Yet another distraction was buying all the uniform, which meant repeated visits to a supplier in Avonmouth as and when funds were available. Eventually I owned a full midnight blue barathea (soft woven wool) uniform with long-sleeved shirts and black shoes, and a full tropical white uniform with short-sleeved shirts, shorts and leather-soled white canvas shoes which looked impressive but proved highly dangerous to walk in. In time I substituted these with tennis shoes, just as official uniform trousers were replaced by contemporary slacks and uniform shoes became anything black from the high street.

Meanwhile, there was still a radar course going on, although my attendance record was patchy. I made a frantic last-gasp attempt to prepare for the exams, playing catch-up yet again and throwing myself into revision despite being told by the lecturer that I had left it too late. At first I thought I might just pull it off; I completed the practical exam on the Hermes in exactly the allotted three hours. A week later I took the second practical exam while suffering some particularly bad after-effects from one of my vaccinations; after being granted a delay I arose from my sick bed and struggled with the Raymarc for three and a half frustrating hours, including multiple attempts at making the two tuning methods complement each other to find the distant hill, before managing to hand over a functioning set. It was kind of someone to allow me the extra time.

There was a hiatus of another week before the two written exams, which gave me further room to study and to cling to some faint hope of making the grade. However the doomsayer lecturer was right all along and although I thought I may have done just enough in the first paper I knew I had failed the second. Getting 60 per cent in each, given how the papers were to be marked, always looked a tough challenge and I had marvelled at the prowess of the few students able to obtain such marks in practice tests. I was able to maintain some faint hopes for a while as the results confirming my fears only arrived while I was already on my first ship.

I was to return and attempt the course again about eighteen months later, with more distractions and similar results. This time I had enjoyed a long summer leave and soon after starting the course I found that my pay had stopped and money was running short. I learned that P & O did not pay for study leave, which I had seen paid by other companies and assumed was the norm. Had I known this I would have planned things quite differently, but at that stage completing the course became a challenge for unexpected reasons and I lost much time and focus just trying to raise enough funds to remain at least nominally in college. Again I passed the practical exams (on the Raymarc and Radiolocator) but fell down on the theory, this time in the first exam.

I have to say I believe I learned what I needed from the radar course anyway, which was the practical experience. I was able to work effectively on the few radar faults I encountered at sea, and after a few years new technology began to reduce the need for component-level fault-finding. While in the USA during my penultimate trip the ship's Sperry radar developed a fault affecting its range rings, concentric circles at set intervals providing an instant indication of how far away certain targets are. I worked on the circuit board in question, identified the relevant integrated circuit on it, and even the leg of the chip leading to the faulty semiconductor inside. I then had to call the maker's local depot and a technician arrived bearing a new circuit board. He agreed that I had identified the faulty chip and more besides but all he could do was sell the new board; this summarised how things were changing.

In practice I needed little of the course theory once at sea, and question why some courses are designed the way they are. In many ways I'm in favour of things being over-engineered, especially structures which for whatever reason are built to take far more than their necessary stresses while enhancing the vistas they sit within. Applying this principle to people can be far less beneficial, especially if the only objective is to qualify and then forget it all while performing work utilising very little of it from day to day.

Back to 1975, we all went straight from the exams to another marathon pub session, joined for a while by Mr Masters although he seemed rather disapproving of our revelry. He may just have suspected how badly many of us had done. I think more than half of us failed the exams in some way, with even that low pass ratio being lifted by students returning to take it for the second time.

I had few regrets, other than leaving on something of a low after doing so much to turn things around and to qualify at all, sometimes against the odds. Roger and I felt we were correct to prioritise the job-seeking and everything which followed; it just seemed to make sense. We felt vindicated when two friends followed us in applying to P & O and found the process more difficult before being accepted. These were Andy, who had dropped a class before we did, and Adrian, one of the few from our Part II class to actually pass Radar. Students started to find securing interviews challenging, and when another two students from our class applied to P & O their applications went no further. Perhaps a large number of newly-qualified people around the country tried to start their careers that spring, taking the industry from under capacity to over, although everyone made it to sea somewhere in the end. Despite not fully focusing on Radar, some of us had done the right thing in aiming for the job market early. I am theoretically very much in favour of giving as much as possible when studying and have worked hard to obtain various qualifications in the years since. However, just then, timing was important and perhaps circumstances conspired against the more technically able.

After days of packing and goodbyes, my Dad arrived and drove me and all my stuff home. Within two weeks I was back in Bristol for yet another party. It was late April and I was due to officially join P & O on 1st May. I learned that one of our class, Tony, was due to start with Union Castle line in mid-May, and that Roger had been asked to wait for *Taupo*'s return around the end of May. No-one else was starting anywhere before June. The following day I learned that P & O had already sent a letter to my old Bristol address asking me to join a ship! After a series of phone calls, I learned that I was joining *Taupo*'s sister ship, *Tekoa*, in Avonmouth on my actual start date, and for a voyage to New Zealand. Eventually, after my rushing home and packing everything, the ship's arrival was delayed by one day, but my nautical career was finally about to begin.

5 P & O

The Peninsular and Oriental Steam Navigation Company is generally considered to have begun in 1837 with the floating of a new company to run a mail route on behalf of the Admiralty from London and Falmouth to Spain, Portugal and Gibraltar. This built upon origins dating back to 1815, to small-scale trade with the "Peninsular" countries of Spain and Portugal, and to supplying the winning royalist sides during both countries' civil wars. The company's flag, with its distinctive coloured quarters, is a legacy of these civil wars and to its being allowed to fly both monarchs' royal pennants.

On the return leg of its maiden voyage the Peninsular Company's ship *Don Juan* ran aground and eventually sank off Tarifa Point, the southernmost point of mainland Spain and of continental Europe. Despite the vessel only being partly-insured the company survived this setback and began to grow. The "Oriental" part of its name was added in 1840, upon winning the contract to take over the ongoing transit of mail eastwards to Egypt. Upon arrival, eastbound passengers and cargo travelled some 150 miles through Egypt to their next ship on canal boats and horse-drawn carriages and carts until a railway was built in stages through the 1850s. Ultimately the company also took over the later stages of the mail service from the Honourable East India Company, running services from Suez to Calcutta. Another route, from Suez to Bombay, followed, although not held exclusively, along with services onwards to Singapore and Sydney. Once all these routes were firmly established and carrying passengers and cargo in addition to the mail, the company began to relinquish its original, and less profitable, peninsular services.

The company also operated subsidiary routes around the Mediterranean, originally for mail services but advertising and providing what may have been the first passenger cruises. Many of these routes ceased when the Crimean War broke out and from 1854 the company was obliged to provide troop ships instead.

The opening of the Suez Canal in 1869 improved voyage times and greatly enhanced the passenger experience. The shipping company became ever more focused upon services to and from the "Orient" and Australia and serving the requirements of the growing empire. One tradition arising from these later services is that they gave the word "posh" to the English language. This is contested and may not be its only origin, but passengers could opt to pay a premium for tickets stamped 'P.O.S.H.' or Port Outward, Starboard Home, thus guaranteeing shaded cabins in the hot afternoons on both their outward and return voyages.

I knew I was joining a long-established company with much prestige and history. As I write, the P & O name is still synonymous with cruising and cross-channel ferries, despite changes of underlying ownership. The company had these to an extent in 1975 too, along with oil tankers, gas carriers, bulk-carrying ships, container ships and their own company independence. However the major business, employing most people and apparently generating most income, was the General Cargo Division (GCD). When applying to P & O, joining GCD was the default entry area although there were many opportunities to transfer, either by application or through circumstance.

A GCD fleet list from July 1975 shows 72 cargo ships and one container ship owned by the company, and five container ships and 18 cargo vessels operated for outside owners. The division was formed in 1971 out of diverse brands owned by P & O. These included British India Steam Navigation (BI), New Zealand Shipping Company

(NZS – some of whose ships continued to trade under the Federal Steam Navigation Company name, an identity retained despite being taken over by NZS in 1912), Strick Line and Moss Hutchison as well as ships already sailing under the P & O name. Some of these had self-evident historic routes of their own although they faced declining revenues due to growing containerisation and air travel.

Tekoa was an NZS ship and still bore much of its old company branding around the ship, from stationery to towels. P & O had begun to rebrand most of its cargo ships into a consistent image, first with blue funnels which bore the company name, then repainting the hulls a distinctive yellow and turning the cranes and derricks sky blue. Some repainting had already begun on *Tekoa* with the remainder completed as we crossed the Pacific during fine weather.

The rebranding also included renaming most of the company's ships with a view to a consistent identity; each new name began with "Strath". This caused some mystification as few people seemed to know what a strath was, even among Scots who the company might have assumed recognised the word as meaning a Scottish river valley. The prefix was not completely new: in 1967 P & O had built three new cargo ships and named them *Strathardle*, *Strathbrora* and *Strathconon*. These were considered highly advanced and known as the "Super Straths", and while at sea I heard them being referred to as such, even as the same people continued to question the rebranding. Gradually the naming system became more accepted, at least as an improvement on names beginning with "Pando" which had been briefly tried a few years earlier. Name recognition often depended upon converting new names to old ones first. Some more cynical seafarers suggested that renaming the oldest and dirtiest ships was a cunning plan to disguise their true nature and reduce the likelihood of officers refusing to join them. If so it could work both ways as the new names were sometimes adapted into warnings. For example the newly-named *Strathaddie* became "Strathbaddie", and *Strathnaver* was referred to as "Strathnever".

The NZS ships, and those from certain other former fleets, were not renamed. This may have defeated the object of a unifying rebranding, and looked as if perhaps someone had run out of possible names before reaching the bottom of the ship list. In fact some surviving names and colour schemes owed their existence to the technicalities of the marketing ventures they served at the time. A fleet of six roaming vessels emulating the traditional tramp steamers had names beginning with "Wild" and retained their white hulls while working on multiple charters. Two other refrigerated ships were moved to the Mediterranean to carry fruit and vegetables between Israel and France; they were given French names, *Vendee* and *Vosges*, along with white hulls and a funnel bearing the Carmel produce logo.

Given the complexities it took time to become familiar with the fleet, and the new marketing name of P & O Strath Services appeared something of a misnomer as well as inviting more parody. However the increased prominence of the company's flag was a more successful symbol of the rebranding.

There was little sense of decline when I joined *Tekoa*, despite some obvious anomalies. The ship was unloading frozen New Zealand lamb, as the tariffs and quotas imposed following the UK's entry into the then Common Market had yet to affect traditional trade patterns. However, it looked strange and archaic, even then, to see rows upon rows of frozen carcasses in open holds, being lifted out one sling full at a time.

P & O was a powerhouse company in many ways at the time. In addition to the above they were involved in oil and gas exploration (P & O Energy Division) and consolidated various haulage operations into a division called Pandoro. The company also owned two ship repair yards, an international shipping agency and the well-known housebuilder and construction company Bovis, which itself owned a number of maritime interests. Ferry services were booming although the separate and very different passenger cruises were at a low point in the 1970s; these only began to improve after years of new investment and evolving customer awareness.

Many of the cargo ships rebranded in the mid 1970s did not see the end of the decade with the fleet; some were scrapped immediately and others sold, usually to foreign competitors. Time was always going to be against many older vessels, but this did not necessarily deter buyers from other countries less constrained by safety and certification requirements than British ship owners were.

New ships were built to replace some of the older fleet. A group of new but relatively basic ships arrived from Sunderland-based shipyard Austin & Pickersgill between 1975 and 1977, collectively known as SD-14s, a name reflecting their standard design. The first of these, *Strathdare*, was sold during its maiden voyage, an ominous sign which conveniently removed a ship with an imaginary place name from the fleet list. The remaining five entered service; I sailed on two of them, and although they had their detractors from those who considered them modern-day Liberty ships they were clean, moderately spacious and easy to work on, even if my first one overloaded me with electronic hardware faults. Additionally six general cargo ships were built in Gdansk, Poland, with the distinguishing feature of 300-ton heavy lifting derricks, enabling them to handle unusual items unsuited to container ships or most other cargo vessels. I worked on these for the final three years of my career. Finally two more ships with similar specifications were built in Japan.

The company was badly affected by recessions and the falling value of sterling in the mid to late 1970s. For a while GCD effectively carried other loss-making divisions, and as bulk shipping and tankers continued to struggle another reorganisation merged them all into P & O Deep Sea Cargo Division. In practice this made little difference to which ships an individual might be assigned to as people were often matched with something similar to their previous ship, but the prospect of working on some different charters and joint ventures appeared. By the late seventies bulk shipping was becoming successful again, along with passenger shipping, and this coincided with general cargo suffering its own downturn. The company began to rationalise, to reduce debts and overheads, and to concentrate on what it saw as its future core businesses. Cargo shipping bore the brunt of this, with much trade being taken up by a consortium of companies, including P & O, operating the growing number of large container ships. One container ship could carry vastly more cargo, and be loaded and unloaded much more quickly, setting new standards for modern and globalised trade.

6 Coastal Tekoa

m.v. Tekoa   Refrigerated Cargo Liner

Built: 1966, Sunderland

Tonnage: 8,226 (gross), 4,478 (net), 11,866 (deadweight)

Dimensions: Length 527'7" (160.80m), beam 71'3" (21.71m), depth 44'6" (13.56m), draught 30'4" (9.24m)

Origin of name: Mountain in Canterbury, South Island, New Zealand

The landmark Friday arrived, and my parents drove me to Avonmouth, with my younger brother also in the car. The joys of 1970s motoring turned this into something epic with tyre and exhaust problems doubling the journey time. And this was in the newest and most presentable car we ever owned, which may not be saying much.

The time did not prove important as I joined a near-deserted ship, with many of the deep-sea company having left including the Radio Officers. We found my cabin, which impressed my family with its large bed and separate day bed, good space, large windows and en suite facilities, confounding some preconceptions of the conditions I was letting myself in for. Day beds were a couch-like feature of many cabins on ships, providing for an assumption that afternoon naps were taken. In practice they were most likely to be used as seating for visitors. The radio room was locked and the bar yet to be restocked, so the first tour of the ship was limited but we all imposed upon the ship's catering facilities for an evening meal. As the dining room, or saloon as I was to learn to call it, was otherwise deserted, the stewards were pleased to serve us a good two-course dinner. There were more course options but we were trying not to look greedy. The food arrived on liveried crockery placed upon starched tablecloths and we ate with silver cutlery; I would learn that the best cutlery in particular was allocated to cargo ships rather than to passenger vessels where it was more likely to be stolen as souvenirs.

I handed in my documents and signed on to the ship's articles as Second Radio Officer, or 2/R/O. The articles were basically a contract between ship and seafarer, renewable at certain intervals or at the beginning of each coastal or deep sea voyage. I sometimes had to sign them on multiple occasions while on a single ship. As for my role, there was a statutory requirement to complete at least six months as a "junior" before becoming a first, or on cargo ships only, R/O.

In total there would be around 35 working officers and crew on board, typical for such a ship and split fairly evenly between the two distinctive levels. Officers were divided into deck and engineering personnel. The Captain's deputy, the Chief Officer, usually referred to as the Mate, took charge of all aspects of deck work. The Chief Engineer, with the same stripes and seniority level as the Captain, held ultimate responsibility for all aspects of the engines, although his Second Engineer, the equivalent of the Mate, usually oversaw day-to-day tasks. The numbers then progressed through more junior officer ranks: second and third on deck, and through to fourth and fifth, and sometimes more than one of each, in the engine room.

The category of "crew" covered non-officer roles on deck and in the engine room, and also the catering team of cooks and stewards. The largest contingent was on deck, supervised by the Bosun, a shortening of the term Boatswain and also referred to in different marine environments as a deck boss or petty officer. The role of

Chief Steward had mostly been amalgamated with that of Purser, an officer rank thus usually noted as PCS. For simplicity I refer to the combined role as Purser in this book. The cooks also reported to the Purser, at least nominally although the Head Cook retained a good deal of autonomy.

The ship, like most I sailed on, also hosted some "supernumerary" people. These were usually wives and children but could also on rare occasions be well-connected individuals within or close to the company, in transit or taking an unconventional retirement cruise.

My new boss, Dave, arrived in the evening along with his wife Kath and young daughter Lisa. I learned that Dave would only be on board around the UK coast, an aspect of the trip I was unaware of; after unloading in Avonmouth it was to load new cargo in Cardiff and London. I had been expecting a long first voyage and in fact it was going to be one of the shortest, just across the Bristol Channel.

Next morning I was keen to see my new working environment for the first time. After breakfast I learned that Dave and family were going ashore so I asked for the keys to the cabin. He was mystified by this and when I persevered he asked 'What, you want to see my cabin?' We finally established that what had been described throughout college as the cabin was in fact "The Radio Room", unsurprising but clearly there was scope for confusion. I was also yet to learn of the tradition of Radio Officers not working in port over weekends, which explained Dave's own plans. In a way it was probably good for me to view the equipment in my own time. Some of it was completely unknown to me, for example the Atalanta and Electra receivers, old models dating back to the 1950s. This was disconcerting at first, especially as I found the Atalanta to be faulty. There was also a broadcast receiver on a separate desk. After a cursory look at the remaining items and a walk around the deserted bridge, I tuned the broadcast receiver to Radio 1 and began to type up a story I had written.

This set the pattern for the rest of that low-key weekend. When Dave returned we left a message with the local Marconi depot requesting assistance. There seemed to be no paperwork to do, which I was yet to learn was an unusual situation, and as it was the weekend we closed the radio room again. This was one of the many positives of my new job: considerable free time in port, especially at weekends but often on other days too.

In the short term this gave me plenty of time to show visitors around, and several former classmates arrived singly, in pairs, groups and with girlfriends in tow, all to witness and share the experience. I was first among them to get a ship and this was everyone's first opportunity to visit one on equal terms, and locally too. I was happy to be visited and to be sociable and demonstrate my new abode. The more technical visitors were interested in the sight of an actual radio room and contemplated the potential challenge of operating it. For others, the bar prices and unlimited self-service hours were definite attractions, especially as we discovered the practical benefits of duty-free pricing. This meant cans of beer for 10 pence and larger-than-usual spirit tots for 5 pence, prices which remained fairly consistent throughout my time at sea regardless of high inflation ashore. There was little sophistication involved; the beer options were usually limited to lager, although some ships also offered a more traditional alternative. Gin was always London style, and "pink" or with tonic. The medicinal traditions of empire thus continued to be celebrated, pending future challenges from artisan and botanical offerings. Whisky was almost always a particular cheap blend, rendered palatable with lemonade or ginger ale; single malt and single cask were still extremely niche terms and decades away from wider appreciation. Vodka, and white and dark rums, completed the standard offerings on display, while a number of other spirits and liqueurs were stocked less prominently. Cocktails were mainly ill-advised experiments with some of the newly-discovered drinks suddenly available to inquisitive teenage minds. Some of my visitors needed assistance down the gangway afterwards, and I know of one visitor with no recollection at all of even being on the ship. Gradually new officers also joined and I spent time socialising with them too, so my new job seemed quite an easy and pleasant one.

Tekoa alongside at Avonmouth

On Monday Dave said he would wait in case the Marconi engineer arrived, and that it was fine for me to go into Bristol for the day. I visited friends, enjoyed meals out, went shopping and saw two films. When I met up with Dave again next morning he told me off for going ashore! He had had a bad day, finally venturing into the radio room and onto the bridge himself and finding, and being unable to fix, faults on the radar, echo sounder and direction finder. He had been chasing Marconi but now could only continue to wait. We were soon friends again and moved on. We were approaching the ship in very different ways; I was keen to learn but knew very little in advance and could only fit in with him; he knew he was only passing through the ship and perhaps hoping to have little to do, remaining free to keep his family entertained.

We gradually discovered some actual tasks we could attempt ourselves, and which introduced me to unexpected features. I learned of a communal aerial system for sharing conventional radio station reception around the ship. The radio room hosted a broadcast receiver with its own aerial and an outlet into an amplifier box called a pantenna. From this, co-axial cable led into public rooms and crew cabins, each room having its own output box and socket where users could connect their own radios. I was to discover that these seldom worked well due to so many points of possible failure, and *Tekoa*'s was no exception, but we spent time trying to improve it and fixed several breaks. The officer and crew bars also had broadcast receivers of their own.

There were also issues with the ship's TV reception, as an aerial on the highest deck level had to be pointed in the best direction. Coaxial cable ran through the ship down to the multi-national TV sets in the officer and crew lounges, but trial and error with a metal coat hanger by the window was often just as effective. We received an amplifier for the TV signals and engaged the ship's carpenters ("Chippies") to run new cabling from the aerial via the new box in the radio room and on to the public rooms, which filled our workspace with noise and bustle for a day. After experimenting with the amplifier settings, and probably benefitting from new cabling too, we could provide the officer and crew lounges with better TV reception, including BBC2 for the first time.

I also learned that ships were sent libraries of books by the Seafarers' Education Service, and several crates arrived. I unpacked these, loaded the old books into them for return and arranged the new books on shelves and into categories. I found something of a librarian's approach within myself and enjoyed this task, as well as being able to choose some reading material. The shelves were arranged into a partition around a large tropical fish tank, with small rails which stopped the books from sliding off when the ship rolled. The partition separated a large lounge and bar area from a more open space known as the dance floor but which in practice mainly hosted darts matches.

Films also arrived and had to be exchanged; a ship received up to six movies, each one usually occupying three reels within a bulky package although long films could fill four or even five reels. I learned how to use the ship's Bell & Howell projector and, just as important, the repair kits for splicing together broken film celluloid as the movies tended to break frequently during showings. Film shows turned out to be the R/O's job, and as the junior it would be mine. It soon transpired that showing the six allocated movies was only a small part of this "responsibility" as people from other ships would visit seeking overnight film swaps. After exchanging films and sharing beers, each ship then had something new to watch. I was also expected to walk onto other ships requesting the same.

The port area seemed rather bleak but on a walk around I was introduced to the seaman's mission (now The Mission to Seafarers), a feature of many ports worldwide. They may have gained a slightly melancholy reputation since being mentioned in Ralph McTell's *Streets of London*, if not before, but in practice they tended to offer pleasant, if spartan, environments in which to pass time and enjoy some welcome recreational facilities.

On Thursday the Marconi engineer arrived and fixed each item in a long working day. I was tasked with tuning the newly-operational radar. It was a different model to those in college, an Argus, but I made it show the distant hill on the display. It was satisfying to accomplish this successfully in the real world. The Atalanta receiver was to fail several more times during the trip, but for now we had more free time. Being in Avonmouth we were near to Portishead Radio, the UK's main coast station for long-distance ship to shore communication, and decided we should go and see it. I was having to make sure I pronounced it properly rather than using the Bristolian version, 'Port Zed.' Their control centre was near Burnham-on-Sea and we endured a longer journey than expected, arriving late in the day but we were welcomed and shown around. There were relatively few operators on duty, perhaps due to it being a Friday afternoon and possibly a time of shift changes, but it was fascinating to see how messages were handled, circulating on conveyor belts and carousels to and from operators. I think I was expecting scenes from a science fiction film set and seeing the place in action revised my view to that of a more homely operation. As we were about to leave, a door opened and someone familiar stepped out. He had been at my college for a while, studying to upgrade his ticket. We chatted for a while and I looked into the room, full of radio consoles and desks bearing Morse keys but now devoid of operators. 'What happens in here then?' I asked. 'Oh, this is 12 and 16 MHz,' he replied cheerfully. These were two of the main long-distance bands, but I didn't ask anything further or recognise the significance of what I was seeing. This was to dawn on me a few weeks later while trying to contact the station, mostly unsuccessfully, when crossing the Pacific. I was about to learn the differences between communicating in class and doing so in the real world.

Another weekend arrived and this meant more free time, and in the knowledge that everything was now in good order. Dave learned that upon arrival in Cardiff he was transferring to another company ship, *Essex*, which was due in Liverpool. This was a much older refrigerated cargo ship, operating on the same New Zealand route. It seemed strange for him to have to transfer at all if the end route was the same and if he had not been expecting a deep sea ship yet, but perhaps there was a bigger plan and he did not question it.

Monday was our last day in port and another company ship had arrived. I knew my former classmate Martin was on board so I went over to say a quick hello. Social call over, Dave and I checked all our equipment again. Our sole responsibility during the short voyage would be to send a message called a "TR" to a radio station, advising them of our departure from port, and another similar message soon afterwards as we arrived at the next one. We joked that we could send them to nearby Portishead using semaphore flags. As we were not sailing until 7 pm, Dave and Kath decided to go ashore for the day, and surprised me by asking if I would look after their five year old daughter. Perhaps they had seen me showing my then-seven year old brother around and recognised an experienced child minder. I sat in the officers' bar for much of the day, keeping her occupied with games and toys and watching the tropical fish.

Just before 2 pm I was suddenly asked to work, as the Mate (Chief Officer) requested a time signal on the hour so the bridge timepieces could be checked. I led my young charge to the radio room and sat her on the deck with some toys while I tried in vain to get the time signal. I found that the receiver had its own eccentricities and the frequency I was looking for was not where I expected it to be, even if it looked correct. I knew there were other stations which sent continuous time signals and told the bridge I would find one of those and link it through to them soon. As I struggled to find one, an older man than I had seen on board so far walked into the radio room. He stared quizzically at the girl playing on the deck and at me as I thumbed through one of the manuals of radio station frequencies while grumbling quietly. When I looked fully at him and spoke, he introduced himself as Cyril, the new Radio Officer. We were going on a two hour voyage with three Sparkies on board.

Cyril helped me to find the time signal and then we were able to introduce ourselves more fully. He was 51 years old and had been at sea for 33 years. He was not expecting to have a "second" on board and did not seem completely enamoured with the idea, which made me wish things had been arranged differently too. I expect he was accustomed to doing things his own way and that the prospect of spending the next few months explaining so much to someone new held little appeal. However we each knew we had little choice but to work together.

Finally Dave returned and after more introductions the ship sailed. I had visions of sitting at the Morse key for my first real radio watch, however briefly. Instead I was asked to look after Dave's daughter again while they packed. The reason for carrying three R/Os was now clear: one to communicate, one to pack cases and the third to provide childcare. We sedately crossed the Bristol Channel, the water calm and the then single Severn Bridge in clear view for much of the crossing. While watching these scenes I taught Lisa how to play darts, although after a while she threw a bullseye and a treble top, and I was no longer sure of being the better player.

Once in Cardiff, and after a casual evening in the bar, we said goodbye to Dave and family and they loaded huge amounts of luggage into a taxi. I never saw them again. There was little more work for Cyril and I, but I briefed him on the repairs carried out before his arrival. We did what we could to improve the TV reception, turning the aerial around and hoping some of the amplifier settings made a difference. This accomplished, we had plenty of time to just talk over coffees and later beer (me) and gin (Cyril). Despite this we were always going to move in different social circles and in the evening I went ashore with some of the officers closer to my age; the more junior deck and engineer ranks.

Cardiff made a poor first impression upon us. In the years since, it has become an attractive city to visit, and even in 1975 its natural setting could be appreciated, but like many British cities at the time it appeared very run-down, and especially near the docks. We were warned that the pubs by the docks had a dangerous reputation and to either drink on board or go into town. We were determined to have a night out and someone familiar with the place led us to a house near the docks which sold drinks under cover, which was reputedly safer but seemed a strange situation as we sat around in seedy rooms being served with cans. We moved on to the town centre and eventually to a nightclub. However the evening turned sour as we left; most of our little group were out on the pavement looking for a taxi when we turned around to see our fifth engineer being beaten up in the doorway. We rushed over to help him and his assailants fled. As we supported him and blood poured over the ground a police car appeared; they took him away with them, first to the police station to clean him up and then to hospital where he received six stitches.

Other than going ashore in broad daylight to buy music, we avoided further trips into Cardiff until our final full day in port, a Saturday. Home international football matches were still a highlight of the sporting calendar, and several of us decided to go to Wales v Scotland at Ninian Park. It was normal to just turn up and pay on entry into games at the time; all-ticket matches were rare. Once near the ground we inevitably went into a pub. It was packed with football fans and just as we had squeezed through to near the bar a massive fight started. I didn't see the cause but heard a glass drop and someone cry out; then within a second, everyone seemed to be either fighting or diving for cover as chairs and glasses flew through the air and the place filled with sound. I was close to the overhanging bar counter and crouched down beneath it, other bodies hiding most of the action. Seconds later the pub was suddenly still, and along with many others I gradually rose to my feet. The pub was completely wrecked, with windows, lighting, furniture and bar fittings all smashed. There was no sign of whoever had been fighting, just groups of friends finding each other and getting out as fast as possible. We had lost one colleague, our electrician, and found him a few minutes later; when the trouble started he had crawled on hands and knees through the melee and escaped outside. Another car from the ship arrived, and we all managed to meet among the chaos outside the pub. Our impressions of Cardiff had been confirmed, but we still went on to the match, fairly confident of our safety in numbers. It was the classic game of two halves, Wales going 2-0 up in the first half and Scotland scoring twice in the second to draw the game. But unsurprisingly the football was not the main talking point when we returned to the ship.

One more day remained, and Cyril and I actually worked for a while, listing the deficiencies in the ship's spares which we hoped could be rectified at our next port, London. This completed, we could relax until departure late that evening. I would take up real-life watch-keeping the next day.

7 Watch-Keeping

A little more detail now on watch-keeping, since this formed the R/O's day-to-day duties while at sea. All this was documented in scattered areas of the Post Office's Handbook for Radio Operators, which formed the basis for the procedural exams within the Part II examination.

The main requirement was to maintain a listening watch on the standard distress and calling frequency, 500 kHz for radio telegraphy. This enabled any distress or other urgent messages to be heard and acted upon promptly, and for contact to be made readily between ships and local coast stations, or with other ships. To maximise the safety aspect, stations keeping watch had to observe two silence periods per hour, each lasting for three minutes and commencing at 15 and 45 minutes past. These were marked on the face of the radio room clock.

Watches were kept for prescribed numbers of hours depending on the number of qualified operators on board, which reflected the type of ship; a cargo ship with one Radio Officer had to maintain a watch for eight hours per day. There was some flexibility in these but typically the hours were 0800 to 1200, plus two hours in the afternoon and another two in the evening. Having some discretion helped the operator to manage their workload and consider the most favourable conditions.

All radio-related times were sent and recorded in Greenwich Mean Time (GMT), regardless of actual locations. If there was any doubt at all, a station would clarify that a time they had given was GMT by adding a "Z", for "Zulu Time" after it. This term was a short phonetic expression, not at all connected with Africa but simply referencing the fact that the time in question was Zero hours different from that at the meridian. It is now more commonly known as UTC, or Universal Time Coordinated, which hardly simplifies or abbreviates it. The R/O often had to think in both GMT and the ship's own time, depending on what was due to happen in each environment. Wristwatches showing multiple times were quite rare at the time and R/Os often kept two timepieces.

Each ship and radio station had a unique call sign which was used in place of their names; four characters for ships (which has become more variable since) and three for stations. The first digit usually denoted the ship's flag or station's country; for example the UK was "G". My first ship, Tekoa, was GRNU, and Niton Radio GNI. Messages were described as "traffic". R/Os listened to coast stations' traffic lists to discover whether any messages were waiting for them, sometimes scheduling their watch-keeping accordingly. A ship expecting British traffic would tune to Portishead Radio's lists every two hours, listening for its own call sign. These were sent alphabetically and the scale of Portishead's operation could be seen in the list taking up to an hour to transmit. Operators would combine listening to this with other tasks depending on their expectations and place in the alphabet. When near coasts, ships would also listen to the much shorter traffic lists sent by local stations, or even call them direct to ask if they had any messages for them.

I usually wore headphones when communicating. All my ships had "sidetone" which enabled me to hear the Morse I was sending; this was a feature not always available on older ships. When listening I was conscious of possibly causing undue disturbance on the nearby bridge, especially as doors were often kept open. A headset also helped when poor conditions or interference forced an operator to apply additional mental focus in order to receive; it was then possible to pick out the required signal and transcribe the Morse from within a crowd of other competing transmissions. This was one of Morse code's most useful attributes, compared to how understanding soon becomes impossible when crossed lines affect voice communications. When simply keeping watch, and especially at quieter times of day or night, I would usually keep the loudspeaker on instead.

Exchanges between ships, or ships and shore, usually included Q codes, including those for number of messages, turn in the queue, changes of frequencies and any interference and requests. The R/O would find the required station's signal, which was usually on a tape giving their call sign, tune the transmitter to the correct frequency and send, as many times as necessary, a short message giving their identity and working frequency. A typical call from a ship to a coast station followed this format:

1. The coast station call sign, sent up to 3 times
2. DE, an expression of "from" which was short and rhythmic in Morse (DAHDITDIT-DIT)
3. The ship call sign, sent up to 3 times
4. The Q code "QTC" (I have a telegram for you…) followed by the quantity if more than one
5. The Q code "QSS" (I will use this working frequency…) followed by the intended frequency, or the last three digits of it if on a higher band. Other very similar Q code options were also available!
6. K (one of many shorter codes also used; this was an invitation for the other station to transmit back)

Every attempt at this was the hopeful one, like having the conviction that this week's lottery ticket would be the winner. On a good day it would indeed be easy to make contact, but there were other times when it took hours, or even days. Sometimes the required station would be audible but sending a tape with a code indicating they were busy and thus not listening for more calls from ships. There were times when a station was audible and answering ships but unable to hear everyone, either due to interference, poor signal strength or atmospheric conditions. Sometimes there was just too much competition.

A variation in the calling process was necessary when a station was silent, as some were, not sending a tape at all but (hopefully) maintaining a watch. In these circumstances the operator would simply transmit the station's call sign, pausing and hoping to receive an encouraging "DE". If and when this response was heard, the above sequence could be sent, with less need to repeat the call signs.

Upon making contact, the coast station might allocate a turn number to the ship, especially during busy times. When the turn was reached, whichever station had messages for the other would send the "QTC" code followed by a number confirming how many messages they had, and these could then be sent and received. If the receiving station was unsure about any of the words received or had missed some, perhaps due to interference, there was a process for confirming or asking for repetition as necessary. Additional communication pre-empted today's text speak. Many operators politely called each other "OM" (Old Man), and used abbreviations such as "GM" or "GE" for greetings at different times of day and "CFM" for "Confirm, "PSE" for "Please and "TU" or "TKS" for "Thanks". Sometimes operators would compliment each other upon completing some particularly smooth communication, adding "FB" (Fine Business). Other shortened words and phrases were invented, sometimes wittily, on the spur of the moment during constructive communication.

Inevitably there could also be bad behaviour on the airwaves, mainly from anonymous operators intruding on other ships' communications or compromising the half-hourly radio silence periods. This led to abbreviated insults, some entirely predictable, while sending the Morse code comma (DAHDAHDITDITDAHDAH) was also used to tell someone to go away.

Most communications, especially in good conditions, were simple activities requiring little more than basic details and a methodical approach, rather like arranging a meeting or ordering a pizza: "what, where and when", leading to a transaction. Over-simplified or vague representations in movies or performance can raise hackles, even many years later. For example, in the film *The Dambusters*, a buzzer prompted the operator to lift a telephone receiver first, which was really a trigger for the watching audience, before listening to the Morse and shouting out the code words. At least that film used actual Morse code, even if we only heard very little of it, unlike many movies which used either random letters or even sounds which were not Morse at all. They don't seem to realise that there are people who can tell the difference. In a more curious example, Kate Bush's wonderful 2014 *Before the Dawn* live show included an astronomer alerting the coastguard to a ship's distress message, which he happened to have heard while observing a meteor shower. As you do. I struggled to understand the thought process behind this, but it probably stemmed from being a late addition to introduce the next sequence of songs, centred on a woman lost at sea.

Messages to be sent from the ship were usually hand written and given to the R/O or left on the radio room desk. These included official telegrams from the ship's master to the company's head office's telex address, and weather observations made and encoded by bridge staff every six hours. The latter could be decoded by the Met Office and counterparts in other countries to provide an accurate report on surface conditions, something not always discernible from weather satellites. Anyone on board could have personal telegrams sent, which the receiving coast station phoned through to the destination's nearest post office, written out and promptly delivered to the addressee's door. A "greetings" telegram could also be sent to mark a special occasion; in this instance the recipient's local post office would transcribe it onto a more colourful template. When receiving a congratulatory telegram for someone on board ship, the R/O could add a slightly colourful sticker to a space down the side, which in my experience often caused some amusement due to its austere and inexpensive appearance. One example showed cartoon seagulls on a royal blue background.

A slower and cheaper medium, for lower-priority messages or those sent with sufficient notice, was a Ship Letter Telegram, or SLT. These were received and transcribed by the receiving station and then sent to the addressee by post. SLTs were also used for recreational messages, such as pools syndicate entries for which Vernons provided a service contactable in this way. It was also possible to give gifts or flowers by sending an SLT to Kays, a mail order retail business (and another company to have seemingly ditched their apostrophe) or to Interflora; the Radio Officer kept small brochures of items available from each.

Telephone calls were often more difficult, sometimes due to the service offered by coast stations being less readily available and sometimes because interference often affected call quality. In all honesty the lack of demand for this service on ships other than passenger ones could also mean the R/O becoming less familiar with the frequencies involved or the best use of the equipment's telephony capabilities and having to relearn in a live situation. Some people would be deterred from requesting calls by their apparent difficulty or because poor connections restricted them to "simplex" calls in which each party had to speak and then say 'over'. Another concern was that their spoken words could "break through" onto radio sets elsewhere on the ship and compromise the caller's privacy. This phenomenon also occurred with Morse transmissions but few on board would have been able to decipher anything, especially at the speed involved. This reinforced the likelihood that any leakage of information from telegrams would be directly traceable to the R/O, who was bound by regulations to maintain secrecy. This requirement meant being party to some sensitive company and personal information at times, and handling it carefully.

The weather messages were handled free of charge but all commercial traffic had to be paid for, both to the company (with some exceptions, below) and the organisation running the receiving station. These were "per word" for written messages and "per minute" for phone calls. The preamble to written messages included the R/O's calculated word count, a figure the receiving station could either query or tacitly accept by acknowledging receipt. The R/O could try to minimise the costs; there were maximum numbers of letters or characters chargeable as one word, but sometimes two short words could be combined into a single chargeable one, provided it still made sense. Ships or other receiving location names counted as a single word regardless of their length.

Messages on ship's business and personal ones from the Master and Radio Officer cost less as they incurred no company charges, but the land charges remained. The cost of any goods or services ordered was added to the sum chargeable on board. Thus another part of the R/O's job involved calculating all the charges, confirming them to senders and completing a detailed monthly summary on what would now be a spreadsheet but which at the time was an A3 size form to be completed neatly by hand. Carbon copies had to be carefully aligned while making entries. The ship's Purser had to be notified of the charges to collect from individuals, and the original of the large form was sent to the company for reconciliation and the allocation of charges to be paid out to land stations and other companies.

It was expected that a weather forecast would be received at least once per day and written up for the bridge;

these were usually sent out by coast stations, scheduled in the same manner as traffic lists. Relatively local forecasts were transmitted in plain language. The information for the seas around the British Isles and Western Europe matched the areas and format within the shipping forecast familiar to broadcast radio listeners; it could be transcribed from the spoken broadcast or from the coast station's Morse version. How many geographical areas' worth of information to pass on to the bridge required a subjective decision, or guidance on preferences, depending on the ship's location and heading. Other countries had their own approaches to dividing forecasts into areas within their scope. Additional larger-scale forecasts, e.g. for the Atlantic Ocean, were sent by long-range stations as groups of numbered code, reflecting the R/O's training in receiving these at college. Bridge officers decoded the numbers into a rudimentary weather map showing systems and pressures. In the second half of my career, radio rooms began to be equipped with fax machines and it became possible to receive scheduled facsimile weather maps printed onto smudgy thermal paper. These held some novelty value due to the "new" and unexpected technology but also because successful receipt could be rare as the transmissions were very susceptible to interference.

Any activity had to be entered by hand in the radio log, as the old wireless log had become known, including signing in, recording each communication attempted or completed and each frequency used, distress or other important messages heard, traffic lists or forecasts received, silence periods observed, time signals taken to check against the radio room clock, and signing off at the end of each watch. If the R/O had no activity of their own to record, they would usually note another ship or shore station's communications occasionally, typically at ten-minute intervals, as evidence that they were on watch and paying attention even while reading or drinking coffee.

When signing off at the end of the day, a space was left for the ship's Master to sign, something usually carried out in a weekly batch on Sunday mornings.

There were three types of distress or other alert message. In ascending order of priority, especially over the handling of normal traffic, these were:
- Safety signal. Message preceded by three repetitions of TTT, with each letter separately identifiable. Message involving safety of navigation or important meteorological warnings.
- Urgency signal. Message preceded by three repetitions of XXX, with each letter separately identifiable. A very urgent message regarding the safety of a ship, aircraft or person.
- Distress signal. Message preceded by up to three repetitions of SOS, with the three letters joined together to form a single character (DITDITDITDAHDAHDAHDITDITDIT, not DITDITDIT-DAHDAHDAH-DITDITDIT). If sent by a ship, this would be followed by its call sign, position, name, nature of the distress and any other useful information. All stations hearing such a message were duty bound to acknowledge it, either immediately if nearby or after a short interval if further away than other vessels.

  Each of the above had an equivalent for use on telephony frequencies: Securité, Pan-pan and Mayday respectively, spoken three times at the beginning of the communication.

There were variations on the Morse distress signal, for use in other circumstances:
- A longer version of the distress message could be sent in order to activate other ships' auto alarm devices. These devices were permanently tuned to distress frequencies and built to recognise long dashes of ten to fifteen seconds when sent within a

distress message. They would then activate a bell in the radio room as well as others in the R/O's cabin and on the bridge, drawing attention at times when no radio watch was being kept. A ship's emergency transmitter could continue to send such a message automatically after the vessel had been abandoned.
- A distress message could be relayed by another ship or coast station; this would be prefixed by DDD SOS SOS SOS DDD, with the letters in each group being joined together. These were heard much more often than messages direct from actual vessels in distress.

This summarises a job description which was mostly humdrum and routine with occasional moments of incident or drama. As *Tekoa* sailed from Cardiff to London it was all new and exciting to me.

After six slightly edgy days in Cardiff we left at around 11 pm. I had already received a weather forecast from the nearest medium range station, Ilfracombe Radio, and now I sent them a TR message, closely watched by Cyril. Once this was acknowledged we signed off and retired to the bar for nightcaps.

I slept soundly, and later learned that Cyril was disturbed by the Lifeguard auto alarm sounding at 1.30 am. He confirmed there was no distress message, checked the device and concluded it was a false alarm. During the day we jointly kept the radio watch, two hours on and two hours off, with me performing under supervision some of the tasks I had been trained for. I sent and received telegrams through Niton Radio, and received another weather forecast and my first safety message. I was just finishing an exchange with Niton when I realised Captain Holmes was standing at the back of the radio room watching.

'How's he doing?' he asked Cyril.

'Doing a great job,' Cyril replied, which pleased me.

That evening the auto alarm was behaving strangely again; we tried to reset and then to fix it but the symptom kept changing, and after our final watch Cyril switched it off.

We entered the Thames estuary soon afterwards and berthed at London's Royal Albert Dock very early in the morning. Combined with its neighbouring docks in the Royal Group, Royal Victoria Dock and King George V Dock, the three formed the largest enclosed docks in the world when they were completed in 1921. I only experienced them in their final years when the effects of long-term decline were all too apparent. They looked another depressing sight and I wondered if all cargo ports were going to be like this. I was also coming to terms with the realities of their nearby inner city neighbourhoods and their different levels of deprivation from where I had lived and studied.

We soon received a visit from the company's radio superintendent, who maintained a depot nearby. Mr Merry was a shabby middle-aged man, possibly younger than he looked, and cursed with a highly inappropriate surname. Cyril told him about the auto alarm fault and was promptly given a severe reprimand for not maintaining a continuous watch in the Channel overnight. He was as surprised as I was, perhaps expecting a more constructive response, but seemed to accept it. There is a regulation in the handbook regarding this situation; I don't know if it was there decades earlier when Cyril trained, and since it was my first day at sea I was evidently not held responsible. In mitigation I can imagine Cyril thinking that we were in an area where many ships would receive any new distress message and be close enough to help, and that our ship would be contactable in other ways if necessary, being so near to the coast and to the local coast station at North Foreland, in Kent. Also we would have been under pilotage in the Thames soon after completing the evening watch, and closing down anyway.

Whatever the rights and wrongs, I was hardly going to be pleased to see this treatment being thrown at Cyril, and my disapproving looks earned me a Merry glare, as I came to know it.

Another auto alarm was produced from Mr Merry's depot but embarrassingly this also proved faulty and an engineer had to be called. There was a notorious tradition of spares being held which were marked, or known to be, "used but good". Sometimes this made sense but it always introduced some uncertainty, and this was one such instance. Along with this dubious kit came a demand from Mr Merry that I should make time to go and tidy up his nearby depot. However such good will was now in short supply and it was decided that I was not going. My absence was not remarked upon, but probably noted.

8 Deep-Sea Tekoa

It was all change in London as many of my newly-acquired friends and colleagues left, to be replaced by people who considered *Tekoa* their second home, veterans of repeated runs to and from New Zealand. These included two officers' wives. We also carried two supernumerary "cowboys", travelling to care for some live cattle, kept in pens on a sheltered deck area and being exported to New Zealand.

I began to hear stories of the beauty of New Zealand and the wonders of its nightlife; also that the Third Mate and Purser had long-term girlfriends there, with the latter planning to become engaged on arrival. The others simply and consistently expressed a grim determination to remain on this route to avoid being sent to "The Gulf", which was already the focus of many shipping routes. They began to talk of 'Coming Back' next time before they had even gone away, and to ask new faces like myself whether we already planned to do the same, however unanswerable this was.

The tone on board changed, certainly within the officers' areas. I accompanied one junior officer ashore to buy more fish for the tank and cassettes for the bar, and was surprised to find him buying music selections suitable for a much older generation. He was adamant that it was 'good stuff' and I soon realised that even if his musical tastes were older than his age he was also choosing appropriately for his familiar comrades. Cyril professed his liking for Perry Como and found that he was well catered for, and that several relatively young officers harboured tastes much more conservative than their years, not only musically. I came to recognise this as a common situation at sea and that it occurred within me too over time. Looking back I can identify with Bob Dylan's hook line in his song *My Back*

Pages. Over the voyage there were many times when the younger element surrendered the officers' bar and its music, retreating to play darts behind the partition or descend the decks to visit the more basic but relaxed and hospitable crew bar and socialise there instead.

Bar and dining table conversation became stilted, especially between the "Regulars" who may have sailed together for too long. We "Newbies" began to form our own groups at dining tables and talk more freely, aided by our taking turns to buy table wine to supplement dinner, but sometimes drawing disapproving looks. I sensed Cyril would rather sit at a table like mine but he was doomed to sit at the Captain's table, where the Old Man's booming voice intimidated his neighbouring officers into cowed mumbles. On later ships I would sometimes sit at captains' tables and sometimes at adjacent ones, depending on factors such as layout and any additional people travelling on board.

Breakfast offered a degree of excitement with its hotel-style cooked options. Lunch and dinner brought a range and quantity of courses hitherto unimaginable to someone who had recently been a student. There was soup, a starter course, main course, optional alternative "main" of cold meat and salad, dessert, cheese and biscuits, and coffee. Each officer usually managed two or three courses but would occasionally "go through the menu", either due to a particularly enticing range of food that day or just to remain at the table and prolong a sociable meal. Officers on watch could only indulge to a lesser extent, taking plates direct from the galley into a neighbouring small room without having to change into smarter uniform. Meanwhile the crew served themselves to all the same food options in their separate mess, out of sight on the opposite side of the galley. If anyone had still not eaten enough, some leftovers were sent to pantries on each deck, to be found when making teas and coffees overnight.

The bar more or less reflected the Captain's table, especially when the Regulars dominated; mostly silent but for the sound of crooners on tape and occasional comments on which fish was chasing which around the tank. The music may have been relaxing but the atmosphere was not. Sometimes even the idea of casually sitting down and talking was terrifying; what could I say to these people? Stepping out of the bar also became a source of tension. Leaving a glass unwashed for any reason, even to just show a seat was spoken for while arranging food or dealing with sudden work requirements, was punished by having to "shout" a round to all present. This was not universally enforced, the main burden usually falling on the younger and less-established personnel. The Regulars covered for each other but ensured they were all alerted and present to neck a free drink from someone new.

The divisions were not exclusively between the officers. The Bosun (the most senior of the deck crew) and the Cook were Regulars and often came upstairs to sit in the officers' bar. They were relatively outgoing but the unusual situation prompted some disapproval from the rest of the crew.

I also met cadets for the first time, two aspiring deck officers gaining experience at sea within their sponsored training programme. They were rather resentful that someone their own age and with zero sea time could be an officer already. It felt a little like arriving at grammar school all over again, except I had already been on board for a few weeks and felt more secure. More galling for them was that cadets often got the dirty jobs on and below decks, while I did not look very busy to them. This was a recurring theme on each ship, and not only as a junior. People saw the R/O's job as one of sedentary ease, and while this was sometimes true there were also times when the notion was patently unfair. It was also the case that the R/O was the only officer on board who had to fully qualify, at their (or their family's) own expense before going to sea. Deck officers started as paid cadets, as did most engineer officers, while electricians and any non-cadet engineers had served apprenticeships and worked in industry. However this argument could never win everyone over.

Things began to improve when I was asked to produce a news sheet. I scribbled and typed up stories from the BBC World Service and managed to deliver something I considered readable. In fact it was acclaimed as a 'beautiful job', initially called the *Daily Sun*, since sunshine was appearing as we sailed southwards, and later renamed *The Austin Telegraph*, just to remind everyone who I was.

I then had to produce other important information on a weekly basis: the football results and the critical score-draw numbers for the football pools. These would be a feature of every ship I sailed on, with officers and crew forming syndicates and compiling standing orders of numbers and dates which I sent to Vernons and organised the charges and payments for. Each week I typed up the fixtures on two pages separated by carbon paper, one copy for each bar's notice board. I then wrote in the results as they were announced, along with the fixture numbers to identify the winning draws. This was much simpler than it might be today as almost all league matches were played on Saturdays, and at the same time. The task also made it fully acceptable to listen to the BBC World Service's rolling football coverage, similar to that on Radio 5 Live now, on a second receiver while maintaining a radio watch on Saturday afternoons.

Watch-keeping resumed and having cleared our radio traffic we connected our broadcast receiver through to the bridge to enable them to listen to the European Cup Final while they also kept watch. We fixed the crew bar tape recorder and a new fault on the VHF. Then the broadcast receiver also failed, and I worked on it during one evening watch while Cyril manned the desk. Trying to fault-find around the main board and looking for test points I reached down and wiped away some thick dust from the chassis to try to read a label there. The electric shock made me cry out and recoil sharply across the room. After some choice words, from myself and a disturbed Cyril, I turned the receiver off and cleaned the label, to find it read 'Danger – chassis live!' More words followed as I cursed whoever had designed the evil device.

Recreation also included some elements of work. I had to run movie shows most evenings, setting up the projector and screen in the bar, ensuring each reel had been rewound ready for seamless changes, and repairing broken film at intervals which served like commercial breaks on TV, as opportunities for new refreshments. Sometimes there were other pitfalls. One film saw the hero killed and the titles rolling at the end of what had been marked at reel one, generating some derision and terminating the show early. Despite such unpredictability there seemed to be an insatiable appetite for repeat showings of our six films. This was partly an appreciation of the medium of cinema and equally another opportunity to sit in the bar in silence.

As the British and French medium wave stations started to fade away I became more familiar with calling Portishead Radio, choosing the best HF wave band and calling repeatedly until gaining a place in a queue. At first this worked well, as still being "local" in world terms seemed to give us an edge. Once we were half way to Panama this began to diminish until we were just one of many fading voices clamouring to be heard. While still working through Portishead when necessary for telegrams, I began to call American Coast Guard stations to clear the six-hourly '"OBS" weather messages. These seemed to be incredibly efficient, responding quickly to calls and communicating in immaculate Morse. San Juan, Puerto Rico (NMR) and Portsmouth, Virginia (NMN) became my new favourite stations for a while, especially at times when longer-range stations were relatively busy.

Across the Caribbean the seas became smoother and teemed with flying fish. The evenings were magical, luminous with background stars not normally visible on land, and decorated with unfamiliar constellations.

The uniform dress code changed to a combination I was unaware of, known as Red Sea rig. This was a compromise between the full jacket-and-tie uniform and tropical whites, consisting of the short-sleeved tropical shirt, open-necked, with dark trousers and shoes. Cyril and I wore uniform during the day and reverted to casual attire for evening work.

As we approached Panama, those of us new to the route stood outside at dawn to view the first visible land: islands and a peninsula to the northeast of the canal. We followed the coast and entered Cristobal harbour, bunkered (took on fuel) and waited to join the next day's convoy.

I was spared a well-known practical joke as first-timers were often told to collect food from the galley to feed the mules. In practice the mules are small electric locomotives which pull ships through the canal's locks. I was free to watch the green and wooded landscape as the ship spent the day slowly passing through the lakes and locks.

We sailed under a large bridge, past the tall buildings of Panama City and into the Pacific. The ship stopped for a while to complete an engine repair, having found that a part fitted in Avonmouth had been installed upside down. The Atalanta receiver delighted us with another new fault; a drive cord in the tuning mechanism had broken. I was half way through replacing it when the whole assembly collapsed and I had to rebuild it from scratch. Still, the next stop was New Zealand, which the Regulars continued to praise at every opportunity as we lounged in our newly-adopted tropical "whites" and looked out upon the Pacific.

Things became more relaxed for a while. A large-scale team darts match ended in a sea of alcohol. The Purser was first to retire at 1 am and somehow it was decided to fill his cabin with all the chairs from the dining saloon, which was easily accomplished without disturbing him. Next morning saw many severe hangovers, the Purser still trapped in his cabin and repeatedly phoning for help, and the Mate's wife angrily refusing to speak to him all day. The stewards rescued the Purser by taking all the chairs back to the saloon so they could serve breakfast. By evening dinner, the "hair of the dog" theory was being tested. It was my turn to buy the wine for my table of four. An engineer summoned a second bottle, and suddenly the others had ordered more and we polished them all off. I still managed to complete my evening watch, competently as far as I remember; perhaps I was becoming immune to this lifestyle's trappings already. Not so the engineer who initiated the flood of wine; he collapsed insensible onto a bench in the engine room during his subsequent watch and someone had to cover his work for him. Somehow the ship kept moving at a steady 20 knots.

This approach to alcohol consumption was mostly accepted on board, in contrast to today's restrictions and testing regimes. I was to find that drink played an even bigger part in daily life on most of my later ships. On this and every ship, people would meet in the bar before and after every meal as well as stepping into the bar for "quick ones" after their watches, and pass at least some of each evening in there too. They had few other options while at sea and most people found their own balance which still permitted them to work effectively. Inevitably a few people did not, and I was to sail with people who frequently drank one or even two bottles of vodka or gin per day. When running the bar, as I often did, I would see the evidence in stock levels and the barely legible chits or book entries left behind. At least it was visible and people knew of situations and when to provide assistance if anything urgent arose, unlike in the few instances I saw of senior officers clutching bottles while alone in their cabins. I actually saw very few instances of someone clearly unable to perform any of their duties as a result of alcohol, although an emergency may well have highlighted more. Being incapacitated would certainly not have been tolerated on any kind of frequent basis. Not from the junior officers, anyway.

On a similar subject, I never witnessed any drug or solvent abuse on ships, at least as far as I knew. There was smoking, just of tobacco, with cigarettes being cheap just as alcohol was. We non-smokers just had to put up with the occasional fug in the bar.

We reached the equator and I was due to be subjected to a Crossing the Line ceremony. On passenger ships this traditionally involves a friendly encounter with "King Neptune" and the presentation of a certificate; on merchant ships it is more likely to include some degree of humiliation. In my case, the occasion was scaled down to a requirement to buy drinks, and I took a proactive approach to head off the possibility of any unpleasant tricks. As we crossed into the southern hemisphere close to midnight only a few officers populated the bar, so I knocked on cabin doors and managed to lead some of the remainder into the bar for bleary drinks. I held a second "shout" before dinner the next day and that seemed enough for everyone. It was the most subdued marking of the occasion I would ever see, and that was probably something to be grateful for.

Gradually the radio stations of the Americas began to fade and the only options were long-distance ones. Company messages became sparse for a while but the OBS messages continued to flow, sometimes building up until we had two or three before successfully making contact and clearing them. I was reaching new stations all the time; Los Angeles (KOK) one day, Sydney (VIS) the next.

In addition to collecting and sending the weather data, ships kept a weather log including additional phenomena and wildlife, which was submitted to the Met Office at the end of each trip. It was known that the Met Office awarded prizes to the officers involved in producing and sending the best information, and a few years later I won a prize two years in succession. It was nice to receive some recognition, even if the awards did at least partially depend on the optimum combinations of people and actions, and of being in the right place at the right time. On this trip, however, some irreverent entries may have affected our chances. One evening's entry from the Third Mate read 'Deadly six-fanged two-horned man-eating twin-titted moth captured by that great deadly moth killer Dick.' A few days later he had completed his qualifying time as Third Mate and would be on Second Mate's pay from then on. The weather log, completed just before embarking on a late-night bar shout, read '3/O completed his time then went on the piss heavy.' Maybe all this was a good test of whether anyone ever read the books afterwards.

The airwaves became extremely quiet, and with nothing at all within range we began to punctuate the silence period entries in the log book with 'nil heard' every ten minutes or so. Sometimes we were actually glad to be presented with faulty radios or cassette players for investigation. We could still hear Portishead's traffic lists but making contact to actually receive the telegrams became challenging, taking up whole days and evenings of calling on different frequencies. I remembered the unmanned room I had seen when visiting Portishead and began to feel a sense of futility over even trying. I hit some kind of psychological barrier and my Morse began to disintegrate, as if I could not string the dots together unless there was some prospect of their being heard. At times this hit me hard, and for a week or so I dreaded sitting at a Morse key.

In addition to being quiet, it was also flat, empty, and at night very dark. Once past the Galapagos Islands two weeks elapsed before I saw more land. I spent some free time, and watch time, on the bridge talking with deck officers and crew to break up the days, and also consulting the nautical charts on the table. These showed huge numbers of islands as we passed through French Polynesia near the evocative-sounding Tuamotu Archipelago, all looking so tantalising on paper but remaining out of sight. The charts were also interesting for what they hinted at; there were numerous entries such as 'land reported, 1902' which we could only speculate on. Perhaps they were the result of navigational errors, or low islands were observed which had since become submerged by seismic movements. Whatever the truth, they were more places to avoid while crossing what appeared to be clear blue ocean.

After a week of almost total radio silence, one evening we suddenly heard a British ship on the calling frequency. They received no reply from the ship they were calling, so we replied and had a long chat with the R/O on a ship called *Larchbank* on its return voyage from New Zealand. We had no particular reason for calling them except it broke the monotony, for them as well as for us. Ships did not always just pass silently in the night.

Bank Line was another major British shipping line at the time and quite long-established, having been founded in 1905. All their ships' names ended in "bank", in this case preceded by trees and in a later class of cargo ships fish, e.g *Troutbank*. The company's later history was similar to that of P & O, of cargo ships being superseded by containers and of historic routes across the Pacific gradually shrinking. The company brand was sold in 2003 and its operations finally ceased in 2009.

As we sailed westwards we had been putting back the clocks, an hour at a time, and thus enjoying longer days without really being conscious of it. We would surrender these hours on our return voyage. Another such adjustment occurred when one day did not exist at all as we crossed the International Date Line. We went from being 12 hours behind GMT to 12 hours ahead, a situation we would reverse when sailing back towards Panama.

We began to hear faint Morse chatter in the evenings, indicating our closing in on busier shipping routes and our destination. It became easier to call regional HF stations too, and with this my Morse sending began to improve, helped further as local communication became possible. I was coming through the other side and feeling stronger for it; that strange affliction of my Morse would not happen again.

Another torment duly arrived, in the form of major seasickness. From the forecasts we continued to receive, severe weather had hit the Sydney area. Now it moved east and we sailed through it for about 36 hours, pitching heavily and rolling through a corkscrew motion which I now learned was a recognised issue with this class of ship. I managed to turn up for work but was clearly incapable of much and Cyril sent me back to my cabin to try to sleep through it. After a miserable day I finally managed to eat and hold down an evening meal and was never seasick again.

After one more day at sea we arrived in the port of Wellington, appreciating its setting in the bay and dreaming of the nightlife we had been promised. I was keen to get ashore and arranged an excursion along with the other junior officers and cadets. The response to this idea from the Regulars was 'Can't you set up the TV first?' Cyril and I battled with the aerial and the mysterious amplifier and managed to find some stations which appeared spectacularly uninteresting, but they seemed to be enough to please the old hands. It appeared that the Regulars' threshold for labelling somewhere a paradise was very low; just then it boiled down to "Not the Gulf" and "Got TV and beer".

Tekoa battles wild weather in the South Pacific

After taking a day off to see some of the sights of Wellington, some unexpected work appeared, and I was introduced to the purgatory of Admiralty corrections. Each radio room kept a set of manuals forming the Admiralty List of Radio Signals, which we used on an almost daily basis to find the correct frequencies for any radio station around the world. The details changed more often than might be thought possible and booklets of revisions were issued every week and sent to ships. Each change had to be literally cut out and glued over the old entry. This was quite tedious and time-consuming, and while almost welcome in some ports as something to do they were mostly the last thing an R/O wished to see. Obviously their arrival coincided with the ship reaching port and receiving mail, which usually also meant that any R/O leaving a ship might face the slightly awkward task of presenting their replacement with some corrections and explaining why they had not been done. Suddenly *Tekoa* received a backlog of several weeks' worth, not something my nineteen year old self was temperamentally well-equipped for but the power of delegation compelled me to spend a day over them. Nothing was ever fully accurate or complete, even afterwards, as I would find when trying to send an OBS to Bermuda on the return voyage. The station told me they had discontinued the service, and when I told Cyril of this he said they had stopped accepting these messages in 1963!

More corrections arrived, this time for ITU (International Telecommunication Union) publications, which required similar processing and I set aside some time each day for them.

It was then deemed a good time to paint the battery locker, which housed our backup power source for whenever the ship might be in distress and/or need to keep the emergency transmitter and receiver functioning after losing generator power. The batteries were large lead-acid units which had to be kept in good order by being topped up with distilled water and having their specific gravity checked regularly with a hydrometer. These were some of my routine tasks, and the reason my first and only boiler suit was becoming punctured with small holes from spilled acid droplets. We disconnected and removed everything and painted the walls and floor. When they were dry I painted the wooden shelves yellow, which was brighter than Cyril was expecting but it was at least clear we had taken a degree of care over the room. Eventually we installed the batteries again and tested the emergency equipment using them. It was all very workmanlike but not the stuff of travel dreams.

I was then offered more time off, for the purpose of finding girls to invite to a party. This was said to be the lot of someone on their first trip and at first I thought it was a new starter joke but found it to be serious. I suggested in turn that surely some of the Regulars must know people to invite, based on the stories they had told over the previous few weeks, but this was met with monosyllabic grunts and excessive concentration on whatever TV commercial was on. Cyril helpfully added that I would be working all weekend if I failed to find any ladies…

I went out and gave it my best shot, managing to chat a little with girls in shops, cafes and parks but never generating interest in ship visits or parties. I began to suspect that the Regulars' portrayal of life in New Zealand might have been based on the past, as either experienced or told, since until 1967 the pubs had closed at 6 pm and ships in port represented the only available nightlife and alcohol. Now the bars were open until the sinfully-late hour of 10 pm and people had found at least some options in the evenings in place of the binge drinking of the "six o'clock swill" and the quest for places to move on to afterwards. And perhaps I had not met the kind of girls I was expected to somehow find, especially during the day. When I returned to the ship I claimed to be awaiting phone calls and was met with no more than apathetic shrugs. I wondered if my task had been a prank after all, but there was no "gotcha" moment of laughter afterwards. At least Cyril did not follow through on his threat of weekend work.

Another surprise followed as two women actually did visit the ship, but of their own volition. The first I knew of them was when one saw me and addressed me by my predecessor's name, which had been a common and increasingly annoying issue with some of the Regulars earlier in the voyage. These ladies only seemed to remember that he had worn glasses, and once I had groaned dismissively they settled down to spend an evening talking with the Regulars. I gathered that they had been frequent visitors to ships in more lively times, and that this visit was to meet up with familiar faces for old times' sake. They at least managed to get some of the old hands talking, which was an achievement in itself.

In the circumstances we Newbies had to find our own entertainment. Friday night arrived and we learned with interest of a disco at the university, obviously a chance to meet people of our own age. We paid our admission, bought drinks and then stood in a large hall, gradually realising that it was a gay event. Also in contrast to the colour and fun of modern Pride events this was the most joyless function imaginable as people stood around barely muttering to each other, even less than we had seen in our officers' bar, or at funerals for that matter. We tried casually chatting to nearby people just to be sociable but this was clearly unwelcome. Then the music started and we edged closer to the dance floor where a group of more attractive ladies seemed to be visible. After some confusing exchanges, mainly thanks to the blind persistence of one of our cadets, the lyrics of the Kinks' song *Lola* gradually made more sense to us, and we decided to retreat.

Ever optimistic, we still relished the prospect of a Saturday night out in Wellington, but looked in on several pubs with rising disbelief at how quiet they were. We returned to the ship via a burger van at 9 pm, dropped in on the Purser's engagement party until even this ended at 10 pm. Determined to see as much as we could, five of us hired a car on the Sunday morning and drove out of town. We found a small wildlife park and then visited Waikanae, a seaside town about 40 miles north of Wellington. We drove back to drop off two engineers for their afternoon work shift, then took the car north again to the waterside city of Porirua for the evening. When we returned to the ship we found the Regular crowd gathered around the TV watching Morecambe and Wise, which at least left the bar clear for us to enjoy a nightcap and some relatively new background music.

A new week, and preparations for departure, reduced the scope for more travels and eventually we sailed for an overnight journey around the coast to Gisborne. This was of some historical interest as the location where Captain James Cook first set foot on New Zealand soil in 1769, although the settlement there predates this by up to 500 years. Cook was looking for fresh supplies but meetings with local Maori led to a number of their deaths and he sailed almost empty-handed, naming the area Poverty Bay. The port itself was very small, a single berth protected by twin breakwaters. A neighbouring hill featured two monuments to Cook's landing.

Tekoa alongside in Gisborne

Downtown seemed to match the port, with a single main street reminiscent of film sets for (very) small town America, a few shops and a couple of bars with pool tables frequented by men with nowhere else to be. Things improved in the evening as we learned of a hotel and music venue called the Sandown Park, which became our go-to destination. We enjoyed the live bands and the nightclub atmosphere over successive evenings, but unfortunately also discovered the "Kiwi" approach to drinking spirits, which was to buy jugs containing 26 tots and repeatedly fill and drink from shot glasses. Having left his new fiancée in Wellington the Purser showed us the way by consuming two such jugs of vodka in an evening. The rest of us discovered a drink called Jellybeans, which was made up from vodka, Bacardi, ouzo, raspberry cordial and lemonade. This tasted like a sweet and moreish soft drink which implied a degree of safety while getting us drunk very quickly. We thought we had learned our lesson after one evening there and enduring the following morning's suffering, but we returned for a second night, pointedly drank much less yet suffered all over again. On our third night there we limited ourselves to a couple of beers, chatted more with the locals and got invited to a party at closing time.

I was subsequently told that we must have been somewhere fancy to get the soft drinks mixed into the Jellybeans, and that more basic versions existed made up only of spirits. The latter sounded difficult to drink so much of, but that may have been a blessing.

I understand that the Sandown continued as a successful music venue throughout the 1970s and 80s, and I see from the *Setlist* web site that the well-known Australian band Midnight Oil performed there in 1979. Sadly it no longer exists but retains some lingering nostalgia. Archive pictures show some distinctive architecture with multiple towers. In 2020 an event called *Sounds of the Sandown* was held at another Gisborne venue, recreating the original place with a glass dance floor and the Sandown's original disco lights.

Two quiet days followed, punctuated with small jobs around the radio room, walks along the beaches and learning Mahjong, courtesy of the Second Mate's Japanese wife. Eventually the loading was complete and a sailing time set, then postponed for 12 hours due to high seas.

When we finally sailed, we met a heavy swell as soon as we passed the breakwaters, and after six hours of rolling we arrived at the port of Napier, docking near the foot of the prominent Bluff Hill. This feature was once practically an island, at the edge of a lagoon, until the land was raised during the disastrous Hawke's Bay earthquake of 1931. The timing of the quake and subsequent rebuilding explains the extent of the city's art deco architecture.

On the way we learned that Portishead had something for us, and tried unsuccessfully to contact them. Cyril tried again for three days while in port at Napier, which may have contravened regulations although he could cite some possible exemptions. By the fourth day the message had disappeared from Portishead's traffic list and become the one that got away.

We had more routine maintenance to do. I made checks on the radar and repaired some aerials and their supporting ropes and cables. The latter included making some eye splices for the first time since my Sea Cadet days, which was quite satisfying. These things completed, there was plenty of free time. I walked up and over Bluff Hill, travelled by bus out into the country and back, and enjoyed visits to the local night spots.

There was also an encounter with two company ships as both *Somerset* and *Tongariro*, the latter one of *Tekoa*'s sister ships, arrived in port. I went to visit the two R/Os on *Somerset* and the three of us went on to visit our counterpart on *Tongariro*. All this led to officers and cadets from both ships visiting *Tekoa* one evening for a large-scale darts match and social. More radio socialising took place after we sailed for Dunedin that evening, as we were called by *Taupo*, which was close to arriving in Fiji from Panama. We exchanged crew lists, one of the main outputs from these exchanges, and Roger and I exchanged some Morse chatter on the far side of the world from where we had started out.

After a full day at sea we arrived at Dunedin, sailing up a long sound and docking close to the city. Dunedin is named from the Scots Gaelic name for Edinburgh, and several place names within the city also indicate Scottish roots. It seemed a very likeable city with an identity of its own, and I regret only remembering the Seafarers' Centre and evenings at a couple of night spots. Close by was one of the company's older ships, *Huntingdon*, built in 1948, which was about to sail for scrapping in Taiwan. Cyril, the Purser and the Electrician visited it with lists of spares they hoped to bring away for use on *Tekoa*. Six hours later they returned, completely drunk and without any spares.

Another ship arrived which we recognised, a cargo ship called *Port Launceston* which had also been in Avonmouth, London, Wellington and Napier. We were operating on what was still a busy and close-knit trading route.

I had to tune the radar to eliminate some "spoking" around the display, after which we sailed for the Bay of Plenty, as named by Cook after a more successful landing, and the port described as Tauranga. I made contact with *Huntingdon* which had broken down three times since we saw it sail. We steamed up the coast through heavy seas, while learning that *Huntingdon* had broken down yet again and was stopping in Australia for repairs. Just getting it to the scrapyard must have been an expensive business.

There was some confusion over exactly where we had docked in our final port, resolved upon learning that the city of Tauranga is on one side of the bay and the Port of Tauranga is located on the other, at the town/suburb of Mount Maunganui. We had a day to make final preparations for the longer voyage back to Europe, and a cadet and I found time to walk through the top end of the town and three quarters of the way up the actual Mount, a small volcanic dome at the harbour mouth. I don't recall why we didn't go all the way to the top, and can only think that time must have been short. The not-quite-climbed

Mount torments me very slightly now when I see it in the background from televised cricket coverage nearby.

As we sailed and I watched the coast recede, two of the Regulars stood nearby at the rail. One of them sighed 'And there it be', and the other replied 'That was fantastic!' I just stared at them both in disbelief.

I don't wish to give the impression that I disliked New Zealand in any way; I did enjoy visiting it as a country with some beautiful landscapes and friendly people even if its small-scale cities and different pace of life took some adjusting to. It would probably have seemed even better if just taken as found rather than being misrepresented by a few people who were travelling there too often and for the wrong reasons.

Cyril and I kept longer watch hours to give me more experience, each working two four hour shifts per day and thus providing 16 hour coverage. I made radio contact with three more friends from college on their first ships; it was good to feel connected. The passage across the Pacific was uneventful and lacking the anticipation of the outward voyage. Even the charts were less interesting as we followed a slight loop to the south of our original route, eliminating any proximity to the islands. The weather was mainly cloudy as a series of depressions followed us.

Captain Holmes, who had been a loud but fairly benign presence so far, seemed to change in character as we closed in on Panama. He sent the Second Engineer to my cabin to rebuke me for not wearing uniform in his presence in the bar before dinner. I was on a different routine at the time and not going to dinner, and uniform in the bar had never been a requirement. There had been palpable tension in the bar, especially after the Captain's arrival, as the officers sat and stood waiting for the dinner gong, a sea of grim faces staring into the middle distance. Presumably the dinner did not improve matters and the Captain decided to assert himself that evening; and via someone else, who was clearly uncomfortable with the errand.

I was just signing off the final evening watch when he brought in a message for Portishead, loudly insisting it be sent 'Now!' Even I could see it was a message of no importance whatsoever but had to try, and since my experiences with Portishead were improving I managed to clear it in 45 minutes. In contrast to this level of supposed urgency, when some important engine parts were being requested he downgraded the message to an SLT which would have to be posted to the company from the radio station. Upon acknowledging receipt, the Portishead operator responded with 'P and O must be a cheap company to order urgent spares by SLT', and I could only reply that I didn't understand it myself either. When I delivered a newly-received message he took the opportunity to rebuke me for reading fiction on watch, or, as he put it, 'things that are never going to affect you.' I did read non-fiction too, but saying so would have made no difference; I was simply a visible and easy target. I gathered that his only interests were the news and particularly the stock market, neither of which seemed to bring him any happiness.

The Captain also put pressure on Cyril to relay a personal message to someone on *Somerset*, and we both faced complaints because we could not raise them. This was despite our publishing crew lists and gossip from several other company ships which proved we were tuning to the company "skeds", set frequencies and times for company ships to communicate, and trying our best. He appeared to have been away for too long, or perhaps the routine of the return voyage was having an effect.

If so, I was feeling something similar myself as I couldn't sleep and kept strange, almost nocturnal hours around my watch shifts for a while, hence my missing dinner. I also stopped drinking for a week, returning to very moderate beer consumption only after the bar ran out of soft drinks. This situation was a definite contrast with the outward voyage when we had run out of wine.

After seeing three of the Galapagos Islands on our way past we arrived off Balboa, Panama, and anchored with fifteen to twenty other ships until the evening convoy's departure time. We had passed through thunderstorms all day and now spectacular lightning illuminated the high-rise backdrop of Panama City. After Panama, we had a full European schedule on our way home: Santander, Dunkirk, Antwerp, Rotterdam and Hamburg before returning to the UK at Sheerness.

We approached northern Spain and I called a local station to check the local time, discovering we were still three hours behind them. The Captain refused to believe me and sent Cyril to make enquiries and confirm it before drastic changes were made to our clocks. I wrote my final news sheet, issue number 42, but the football reporting had to continue. Our main transmitter failed. As we tried to fix it I received my first distress message, a relayed one for a Greek ship on fire in the Channel.

On arrival in Santander we again tried to fix the transmitter, and then called in a local engineer. I had some free time in the afternoon and walked into town where a colourful fiesta was just starting. With some spontaneous confidence I ordered wine in a bar and somehow communicated with people there in fragmented words and gestures.

Our steering gear failed as we left the harbour that evening and we drifted for half an hour during repairs before taking on the often-unfavourable seas of the Bay of Biscay. Once under way I received another relayed distress message, about an overdue aircraft off southern Ireland. We rarely got to hear the outcome of situations like this. The main transmitter failed again, as did the Atalanta receiver, yet again. I fixed the receiver but we had to call in more help for the transmitter at subsequent ports as each fix seemed to lead to a new problem.

We were due to spend one day in Dunkirk, but the company reportedly declined to pay for Bank Holiday weekend overtime. This meant that once a Marconi engineer had left after attempting another transmitter repair the planned single day in port became four mostly lazy ones, sightseeing and discovering the charms of sitting outside French cafés and bars. Perhaps Portishead had been right about the company's financial outlook, but there were some upsides for us.

After sailing, Cyril and I worked busy evening watches with messages to and from multiple stations and a string of safety messages in addition to the routine preparations. A long passage up the River Scheldt followed and we docked early next morning right in Antwerp's old town. This stop of a few hours was extended due to a dock strike in our next port, Rotterdam, so after the customary Marconi visit to take away some transmitter parts for testing there was ample time to appreciate the city's historic architecture, and one or two bars.

Marconi returned next day, advising us of a definite fault they had found so they could now rebuild the transmitter. There was an unexpected addition to the bar in the form of a large old sofa, seemingly found by two officers at the end of a drunken night ashore and somehow carried back to the ship and up all the stairs. We sailed that evening and by the following morning the sofa had gone, presumably over the side as it was never seen again. I was just glad I didn't have to send any messages warning shipping of it, or receive any from small craft which had hit it.

At Rotterdam we sailed past the huge Europoort complex in the small hours and moved well upstream to dock at Merwehaven, just on the west side of the city centre. I phoned home from the mission and my parents thought I must already be in England and leaving the ship as P & O had told them I was due in Sheerness. In practice I still had two and a half weeks to go. There was no such confusion for Cyril whose son lived in Rotterdam, and he went ashore for a long visit.

I found some technical checks to do for the rest of the first day and could then enjoy a free day around the city, most notable for the unplanned moments. Soon after leaving the ship I found myself outside a football ground, and as wide gates were open leading through to a goalmouth I walked in. I met a member of the ground staff and learned that it was the home of Sparta Rotterdam, less well-known than their neighbours Feyenoord but the oldest professional team in the Netherlands and dead ringers for Sunderland whose strip they adopted in 1899. We stood on the pitch discussing football for a while. On my way back to the ship from town I remembered that Holland was supposed to be famous for its windmills and surprised myself by asking some people at a bus stop where I could find some. They directed me to a nearby suburb called Schiedam and told me which bus to catch. Upon arrival I walked along a canal enjoying the mills and the views. On my next trip I was able to lead colleagues there and they were impressed at my knowing my way around so well!

After going back to the mission in the evening to exchange a crate of paperbacks, we were under way again on a 24 hour passage to Hamburg. We spent two days there, including a Sunday but everyone's enthusiasm for going ashore was waning by now. I would become more acquainted with the city on subsequent visits, but for the time being we found some new work to do. The much-used and mistreated officers' bar cassette player had gone wrong and we managed to fix it but not before facing complaints over taking too long. Eventually Val Doonican and other similar cassettes were soothing the Regulars again…

Cyril decided we should paint the radar scanner, which sounded fine until he asked me to climb up and do it! I froze half way up the unprotected ladder and he took over and soon got the job done. I found such heights daunting on some older ships built with no consideration of safety. My later ships had protective hoops at intervals along the ladder and I became comfortable with these, but for the time being the scanner was a no-go area for me.

After another 24 hour passage we anchored off Sheerness, our final port. We knew we were going to have to wait, but not for how long. I optimistically collected all the S.E.S. library books and ticked them off the inventory sheets, and the Captain told me to put them back out. Tantalisingly we could see the port about two and a half miles away, and, more worryingly, the masts of SS *Richard Montgomery* only three quarters of a mile in the other direction. This was carrying a cargo of ammunition when it dragged its anchor and ran aground on 20th August 1944. Work was undertaken to remove its hazardous cargo but the hull cracked open after a month and around 1,500 tonnes of high explosive had to be left on board. There has always been some concern over the risk of a major explosion, and we were reminded of it every time we looked just across to the west. Even now, opinions seem to be divided over the likelihood of an incident.

We learned that we were due to unload after *Somerset* had done so; they had left New Zealand after us but were believed to be ahead of schedule. This made some sense until we scrutinised the port through binoculars and could not see its yellow hull. On day five at anchor, just as restlessness was really beginning to take hold, *Somerset* actually *arrived* and immediately docked in the port! We could have been in port for all that time.

Cyril and I had reverted to the minimum of eight hours of daily watch-keeping since anchoring, and we faced constant complaints about the TV reception. Being at anchor meant rotation with the tides, so it was impossible to keep an aerial pointing in the optimum direction, but explaining this was usually futile. We experimented with coat hangers and small portable aerials, and eventually the Purser calmed some of the crowd by bringing his own portable TV into the bar where people huddled around as if witnessing some new invention.

We began to devise new work to pass the time. We cleaned the battery room again and ensured the batteries were in still in perfect condition; painted the deck of our little workshop adjacent to the radio room; cleaned ceramic insulators within the aerial rigs; replaced a deteriorating aerial wire; tested survival equipment, and put through regular phone calls for everyone to phone home. Cyril found that I had quoted the Captain too high a price for his call home, by seven pence, and I was forced to go and tell him that he would be charged slightly less than expected. Breaking this news to most people might simply have led to dismissive laughter but perhaps inevitably not in this case as his angry response reverberated around the upper decks. I was surprised he had needed a phone at all.

A visit from Customs brought us a big batch of Admiralty and ITU corrections, which helped to pass a day or two, and also newspapers and, unexpectedly, badminton equipment. We set up a court in one of the cargo hatches which had been emptied in Europe and played round-robin games.

We heard from *Somerset* that they would be completing after a week, although even this was delayed by a bomb warning closing the port. We continued to keep watch and received another urgent warning, this time because red flares had been seen in the estuary, leading to someone being rescued from the water.

Finally we watched *Somerset* sail, and I collected all the films and, once again, the books. After twelve days at anchor we could dock and go home. The holds were opened and frozen lamb began to be lifted ashore. Visitors flooded the ship, unfortunately including Mr Merry. He rebuked us for not being in uniform despite our being packed and ready to leave. He praised the condition of the batteries, but when he learned they were mainly maintained by me he was disappointed and glared at me repeatedly anyway. Perhaps his depot was still untidy.

I got to meet Cyril's wife, in whose honour he had recently celebrated his 29th wedding anniversary. Cyril and I said goodbye; he told me to make him the villain in a future story. Sadly I still haven't done that, but I don't rule it out and perhaps suitable inspiration will strike one day.

For me it was quite a mixed trip in which I learned much and realised some of the things I didn't know. Despite one wobbly spell with the Morse I had handled the actual communications quite well, and been able to repair many unfamiliar items. On the other hand my lifestyle and outlook must have jarred with Cyril's, and I can't have been the easiest of colleagues for him at times. He had definitely earned a solo trip for his next voyage.

Leaving a ship was referred to as "paying off", a term dating back to a time when seafarers received all their due pay in a lump sum at that moment and promptly spent much of it in nearby dockside taverns. Payment methods had evolved, with salary payments into bank accounts, direct debits taking some of it away and overall finances becoming more even. Sailors were no longer likely, or even able, to blow all their earnings upon stepping ashore but the terminology remained.

We would pay off with time saved, too. The amount of paid leave appeared generous, although it included all the weekends spent on board in addition to the standard allowance. A five month trip would typically accrue around two months' leave, which was a more feasible time for a careless sailor to spend their savings. I was not the most thrifty of people at home or at sea but I did manage to save something, as well as funding some predictable things during my first leave: intensive driving lessons (and the successful driving test) plus a large new stereo. I was still nineteen, after all.

Despite all my pictures, letters and anecdotes there was still bafflement at home over what I did. Sometimes people had noticed fishing boats while on holiday and wondered if they might have seen me at work. Trying to describe the difference between a fishing boat and a cargo ship, even in terms of size, was futile. The shipping company's name seemed to be unknown, even as a passenger cruise business, in my landlocked area and when I spelled it people assumed the Post Office was involved, and not just in the Ministry name on my ticket. Mentioning the Merchant Navy evoked nothing more than vague notions and if anything the second word was latched onto, along with questions of how many years I had signed up for. Saying it was just a normal job was not what anyone expected to hear. Ultimately I became defined by two questions, frequently asked each time I returned from a trip: 'How long are you home for?' and 'When are you going away again?'

9 Somerset

m.v. Somerset Refrigerated Cargo Liner

Built: 1963, Clydebank

Tonnage: 7,602 (gross), 4,056 (net), 10,256 (deadweight)

Dimensions: Length 488'3" (148.81m), beam 66'4" (20.21m), depth 41'0" (12.49m), draught 28'2" (8.58m)

Origin of name: English county (naming ships after counties was an old "Federal Steam" tradition)

I had to wait a long time for my second ship. I had completed four and a half of my probationary six months, and was keen to complete the remainder. I asked Personnel for another ship as soon as possible, and the response was non-committal along with a comment that I would have to pass the radar exam before being promoted. This was a blow as it had not been stated before. It shaped some of my plans, yet I later learned that the person who said this was very junior and that it was not actual company policy.

As the end of my leave arrived, in mid-November, I phoned Personnel again and was told I had leave until the end of December! This was a mystery, or almost certainly an error, but I could only enjoy the extra time at home. In early January they sent me joining instructions for a ship called *Strathnevis*. These were amended a week later with a joining date at the end of the month and an itinerary of British ports followed by several around India. Another week passed and another letter arrived, this time assigning me to *Somerset*, which had been to New Zealand and back again while I was on leave. When I phoned Personnel to confirm I was told that *Strathnevis* was being assigned a newly promoted First R/O and that he might not be ready to mentor a junior.

I was beginning to realise that this kind of uncertainty was the norm, and that nothing was definite until boarding the ship or plane. I would experience sagas like this again, long spells of vagueness and inactivity followed by requests to drop everything and get myself to a port or to Heathrow immediately. Finally, four and a half months after leaving my first ship, I travelled back to Sheerness to join my second.

Somerset was only three years older than *Tekoa* but the accommodation seemed to date from an earlier generation with single cabins and communal toilets and showers. I met my new boss, Brendan, and immediately Mr Merry arrived on board and began asking us questions about the radio room. We knew nothing ourselves yet, which displeased him, and we spent a large part of a day checking equipment and listing the many faulty items we had been left with. This led, several days later, to a Marconi engineer spending two days on board working on the main transmitter, both receivers, radar, depth sounder and lifeboat transmitter. We were presented with a brand new Apollo receiver, a familiar sight which despite being maligned at college proved reliable and good to operate in comparison to *Tekoa*'s older sets and the similar one we had just been relieved of.

I felt I was gaining experience all the time, yet I could feel my lack of worldly knowledge after taking myself on the train to London to see a football match. On my return a steward greeted me with 'Hello Sparky, been up the smoke?' I was nonplussed and he had to explain what "the smoke" meant.

Sheerness in January was cold and grey, with a biting wind which made even walking to and from the shops an endurance test. The pubs seemed to offer little ambience, entertainment or even warmth, so one evening five of us crammed into the Third Mate's Volvo sports car, which seemed to be made for only two and a half people, and drove to a night club across the island. This seemed more promising, with a show from a comedian and then the beginning of a disco, as actual crowds of people enjoyed a night out. Then the club announced that there had been a bomb scare and that the place had to be evacuated. People milled around outside and we decided our evening was over. The following day someone was having a haircut and told the barber about our night out. The barber told him that the club was known to stage bomb scares to clear the place when they had made their takings, and that perhaps it had happened too often for someone since the place had burned down overnight.

We spent twelve freezing days in Sheerness; Brendan wisely only stepped ashore once, to accompany me to a bookshop I had found. On our last day the Marconi engineer returned with more new equipment, and we entertained him with well-earned beers before preparing for the ship to sail. Our next destination was South Shields, for some maintenance work in dry dock. As on my first trip we got time signals and weather information, sent a TR message and planned our watch hours for the evening and the day at sea which followed. Brendan and I seemed to agree on things and we worked easily together.

We sailed up the North Sea, sending messages to the coast stations along the route, Humber and Cullercoats. After anchoring overnight we headed up the Tyne and into the dry dock. First impressions were poor, which I had found the norm so far in British ports. There was a view of docks up the river on both banks as far as one could see, punctuated with cranes, partially-demolished buildings and tangled heaps of scrap metal. People challenged the Geordies on board over their wistful portrayals of the place.

Yet it gradually worked a spell, winning us over with its people, atmosphere and nightlife. I remember the Britannia and Voyager pubs, and the Tavern and Chelsea Cat nightclubs. The latter appears to be famous for hosting many big acts in the sixties, with an emphasis on blues rock, including Rory Gallagher, Family, Cream, and even Jimi Hendrix for one night in February 1967. No such "names" or future stars performed when we were there as far as I recall, but they were good nights anyway.

Somerset in dry dock, South Shields

The ship had two echo sounder projectors, or transducers, and we had to use the time in dry dock to inspect these from above and below. The first task meant going to the bottom of cargo hatches number 2 and 4; we found one unit needed water pumping out while the other was still watertight. Next, we had to descend into the actual dry dock where we felt tiny next to the size of the ship and concerned by it being supported by piles of bricks which looked less secure than we would have liked. There was about a metre of space between keel and dock floor and we had to crouch down and crawl around under the ship to locate the sounders' metal plates and confirm their condition. It was daunting but we managed to find them before returning to the surface as quickly as possible.

The dry dock, Brigham & Cowan's, closed in 1982 and is now the centre of a housing development named Captain's Wharf. Two nearby dry docks have also been surrounded by housing, one retaining its water while the other has been filled in.

As at Sheerness, Brendan only stepped ashore once. I accompanied him and we found the beach and the Roman fort and museum. Thereafter we prepared to sail for London, and when the time arrived the dry dock took five hours to flood. Two cadets who lived locally made a late visit to the ship and became stranded when the gangway was raised; they had to be hoisted off by crane and bucket. One of the locally-born officers propped up the bar and told everyone of his lifelong dream, about to be realised, of sailing out through the Tyne breakwaters. When we finally moved out of the Tyne into heavy seas at midnight, he had passed out in the bar and missed the big moment.

The ship rolled heavily in the North Sea, and in the morning we monitored a distress situation. Brendan was woken up by the auto alarm bell in his cabin at 5 am and from then on we heard a total of eight relayed distress calls in Morse and on the equivalent telephony frequency, advising of a small Polish ship in difficulties. In this kind of situation ships were obliged to minimise any other radio traffic but a nearby Greek ship earned repeated rebukes from the main Dutch and Belgian stations, Scheveningen and Ostend, for persistently trying to transmit. By midday a Russian trawler had reached the stricken ship to provide assistance. I note from subsequent records that the ship in question was 'delivered free of charge' afterwards and then operated by a different shipping line for many more years.

After a quieter afternoon we sailed up the Thames, logged off after passing Tilbury, watched one of the company's ships, *Manapouri* pass on its way out towards New Zealand, and eventually docked in Royal Albert.

A Government inspector arrived and passed all our gear except the auto alarm. These highly mechanical devices were proving particularly prone to failures. We endured repeated visits from Marconi and Mr Merry's even-more-sour assistant, the latter trying to test the auto alarm, pronouncing it still faulty and calling Marconi back again. The engineer said it was working perfectly, as did the inspector and we gained approval.

The stay in London took days longer than planned, and the main reason for this seemed to be because some of our cargo was whisky. When this became known to the port workers, cases were smashed open and drunken dockers lurched around the decks and wharves. Some sacrificial cases were left out for them to find in the hope that the rest of the cargo would be safely loaded, but the second part of the plan was not entirely successful. Stories abounded of artificial "drinking rooms" and access corridors made in the holds by artful positioning of the crates which had actually made it on board. The stevedores in the movie *On the Waterfront* complained of having to work on too many banana boats and dreamt of handling a boatload of whisky; their dreams would have been more than fulfilled on the *Somerset*! One day ended with the Mate exclaiming furiously, and very publicly, that only 50 tons of cargo had been loaded, a pitifully small amount.

At this point I had to say goodbye to Brendan and to other colleagues who had only been covering the UK coast. My new boss, Paul, was a Cornishman a few years older than me who carried an air of seniority while remaining approachable. However he was a little wary of me at first and it turned out that he had been warned about me by Mr Merry. This led to our having a long discussion to clarify things, especially those which Mr Merry seemed to have made up. While subsequently working in Wellington we were regularly amused by a daily radio show's segment called *Air Your Beef*, in which residents could phone in their grumbles and the best complainant won a brace of chickens. I was tempted to call in and rant about Mr Merry, although I don't know what I would have done with the chickens.

Some of the deep-sea officers were making return trips to New Zealand like those on *Tekoa*, which concerned me at first but they were a younger crowd who maintained a relaxed atmosphere on board. At first this seemed to apply to the newly-joined Captain Harris too, and after Paul and I had rigged up his personal radio aerial he invited us and some other officers for drinks in his cabin. However he proved quite erratic in nature as the trip unfolded.

As we sailed out of the Thames, Captain Harris decided he would like to make a personal telephone call, a fairly infrequent request on ships like ours and surprising as we had only just left port and it was 10 pm, the usual end of watch-keeping hours. We wondered what he could have left switched on at home. It took us an hour to get a response from a coast station and have the call connected, after which he told us we were to provide 16 hour cover, eight hours each per day. On the next day he reversed this and told us to cover just eight hours.

This coincided with a reminder of our main, safety-related, role at sea, as we received two urgency messages within as many minutes. One was for a British cargo ship, *Wittering*, which had collided with a container ship. It later sank near Beachy Head, with fourteen crew picked up by the Hastings lifeboat. The other was from a French station advising of a missing trawler nearby, and soon afterwards a search plane passed overhead.

The auto alarm failed three times in one night, understandably irritating Paul as the alarm bell was in his cabin, and we spent a long day trying to find the cause. We decided it was something mechanical for which we carried no suitable spares, and carefully took it apart while cleaning contacts and bending armatures. This seemed to fix it except for our having to repeat the process in New Zealand. The Apollo receiver began to cause concern as one of its digital numbers kept blanking out, and eventually the same kind of mechanical cleaning as with the auto alarm seemed to clear the fault. All this was probably good preparation for the computer and printer faults of a later age.

Once in the Atlantic, darts became a dominant recreation on board, much more so than on *Tekoa*. As well as the usual casual games there were matches between teams of officers, and between officers and crew, with hospitality in one bar returned in the other. There was a league and a knockout competition, a large-scale "Around the Clock" competition and an even larger-scale challenge involving multiple random targets and accumulated scores for hitting them with darts. Paul was tasked with drawing up tournament fixtures. A table tennis league was formed, between ten of us, and a table set up for a while. Deck golf also became popular as the weather improved, particularly in the Panama Canal and beyond.

The captain forbade the change into Red Sea rig as he personally disliked it, and people complained for a few days until permitted to transition directly into full whites. We saw the hat-shaped Sombrero Island, passed the Virgin Islands and saw the cruising *Queen Elizabeth II*, or *QE2*, in the distance. The latter attracted much attention and Paul and I heard their R/Os responding to friendly calls from a number of nearby ships, including a British warship.

Arriving at Panama we docked in Cristobal to take on more fuel, which also provided an opportunity to go ashore for a look around. It was the less-developed end of the canal but at least enabled us to say we had set foot in that country. After bunkering we moved to an anchorage overnight before passing through the canal, the transit punctuated by deck golf and a darts tournament. Once in the Pacific the weather became much warmer, with calm blue seas.

Somerset alongside at Cristobal, Panama

The fine weather was an invitation to sunbathe, and I went outside with a pillow and one of my cabin's spare blankets. Captain Harris saw me and told me I should get a 'proper' blanket for the purpose from the Purser. The Purser had nothing different and said I should use what I had. The captain still forbade me to sunbathe, which annoyed me and mystified my colleagues who also planned to use the same blankets. From the following day we all simply made sure he did not see us setting off outside. I gained some covert revenge on the Captain about three days later when I found him sunbathing, on a standard blanket, on the bridge wing, which must have been an unpleasant sight for the officers on watch. I took a picture of him spread-eagled on the deck, his huge stomach obscuring his trunks and giving the impression, God forbid, that he was lying there naked.

When this picture was developed in New Zealand it caused much amusement around the ship, and fortunately he never saw the picture himself.

He also became very agitated over our broadcast receiver. Despite the radio he had brought on board himself and our setting up an aerial for him, he chose to listen to the BBC via the communal system, which could relay into the cabins whatever the radio room's broadcast receiver was tuned to. We tried to keep the receiver tuned to the BBC World Service but while on watch we were not normally listening to it ourselves, and different times of day or night meant changing to different wave bands. He frequently burst into the radio room while we were dealing with actual work messages, angrily complaining about the radio reception and trying to adjust the tuning himself. This was a feature of the outward and return voyages, becoming virtually intolerable later.

Crossing the Pacific we saw two of the Marquesas Islands, presenting high faces of rock. A few days later there was a reminder of the phantom islands I had noticed before on the charts. We observed an island where the chart suggested there should not have been one, even after some hasty checks of the calculations which fixed our position. There was no satellite navigation yet, and the navigational systems relying on land-based radio beacons did not extend to where we were, so our position was based upon traditional sextant sightings and the mathematics which followed them. In poor visibility there was always dead reckoning, extending existing pencil lines further along the chart and making educated assumptions. The bridge was quite certain of our position. One of the cadets present claimed to have seen the island first and suggested it be named after him.

Our schedule featured stops in Apia (Samoa), Suva and Lautoka (both Fiji) before unloading our general cargo in Wellington. Before reaching Apia we were told to cancel our stop there and head direct to Suva. Presumably relaying Apia's cargo from there was more cost-effective. Or perhaps there was no longer enough whisky for everyone. The remainder of our schedule unfolded: from Wellington to Picton and Timaru, returning via Panama to Dunkirk, Antwerp, Rotterdam and Avonmouth.

The sighting of islands became more frequent as we closed in on Fiji, and one morning we docked in its capital and main port, Suva. Beyond a busy market this was as verdant and lined with palm trees as we had imagined. Fiji had a reputation for being a good place to buy a wristwatch, and several of us went shopping, going from one shop to another in search of the best deal. Eventually I bought the seafarer's default watch of that time, a Seiko 5, for what seemed to be a good price. This accomplished, we spent a predictable amount of time visiting bars and a nightclub, returning to the ship very late.

When I woke up the ship was already on its 120 mile passage around Fiji's main island to the smaller port of Lautoka. After two short radio watches we arrived, gazing upon sapphire blue seas and green hills stretching towards clear sky. We expected to anchor until a French ship left, but found we had beaten it to the port by a few minutes and were admitted instead. There was time for a short trip ashore to stroll through a smaller-scale version of Suva's retail district and buy small gadgets. Back on board I went to my cabin for an early night at 9 pm, and woke after midnight as the ship was under way again.

A heavy swell prompted everyone to refer to the weather as New Zealand's first line of defence, but we battled through and reached the shelter of Wellington's fine harbour. We still saw the evidence for its being known as "Wet and Windy Wellington" at times. Following my first visit my expectations for the stay there were low, but being there with a more sociable and well-connected group of people meant that this time there were parties, on board and ashore.

The Met Office visited us one day and invited us back for a look around. The ship we had seen leaving London, *Manapouri* was in port at the same time and after the inevitable darts challenge we played them at football too. An additional match was arranged against another nearby ship.

Live music was also a significant feature of our stay. The singer Melanie was due in town, and the local radio station mentioned her every day. Despite her being a big name at the time, thanks to hit songs including her emotive cover of the Stones' *Ruby Tuesday* and her own *Brand New Key*, each radio feature ended with the playing of a song called *Alexander Beetle*. This novelty song about a little girl losing and finding her pet beetle, punctuated with some quirky high-pitched calling sounds, was evidently the main reason she was celebrated in New Zealand, and we rolled our eyes every time it was played. Despite this, and since I knew and liked several other songs of hers, I bought a ticket to the show and duly sat in the Town Hall stalls as she performed with a full band. After about half an hour she made a near-fatal error and asked the audience for requests. There was a tumult of cries for *Alexander Beetle*, and when these had died down a surprised Melanie said 'All right, let's get the little children over with first!' The song was played, there was huge applause, and large sections of the audience began filing out of the theatre. Melanie called out 'Hey I haven't finished yet!' but she lost about a quarter of the crowd, who presumably went home happy regardless. She recovered to play the remainder of an excellent two hour set, but I wonder if she ever did requests again, at least there.

The other live show of note was that performed every night by a band called Mother Goose, at the Lion Tavern. These were a catchy rock band whose shows included some novelty songs and comic routines, their quirky style not at all out of place in New Zealand then, having much in common with early-era Split Enz. Each band member dressed in distinctive costumes, with varying degrees of success: sailor, ballet dancer, baby, pixie, bee and mouse, before Village People became successful with a similar approach. Dropping in to see them became an essential part of evenings out, and I saw them seven times within two weeks before their residency ended. They went on to release three albums, and the Australian bands Men at Work and Midnight Oil, both later to become much better-known, opened for them on tours. YouTube has a video of their best-known song, *Baked Beans*, which sums up their style as well as offering a nod to the choral section of Queen's *Bohemian Rhapsody* and perhaps paving the way for Paul Young and Streetband's song *Toast*!

Finally we left Wellington and followed the route of the North to South Island ferry, to the small port of Picton. This lies surrounded by hills at the head of Queen Charlotte Sound, now co-named Totaranui, a fjord-like inlet from the Cook Strait.

After briefly investigating the town's three pubs our attention turned to the water. Ten of us took one of the lifeboats out for an afternoon around the sound, carrying several cases of beer. We stopped and relaxed at a picnic spot and then sailed further out towards Cook Strait. At the furthest point from the ship the engine failed, and the combined efforts of the engineers on board failed to restart it. We were carrying portable radios from the ship but seemed to be out of range. Eventually we managed to flag down a passing cabin cruiser and ask the family on board for a tow back to the port, for which we gave them a case of beer.

A Danish ship was berthed beside us and, as ever, we invited them over for a darts match. Fixtures for games were drawn up and we were soon comfortably ahead. Then

I found that my match was against their nineteen-year-old female R/O, and as I threw a double and began to score it became clear that she had never played before. I said she could start without needing a double, which was seen as a nice, harmless gesture since I was soon aiming for my own double to win the game. Somehow the winning double just would not happen, and after several very near misses on my part she had one wobbly throw at a double herself and made it! After huge cheers of derision (from my ship) and delight elsewhere, I was surrounded by Danes hugging me, shaking my hand and saying things like 'You are lovely bloke, thank you for letting her win!' I went along with the celebrations. Part of me felt crestfallen but I was also slightly pleased at the kind of sporting upset people enjoy, at least when it happens to someone else.

It was decided that I should help one of the electricians to carry out some routine maintenance in the engine room, stripping down motors, cleaning them and rebuilding. I spent two days down below, emerging looking extremely dirty each day while my white boiler suit became unrecognisable. The company issued boiler suits at intervals, with engineers and deck officers receiving six at a time. R/Os only got one, and mine for that year was unusual in becoming less than pristine; my working in the engine room could not have been anticipated. Later I was told off for wearing a dirty boiler suit on lifeboat drill, although I still only had one and was expected to wear it then. I tried to wash it and was told the washing machines in the accommodation were off limits for boiler suits, which had to be washed in the engine room. I could not enter the engine room to wash it without wearing a boiler suit, so it remained dirty and it was suggested I was somehow being difficult.

Modern health and safety did not really exist at the time, even at a basic and uncontroversial level. I don't recall seeing many safety boots, other than those worn by the engineers when working on heavy equipment "below". I ruined a pair of plimsolls in the engine room, a situation unimaginable today when boots would be mandatory. I have pictures of officers and crew working on deck in boiler suits and ordinary shoes, or shorts and plimsolls, and rarely if ever wearing hard hats even though each cabin did actually have one provided. Life jackets were donned for statutory lifeboat drills but never for casual boat trips which covered much greater distances. Harnesses for high working were unknown; I would have welcomed access to one. I also have a picture of two crewmen on one of my ships suspended overboard on a small platform to repaint the draught marking numbers on the bow, each wearing just their shorts and holding the supporting ropes with one hand.

We sailed out of the sound and down the South Island coast. Within 24 hours we had docked in Timaru, an agricultural town built on the lava flows of a nearby extinct volcano, Mount Horrible, supposedly named after a surveyor was asked about his day in the hills. We took on a full cargo of lamb from mechanical loaders which loomed over the ship's decks. The town seemed smaller than expected and perhaps, as per Hamburg on my previous trip, we were looking ahead and less inclined to explore the last port. There was controversy some years ago when it emerged in a book that two British Lions rugby players had given unflattering quotes about the town after playing there on tour. These referred to tumbleweed and the lack of entertainment available, and may suggest that the team saw even less of the town than we did. In response, local food and drink producers were photographed promoting their products, aiming to show the town in a better light.

It was certainly not the most bustling or lively town but in addition to the usual facilities we found a pub which stayed open after closing time, made visits to a very good seaman's mission and enjoyed a superb meal in a restaurant called Sorrento. They returned a good tip, saying they did not accept them. I always found the food in New Zealand excellent, from the burger vans to the restaurants. I was sent down the engine room once more to work on another group of motors and unusually worked along the propeller tunnel for a while. After a separate task connecting aerial fittings to the top of the funnel, I could definitely say I had seen the ship from top to bottom, inside and out.

We sailed into two days of heavy seas, punctuated with falling objects until every loose item had been safely stored or wedged into corners on the decks. We crossed the Date Line, living the same date twice over. This happened to be one officer's 21st birthday and he talked of forming a special club for people who had had two of them.

We followed a southern route back across the Pacific, distant from any islands. We sailed close to the Oceanic Pole of Inaccessibility, the point in the Pacific Ocean furthest from the nearest land (an uninhabited reef 1,670 miles away in the Pitcairn Islands group), feeling very conscious of our isolation from the human world and of how limited our outside options might be in an emergency.

Three days before Panama, our Refrigeration Engineer was taken ill and diagnosed with appendicitis. Paul and I became busy with medical messages from Panama which advised getting him to a hospital within 24 hours. This was not feasible although the ship did manage to speed up to 17 knots in an attempt to arrive more quickly. The situation was serious not only medically but because the "Frosty" tended to carry sole responsibility for the safe transit of refrigerated and frozen cargo, with failures being highly expensive for the company and career-threatening for the individual. Engineers doubled up to cover his duties. Paul and I provided round the clock radio cover, 6 hours on and 6 off while sending updates and continuing to receive medical advice. Finally we anchored off Balboa and a launch arrived to take the patient ashore. Soon afterwards he was back, now diagnosed with acute gastroenteritis which was easing already. The emergency was over.

The Caribbean and Atlantic brought sunny weather and we held a final boat drill, this time in tropical whites so I was spared more boiler suit shame. A final darts tournament was held over a week or so and I made the semi-final. We changed back into full uniform. The captain demanded extra weather forecasts and coded analysis, as if suspecting the fine conditions were some kind of trick. He also demanded Radio 2 on the broadcast receiver, with occasional changes to the World Service for their *News About Britain* feature. When two officers challenged all this during a ship management meeting, he grew angry and demanded we set equal times for Radios 1, 2, 3, 4 and Luxembourg, and with different times every day! I had to draw up a complicated schedule which he rejected before accepting a revised version and apologising for his demands. Somehow we also found time to keep handling the ship's business messages and other necessary information, even if they had become of secondary importance to our captain.

The stressful situation with the broadcast radio continued. I went ashore in Dunkirk to make some phone calls at the mission, leaving the set tuned to Radio 3 as per the schedule. On the way back I met Paul and four other officers who were returning after passing the afternoon in a bar. We found that the ship had been moved along the dock by about five feet, and the gangway was still up. Paul realised it had been forgotten after the move, reached the rail and climbed up in order to lower it from above. The spectacle was not exactly Kirk Douglas in *The Vikings* but effective. The Mate was greatly angered by this and remonstrated with him. The Captain arrived, complained about the radio, which I had been unable to adjust while stranded on the wharf, and then accused *me* of lowering the gangway! Having restored the radio to the schedule I passed the evening in the bar and at nearly midnight I went to retune the set ready for the morning. The Captain promptly appeared and complained again as he was still listening to it. He seemed to be maintaining an almost full-time vigil.

As we reached Rotterdam we went to set Radio 2 as per the schedule and found the Captain had been in the radio room and removed the fuses from inside the set! This was intended as some kind of statement, since he had now decided he wanted the station earlier than planned and chosen to sabotage the set rather than just ask for another change. We managed to avoid saying much in response, knowing everyone's sympathies were already with us anyway but especially after he made a failed attempt at humour in the officers' bar. He put up a notice which was meant to be a jokey comment but his words only baffled people, and the fact that he had meticulously crafted it all in "Olde English" calligraphy, which must have taken long enough for reflection, made it even more bizarre. It somehow took us a while, even after recovering the fuses, to say to ourselves 'Just a minute, he's also got his own radio!' Given where we now were, he could receive medium wave stations himself at any time, if only he tried. It made the situation seem even more strange but no less annoying.

Later I had cause to wonder if Captain Harris had been ill and whether taking medication might have influenced his behaviour. A year or so after this voyage there was a notice in the company magazine announcing his death. I think he was about 60. I was to have similar thoughts of some other captains during my career, upon witnessing disturbing character traits often supplemented by excess alcohol. Their presence on the bridge was often that of an irritable back-seat driver. By contrast I usually found Chief Engineers, their equivalents in seniority, to be relatively well-adjusted. The latter had risen within a more collaborative environment and were seen as the ultimate point of reference and knowledge in their field; this meant recognising the need to maintain that knowledge and continue to learn, each ship having some differences from others. This must have differed in some way from how progression sometimes occurred within the deck environment.

We sailed back through the Channel and around to Avonmouth. Paul and most of my deep-sea colleagues left, while I remained on board for another ten days. Paul's replacement arrived but he did not recognise some of the equipment and I had to host the Government inspector and demonstrate everything. I had far exceeded my six-month "time" by now (I was closing in on ten) and felt in control of everything except perhaps a broadcast receiver and rogue captain combined. Even the newly-reacquainted Captain Holmes, having relieved Captain Harris, seemed happy with my work on board.

I went to Brunel to enquire about the radar course and took the last available place, paying the £40 fee on the spot. At the time I thought securing this was fortunate, but later I was not so sure. A short search for new term-time accommodation followed.

Staying on the ship for longer also enabled me to host a string of visitors from my college days again and to attend some conveniently-scheduled social events in Bristol. Some of my friends brought bad news; Andy had been made redundant after one full-length trip and Roger after two shorter ones. Both decided to take new jobs away from the sea. I can only think I survived through being away at sea on a crucial decision date while they were home on leave.

The contraction of the fleet was already under way, with staff reductions to match. These were not usually announced; people had to interpret the shrinking lists of ships and personnel circulated by the company. I went home for a long summer of leave, and it would be eight months before I joined another ship, something very different and unexpected.

10 Dwarka – New Lands

m.v. Dwarka   Passenger/Cargo Liner
Built: 1947, Newcastle
Tonnage: 4,851 (gross), 2,672 (net), 4,525 (deadweight)
Dimensions: Length 398'7" (121.48m), beam 54'9" (16.68m), depth 41'0" (12.49m), draught 27'0" (8.23m)

Origin of name: Coastal town in Gujarat, India

After my return from mostly-unpaid study leave in Bristol I made myself available for duty and my Personnel contact, Marie, recorded me as an available First R/O. This seemed only right as I knew another of my college friends had already been promoted (by Marconi) before returning to college to attempt Radar again.

Time passed, and I wondered if I should have made myself available while still at college, and thus become salaried sooner. My Radar results duly arrived, confirming my failure and signed with a civil servant's illegible signature. I had to choose whether to keep it quiet and risk redundancy upon being found out, or confess all and risk the same. After some deliberation I decided on honesty and told the company. Two more weeks drifted by and I received a large envelope which I was relieved to find contained only company notes and pension scheme information. Assuming this was a slightly encouraging sign I phoned Marie again. She told me I would be flying to Dubai at the end of February (another month away) to join *Dwarka* as Second R/O.

I knew *Dwarka* was one of the company's oldest ships and that it followed a fixed run between India and the Gulf. Its notoriety within the company had somehow passed me by. It was another ship for me, which was something to be celebrated in itself, and on a different run, so I looked forward eagerly to the experience. Remaining a "second" did not concern me at all just then.

Another two weeks went by and I heard from Marie again. 'Are you in a good mood?' she asked. I half-expected a change of ship, or to hear redundancy mentioned after all. In fact they had sent out my joining instructions, but to my very old Bristol address (where I had last lived two years earlier, and the rodent-infested owners forwarded nothing), and in anticipation of my acceptance telexed Bombay to advise them that I was flying there next day! She was pleased and perhaps relieved when I agreed to do this, and I noted the details of the flight from Heathrow.

I recognise that Bombay has since been renamed, but to write of the city as Mumbai in 1977 would also seem slightly incorrect. I believe some people who call Mumbai home still refer to it as Bombay among themselves, and using its old name here, which is how I knew it then, seems more appropriate to me.

A frantic day of shopping, packing and travel followed and I boarded a British Airways 747 for an overnight flight via Bahrain. I studied clusters of oil well flames in the desert and marvelled at the bright lights of Baghdad on either side of the meandering River Tigris. By dawn the second leg of the flight took me over Dubai and the Gulf of Oman, and I looked upon wide blue sea and the occasional tiny shapes of ships far below.

Cloud cover built over the Indian Ocean and the plane descended through it to offer a first view of the sub-continent. I saw brown, silted rivers looping across parched agricultural land, and villages with clusters of square buildings, roofs as brown as the landscape. A circular pass, low over the city, was made and I picked out the Gateway of India monument, its arch a prominent landmark on the Bombay water front. Eventually the plane landed smoothly, and it was announced that the temperature was 77 degrees Fahrenheit. I wore my jacket to leave the plane but the humidity was an instant shock. Perspiring heavily, I soon removed and carried it through the airport, along with my considerable hand baggage. Worse, I was also bearing a raincoat, a legacy of England in February and now an extra dead weight.

I spent over an hour completing forms, receiving half of each paper back, gaining ink stamps, battling for baggage, being searched by Customs (lightly, once they knew I was joining a ship) and repeatedly asking for the shipping agents as I passed through Immigration and among all the people who seemed to mill around the building. The agents were a well-known company dating back to 1847 and closely associated with shipping in the region ever since.

'Mackinnon Mackenzie?' I asked over and over, falling back upon the traditional English method of communicating in other countries. 'MacKINNon MacKENzie?'

After a while one of the airport staff understood and translated. 'Ah, MACKinnon MACKenzie!' The different syllable stresses made a difference. He waved towards a crowd behind a tape barrier and a casually-dressed local man approached, smiling and nodding in what I took to be recognition. We greeted each other, a clash of very different accents but finding we could communicate quite well.

'Can we get out now?' I asked him.

'Soon. This is much quicker than usual,' he replied.

Eventually I received my final piece of paper, handed it to yet another official twenty yards away and stepped outside. The agent promptly ran down the crowded street in search of a taxi while I struggled with my bags a long way behind.

I thought getting into a taxi was the end of the trial, but soon learned the realities of road travel into the city. The taxi swerved between stationary vehicles at junctions, scattered pedestrians on zebra crossings and seemed to defy every instruction sign. Every other vehicle did the same, leading to numerous near collisions where right of way was determined by who held their nerve and their hand on the horn the longest. In this particular taxi the brakes seemed to be defective and the vehicle needed a long stopping distance, but this did not deter the driver from staying very close to the back bumper of whichever car happened to get in front. If they braked, our taxi had to veer out to the side and risk an alternative collision. On subsequent days I became accustomed to rides like this, but just then my nerves were shredded.

I was also assailed by smells from traffic exhausts, tyre rubber, factory smoke, food, sweat and odours I tried not to think too much about, while beggars reached through the taxi's open windows pleading for currency whenever we had to stop. Approaching the docks I saw people sleeping on the pavements, undisturbed by the passing crowds and traffic.

Acquiring a pass into the docks was another long procedure involving a group of uniformed officers. I completed a form, one of them read it, another one stamped it along with my passport, and yet another officer wrote out a pass. While this took place I studied the signs on walls around the port. The one in the office read 'The Corrupt are not above Justice' while just outside I could see 'There is no substitute for hard work' and 'Courtesy keeps everyone happy.' It was all very commendable but I would have preferred to read them while actually moving towards the ship.

The ship looked and felt like a journey through time into the colonial era, in its appearance and routines. It still bore the British India (BI) Line colour scheme, a white hull and a funnel with two white stripes on a black background, recognisable to anyone who went on school cruises on *Uganda* or *Nevasa*.

Once on board it seemed better than I had expected. My cabin was small but it included a bed, a day bed, a desk and some enclosed wardrobe space. I had lived in a similar space on my last ship, which was a generation younger. There were three visible differences this time. One was the relative lack of privacy as cabin doors were usually kept open when occupied, with a curtain which could be pulled across the space. Next, instead of cool air quietly blowing from overhead ducts, as in more modern ships, there was an individual air conditioning machine extending out through the bulkhead, which I would discover to be noisier than anyone else's; I became a deep sleeper and remained grateful that it proved more reliable than most. Finally there was a metal chest in the corner containing a block of ice, where I was to keep my cold drinks.

I took over from Don, a Mancunian with a goatee beard. He was a First R/O, a couple of years older than me, who had served as a second on board. He promptly left to stay at the BI Club, a company leisure venue which also contained some accommodation, before flying home. I also met my new boss/colleague, another Paul. He was a very straight-talking Yorkshireman, slightly older than Don and I.

Indian stewards (from Goa) and deck crew were hard at work, and I was introduced to both British and Indian officers. I was shown around the wooden decks and through the bar, separate officers' lounge, dining saloon, first class lounge and more other recreational rooms which belied the ship's small size. The radio room hosted some modern equipment beside occasional curiosities, and the dark wood-panelled bridge had a charm of its own, and a Radiolocator radar which I recognised. I was pleased to note the low and accessible height of the radar scanner mast! Cargo was being loaded into holds, and I was advised that passengers would arrive just before we sailed.

Dwarka

There was little time to recuperate as a few of us went to visit Don at his overnight abode. The BI Club was as traditional as it sounds, and we played snooker and ate supper there, served by uniformed stewards who seemed to live in the place. Later we moved on to the city's two smartest hotels, the Taj Mahal and the Sheraton (now Oberoi). We admired the night-time vistas of the city from the Taj's 20th floor bar while sipping Gin Fizz and Screwdrivers, and enjoyed a slightly different perspective from the Sheraton which included the brightly-lit frontages of the ocean and Back Bay.

Walking into each place meant stepping between worlds, leaving behind dark and teeming streets for gently-illuminated calm, air conditioning, uniformed service and drinks which each cost more than many people below might expect to make in a day. The contrast was not a totally comfortable one, although neither world was really our own.

We walked to Cross Maidan, one of the open spaces famous for its multitude of informal cricket games. Fittingly we were often assumed to be England cricketers as a Test series had just ended in the city, and became accustomed to cries of 'Look, Tony Greig!' and requests for autographs. None of us resembled him and we were amused by such comparisons, occasionally playing along with them. The *maidan* was hosting an event called *Crafts India* and we wandered around the stalls, taking in the atmosphere and admiring the imposing Victorian architecture of the railway station, then still called Victoria Terminus. Eventually we took a taxi back to the ship, passing the squalor by the dockyard walls again. It had been an interesting and eye-opening day.

All this established a template for the next few days. The *QE2* arrived on its world cruise and crowds gathered around the Gateway of India, the scene of King George V's arrival in India in 1911, to peruse the street traders and watch the snake charmers. There were more motivational signs on the sides of buildings and buses. We made further visits to the hotel bars and revisited the craft stalls on the *maidan*. Someone expressed interest in buying a pendant, but had second thoughts. 'It's plastic!' he cried. The trader replied 'Not plastic - imitation wood!' No sale was made there, but on other stalls silk ties and scarves were good value. The event was highly eclectic. A funfair section contained a hoopla stall where the only prizes were cigarettes and soap, which I learned were tradeable items; stewards on the ship were pleased to be given any surplus quantities we had. An exhibition by the local State of Maharashtra proclaimed the outcome of its family planning schemes, with 87,000 abortions over the previous year 'the best record in the country'. A telecommunications exhibition was filled with old telephones and models of Post Office radio buildings, of some professional interest despite their bearing warnings to 'Touch me not'.

I learned the routine for posting a letter home from the Post Office. This involved queueing at three different counters: first to weigh the letter, then to buy the stamps and finally to hand in the letter for franking and adding to the outgoing mailbag. I was told of the importance of making sure the letter was franked in my presence, to ensure the stamps were not stolen later on. This always led to an exchange of stares between clerk and customer as each assessed the other.

The ship's officers also frequented the Breach Candy Club, an exclusive outdoor swimming pool and sports club on the prosperous ocean side of the city for which the ship apparently held a block membership. We would spend whole days there, swimming, drinking cocktails, reading the newspapers, eating dinner and watching the sun set. One evening we sat on the balcony of its bar and watched an unexpected sight as ten members of the Caledonian Club of Bombay held their weekly Scottish country dancing session. I understand the Breach Candy, under its full name as a Swimming Pool Trust, has become even more exclusive since, with high joining and membership fees and a waiting list of up to fifteen years. However it also appears to face a number of challenges due to legal battles between old and new management, and also the loss of its prized sea view due to land reclamation for the building of a new coast road.

Late one night someone suggested walking back to the ship, something not normally recommended. 'It's only twenty minutes away!' he said. The next hour was quite educational. As we walked towards the docks along unlit roads we passed through the full extent of the outdoor sleepers: men, women and children huddled on rugs or sacking, while many more clearly lived in shelters or tents made of similar material. Dogs barked sporadically, rats scurried through piles of festering garbage, and giant cockroaches darted around our feet, sometimes in their last moments prior to loud crunching sounds and louder expletives. I would soon look back on this walk as suitable training for my first voyage on board, as it offered a preview of how most of the ship's passengers travelled and of the monsters which teemed behind its brightly polished surfaces.

Dwarka's round trip to the Gulf took in the following ports: Bombay, Karachi, Dubai, Doha, Bahrain, Kuwait, Doha, Dubai, Muttrah, Karachi and back to Bombay. There had been some variation of ports at times in the past, but this route remained consistent during my time except for sometimes omitting Karachi due to disturbances following the controversial 1977 election. Each trip took around two and a half weeks, with one to two weeks in Bombay for cargo handling before the next trip. I was on board for seven such trips, and will mainly focus in this chapter upon the first trip when the places and experiences were new to me, and follow in the next one with some specific moments from subsequent trips.

Cargo was a secondary consideration as the ship's main function was to carry around 1,000 passengers at a time, mostly people seeking their fortunes by working in the Gulf and returning home afterwards. It was said that *Dwarka* was a tenth of the size of the *QE2* but carried more passengers. This was possible because although the ship had some first and second class cabins most passengers were "unberthed", carrying their own rugs or mattresses and sleeping on the floors of unused cargo holds or out on deck. They were provided with food, from a bakery which produced 4,000 chapatis per day and from several galleys with all dietary requirements catered for. People of all religions mingled, yet seemed to make space for each other's ceremonies. Air travel has since superseded all this, but at the time the route was a major business and arguably an instrument of social mobility. *Dwarka*'s surviving sister ship (there were originally four such ships), *Dumra*, had been sold to an Indian company and renamed *Daman*, but it still provided the same service and the two ships were considered to be twins and friendly collaborators rather than competitors.

I gradually became used to the routine on board. I ordered cases of canned drinks from the Purser's office and during the next day they appeared in the chest in my cabin. At 5.30 each morning a steward brought a large block of ice into my cabin and placed it in the chest in readiness for the drinks delivery. I was woken again at 7.30 when the same steward brought me some morning tea, after which I dressed in Red Sea uniform and went to the dining saloon for breakfast. Lunch and dinner were served in the same saloon, where I was served at a long table with several other officers. The Captain's table was adjacent, where he sat with other senior officers – the Mate and the First and Second Engineers – with some places spare to be allocated to any invited first class passengers. During the day stewards brought mid-morning lime juice and afternoon tea. There was an officers' bar, staffed by another steward (who also happened to sell washing powder for some reason), where we could congregate and order drinks until 11 pm. This was only moderately used as longer and more intensive social occasions took place in people's cabins or outside on officers' accommodation decks, fuelled by the contents of the metal chests.

Paul would instigate some events by wandering into my cabin to ask me something. After a short conversation and a pause, he would look around and say 'Good job we're not in t'desert.' This was a cue to offer him a drink, after which any other officers walking past would peep through the curtain, sense the beginning of something and drop in too. They would find themselves reciprocating soon afterwards.

After five days we prepared to sail. The lifeboat transmitter had been away for repair and a Marconi technician returned it in time for the pre departure lifeboat drill. When the alarm for Boat Stations was sounded I made my way to my numbered lifeboat out of the ten available. I struggled to get into its small radio hut and had to discard my life jacket and hard hat first. Finally we were lowered into the water for a spin around the bay while I tuned and tested the transmitter. This was powered by cranking handles, awkward within combined spaces and requiring assistance before I could free my hands to actually operate the device.

We moved across the harbour to another pier and around 800 passengers boarded, scrambling for their preferred places on deck. There were numerous noisy disputes with police and the ship's Security Officer as personal possessions were separated from the larger baggage which travelled as cargo. No-one appeared to travel light. More passengers would join in Karachi. I remembered with a smile that Personnel in London had told me the ship carried 'one or two passengers around the Gulf'. We sailed with nearly 1,000 people on board, including 134 officers and crew. Karachi was 36 hours away and I took up my position in the radio room for the first of my evening watches.

Paul asserted his seniority to claim day watches, with me covering a two-hour evening watch and an unsocial one from midnight to 4 am which called for some adjustment. I suggested some later morning task times to the cabin steward so I could sleep in after my late watch. I was sustained through my first late watch by concentrating on messages to Karachi and from Portishead, and from a pile of sandwiches and pot of coffee served by the night steward. I became accustomed to the routine, which also included reading numerous books and holding long conversations in the darkness of the bridge with the deck officers on their own watches. One of them had been asked at home what his job was like, and his reply was: 'Just imagine getting up twice a day and spending four hours looking out of your bedroom window.' Yet to me the deck watch seemed full of varied sights and tasks, so I wondered how he would begin to describe my job in a room which lacked even a window!

The ship hugged the coastline, passing Porbandar, Gandhi's birthplace, and the ancient city of Dwarka after which the ship was named, each visible just a few miles away while we maintained a leisurely 12 to 14 knots. The latter was the ship's maximum and given its age it was no surprise that there were many breakdowns. When these occurred we philosophically enjoyed the calm, with the exception of the Chief Engineer who frequently had to face the Captain's (sometimes less than polite) enquiries.

We passed Manora's breakwater and lighthouse and on through the narrow Baba Channel into a wide bay and the Port of Karachi. Docking was chaotic in windy conditions and we became wedged between the dock and a mooring pillar for the Naval floating dock nearby. After further manoeuvring we almost hit another berthed ship, while the owner of a small wooden boat alongside swiftly abandoned it in favour of dry land as we drifted again. Eventually we hit the wharf with a hard bump and tied up alongside. After all this there was no time to go ashore and we promptly sailed with another 200 passengers on board but leaving behind one passenger who arrived just too late for the raising of the gangway. I wonder what effect that moment had on the man's life. He or his family must have paid, possibly through borrowing, for the passage not taken, while anticipating future riches from his prospective work in the Gulf.

The next stage was the longest single leg of the ship's route, the run to Dubai being estimated at 703 miles in 54 hours. This was also a weather interval in the form of a cloudy day with a patch of actual warm rain, the first I had experienced since joining the ship. A school of dolphins passed alongside, their bodies arching out of the water in almost telepathic union.

It was the perfect time to show films, and the ship had a plentiful supply, receiving extra movies direct from London in addition to the usual six from circulating stock.

Dwarka's officers also had their own sporting craze. Where *Somerset* mainly had darts, this ship had table tennis. A table was permanently set up in one of the lounges and people often arrived in pairs or groups to play each other, day and night. Kiran, our Third Mate, was particularly good, using his height to shape impressive forehands and smashes, and I learned much from repeated games against him. When a tournament in league format was held about two months later, I won it.

The weather became hot and we entered the Strait of Hormuz, plotting our own course near the rocky Oman hills as today's designated shipping lanes were not yet in place. Oil tankers appeared in the haze, empty and high in the water on their way into the Gulf, and low silhouettes as they left. Fittingly, dhows were also visible at times, traditional wooden trading boats which contrasted sharply with the large modern vessels. We looked down through deep blue water upon jellyfish of different shades and combinations of blue and purple. Rounding Quoin Island, a small triangular landmark at the entrance to the Gulf, we approached the United Arab Emirates and, as night fell, looked upon the lights of Sharjah and Dubai and their interconnecting highway.

Dubai was one of the ports which the officers on my first trip had been anxious to avoid. It was growing rapidly and importing huge amounts of material, which resulted in the port having very long waiting times: typically three months or more. The port, Mina Rashid, had been an ambitious statement in the early 1970s with its ten berths, but on my first visit I also counted 46 ships at anchor outside. Being a passenger ship, *Dwarka* had priority and we sailed straight in. The port was expanded in 1978 and my various ships continued to dock there afterwards, but it was eventually superseded by the newer Port of Jebel Ali, some 20 miles along the coast. Mina Rashid closed to cargo traffic in 2018, becoming exclusively a passenger terminal and permanent home of the retired *QE2*.

The next day was a Sunday and I was keen to go ashore and explore. It was already too familiar to others, some of whom were busy disembarking 413 passengers, and I went alone. The scale of Dubai was very different to today and centred on the Creek, a natural waterway which divided the city into two fairly equal parts. The port entrance more or less marked the city boundary, and all of Dubai's now-famous sights further down the coast were many years away from construction. I walked from the ship to the Creek, a mile or so, wandered either side of the water using traditional wooden ferry boats costing the small sum of one dirham per ride. I bought a cassette recorder and visited the museum, built within a fort in what is now promoted as the Al Fahidi historical neighbourhood and said to be Dubai's oldest surviving building.

Sailing overnight we arrived at Doha, the capital of Qatar, early next morning. This was another rapidly growing city but without Dubai's natural deep water access to the sea. A long and winding shipping route had been dredged through shallows to a four-berth wharf, itself built on reclaimed land at the end of a long pier stretching from the distant city. Arriving was a complicated process and we only stayed for a few hours, disembarking more passengers and cargo and moving on towards Bahrain.

Bahrain was one of the more recognised Gulf destinations at the time, especially since British Airways began a Concorde service there in 1976. Like Dubai it was building rapidly and encountering the same issues. The port, close to the capital Manama, was another small jetty, accommodating about six ships at a time and with US Navy ships sometimes having priority. Arriving at the anchorage soon after midnight I could see no land but the lights from all the other ships waiting offshore created a bright horizon of their own.

I had been warned of the variable service levels of Gulf radio stations, and one of them was the object of something displayed in the radio room, the rules of a spoof game called *Find the Frequency*. This enabled the operator to score points by making contact with the radio station and many additional points through being interrupted, having frequencies repeatedly changed or losing contact altogether. In the game it was 'forbidden' to cheat by using their good operators, but stated that as they were almost never on duty there was very little chance of breaking this rule. Also there was no time limit: 'Some games have been known to last for two days or more.' Given my expectations I was pleased to be able to contact them at all, even if I was shocked at their high charges. One station I had to contact was silent for four hours before replying and granting a turn number, then just as I started to send the first message told me to wait for twenty minutes. No explanation was given, but a long time later they actually did return and continue to receive.

There was also some anarchy on the VHF, and the bridge officers complained of hearing music, animal noises and obscenities being broadcast on Channel 16, the calling and distress frequency. All this broke regulations which were unenforceable in practice, depending instead upon some optimistic ideals of behaviour. On one overnight watch a nearby ship was holding a long conversation audible to every ship on watch in the area; when Kiran told him to shut up, music was broadcast instead.

I was also learning of the more adverse conditions on board, exemplified by its huge cockroach population which manifested itself in drawers, shoes and clothing, and across the interior and exterior decks. Some chilled foods were stored in an area known as the handling room, between the galley and the dining saloon. It became known that this was heavily infested and that food was left uncovered on the floor. There were instances of salad being served in the saloon just as these sometimes unexpectedly large creatures burst out from it and ran across the table. Main courses alternated between British and Indian, and at first I was unfamiliar with some of the Indian dishes and opted for cold meat and salad instead. I soon developed more taste for curries rather than risk the chilled foods.

At least there was only sporadic evidence of rats, although inevitably there were some on board. Food items which had been left out were found to have been nibbled at times, and there was no other explanation. There were plenty of rats on the wharf and in the surrounding streets of Bombay, sometimes popping up and sitting beside children on shop doorsteps, each tolerating the other and contemplating the view. Perhaps the large number of passengers on the ship acted as a deterrent to some extent, filling the spaces the rodents would normally have thrived in.

The Mate, Hughie, constantly threatened to write to the NMB (National Maritime Board) for breaches of agreements over the living and working environments. The NMB was established in 1917 to define wages and conditions for seafarers at a time when they faced daily risks. However it was largely superseded by the Merchant Shipping Acts of 1970 and 1974. None of us knew this at the time and there were ongoing references to it in company documents. Hughie's complaints never made it into writing, and their repeated airing after several drinks remained a good source of amusement.

All this chimed with the perception of *Dwarka* being considered a punishment ship, or at least a ship which required Personnel to work particularly hard to persuade or coerce people to join. I could imagine and understand some possible reasons why I had found myself there. Paul was working on an overseas contract, under which it was possible to work outside the UK for a year and be paid without any deduction of tax. He had been hospitalised in

Singapore with appendicitis and peritonitis, after which he was told the only possible ship for his remaining months away was *Dwarka*. He counted the days and proudly displayed his surgery scars while remaining convinced that the company had treated him unfavourably, or worse. Others on board had their own stories, with different circumstances but the same outcome.

Some claimed that having arrived and seen the ship they would not have signed onto its articles, except for their predecessors getting them drunk first. I later saw this tactic in action, as new arrivals were made the centre of celebration and bonhomie for two or three days, before suffering a long hangover. 'This is all *his* fault!' they would say of someone now safely home in the UK. 'I was going to tell them to put me on a plane straight back!' Whether this would have ever been agreed, or if anyone would really have refused to join at that stage was highly debatable, but it gave some officers a rueful back story and an excuse for their presence which they could just about live with.

Places ashore with good facilities were precious. Bahrain had the British Club, another venue where company employees were welcome, with its swimming pool, tennis courts, bar and restaurant. We enjoyed the facilities and a very British meal of gammon and pineapple, chips and peas while the ship landed its passengers and took on some bound for Karachi.

Kuwait was one of the better-known Gulf destinations at the time due to its early realisation of oil riches and having already built a modern western-style city. However it seemed to hold relatively little appeal for most except there was constant talk of the hospital paying the generous-sounding sum of £22 for blood donations. People supposedly planned to do this but all lost their nerve once we had docked. As it was my first time in Kuwait I went ashore to investigate the city's striking modern buildings, almost the only pedestrian on dusty and sandy pavements while large limousines rushed by. We were joined alongside by *Strathdoon*, one of the SD-14 ships on its maiden voyage, and an older cargo ship *Stratharlick*. We visited both for a quick look around, and it was soon time to sail again.

We steamed down the Gulf for 24 hours and on stepping outside from my night watch I was awed by the sight above as the ship moved within total darkness. The Milky Way fully crossed the sky from Cassiopeia in the North to Scorpio in the South, luminous and shimmering. It seemed a silent experience too, despite the underlying rumble of the ship's engines. Any Zen calm was short-lived as we returned to Doha to pick up passengers returning home, slamming into the dock with incredible force. There was once a radio programme called *The Navy Lark* in which the ship's docking was accompanied by all the crashes and smashes the sound effects department could deliver, and I was beginning to think of it regularly. On this occasion it was quite windy and Doha only had one small tug to provide assistance. I walked up and down the wharf photographing the action as the passenger queueing system broke down into a chaotic scrum. Eventually hundreds managed to board, weighed down with bundles of TV sets, cassette recorders, fridges and fans as well as all their packed luggage.

The next stop was a second visit to Dubai. There was an hour's time difference between Qatar and the UAE, and on our outward trip the clocks had been adjusted overnight. This return journey took place during a single day and there was much argument between the deck officers on how to manage the clock change. Eventually they decided on advancing the clocks by 20 minutes, three times during the day, which ensured they all gained equally on their respective bridge watches. This wrangling would have been unnecessary had they known we would have to anchor overnight on arrival. We took our place outside the port along with 55 other ships and the night was punctuated with table tennis from the lounge and the opening of drink cans from the better-stocked cabins.

Once in port the ship loaded 300 tons of scrap in addition to taking on more passengers. This was a regular but dangerous combination and on a later trip there was an accident while loading similar material. A half-ton drum of scrap metal dropped from a cargo sling, hit the crowded deck and rolled over the legs of a passenger, causing serious injuries which would require lengthy hospital treatment. We were told to expect 24 hours in port but suddenly informed after twelve of them that loading was complete and the ship was about to sail.

One of the passengers gave birth that morning and was removed to hospital, leaving all her belongings on board. We had to itemise these so her travelling companion could sign as having taken responsibility for them. They included an amount in cash equivalent to my gross salary for about three years, along with numerous gold bangles, rings and other jewellery items, which made me wonder what her job had been and if I was in the right business.

The ship did carry a doctor although it was perceived as being a retirement position and people's expectations of him were limited. This was reinforced when some additional booster vaccinations were offered but he appeared to be reusing the needles for multiple jabs.

Given the number of people on board, there were bound to be occasional deaths in transit. I recall two during my six months on board, perhaps a low ratio to the number of people carried. There were no burials at sea; bodies were placed into cold storage until they could be unloaded at the passenger's home port.

The final "Gulf" port was Muttrah, out in the Gulf of Oman in its own natural harbour close to the Omani capital, Muscat. The setting was dramatic, the harbour and town surrounded by angular mountains and crowned with the tower and walls of a fort. This was built as part of a network established by the Portuguese in the 16th and 17th centuries to protect their newly-discovered eastern trade routes.

Muttrah, 1977

Shore leave was restricted, and I was told that this was due to *Dwarka*'s involvement in the theft of a cannon from the fort. This proved to be an incomplete view and an injustice to the ship. Further information revealed that until the early 1970s the fort was open to anyone, although this led to graffiti as a number of ships' names were painted on the castle walls, and to the theft of a number of cannons which subsequently decorated parks and gardens elsewhere around the world. Finally the P & O ship *Manora* (later *Strathmay*) stole the last cannon in good condition, in what seems to have been an outstanding act of manhandling and seamanship, especially as the port was unfinished and the ship was at an anchorage rather than alongside. The plot was hatched in homage to the captain who was known for his interest in cannons which included producing technical drawings and wooden models. Locals reportedly watched the complex manoeuvres down the hill and across the water while, as with the removal of previous cannons, appearing completely indifferent. However this time a diplomatic incident followed, resulting in written apologies and *Dwarka* having to liaise with *Manora*, transfer the cannon by lifeboat (another difficult operation, at sea and in the dark) and return it to Muttrah on its next visit.

Another 161 passengers boarded and we sailed with 1,075 passengers on board: 54 in cabins and the remainder on deck. As we left I saw, for the first time, the phenomenon of bioluminescence: a luminous green and blue effect on the water as the bow wave disturbed light-emitting organisms below.

While company ships usually carried at least one electrician as an officer rank, *Dwarka* employed Indian wiremen. I was unclear of exactly what qualifications they held, although the one covering the bridge deck was certainly industrious. He stepped into the radio room during an evening watch waving his test equipment and telling me he had 'detected a short'. I assured him that my equipment seemed to be in order but showed him a faulty outlet just outside the room. He was not interested, saying he had not detected anything wrong with that one.

In the morning Paul woke me early with 'Do you know anything about Radiolocators?' This was followed by 'How do you open the display unit?' The radar was apparently completely dead. I thought this was a chance to shine and stepped onto the bridge to begin checking the unit's power supply. The fault was simpler still; the wireman had 'detected a leakage' and turned off the power to the radar! He was told to reconnect it and to keep it that way.

After a 564 mile passage we returned to Karachi. Hundreds of relatives and porters waited noisily as we docked, and as the gangway was lowered they surged towards the ship as customs and police tried to push them back. Some tried to climb the mooring ropes, and eventually the separate passenger gangway was hoisted into place. This prompted another charge of porters and within a few minutes some two hundred had squeezed onto the deck, scrambling to pick up suitcases and bundles of bags.

It was election day and our time in port was extended, so Paul and I hired bicycles from outside the dock gates for two rupees an hour. The shops were closed and the roads mercifully quiet, and we were hailed by groups of small children at the roadsides. We visited hotels to swim and enjoy drinks, and toured the city until my bike began to fall apart, with the brakes failing, the saddle disintegrating and a pedal falling off.

Returning to the ship in the evening another company ship, *Strathmore*, had docked nearby. We exchanged films with them and arranged visits for the following day, which became compromised by confusion over the sailing time. This was already a recurring theme, and an unlikely one as passenger ships are normally expected to keep to precisely-defined schedules. There will be more on this subject in the next chapter.

On the run down to Bombay the night sky was magical, with Orion high in the sky and the Southern Cross clearly visible ahead. Eventually a dull red quarter moon appeared over the Southern horizon, becoming creamy and casting a bright sheen ahead of the bow. We were called by a Sri Lankan ship, ten years older even than ours and apparently lost, with no navigation devices except their radar which was faulty. They asked for their position, which was given to them. They were only moving at 5.5 knots and we soon overtook them, a rare event for *Dwarka*. We continued watchfully through hundreds of fishing boats, most of them too small to register on the radar and unlit except for being outlined in the moonlight on the water. There was a constant risk of fishing nets snagging in the propeller and causing damage, not to mention the collision danger to the boats and fishermen themselves.

We arrived in Bombay soon after my overnight watch and I was woken from a deep sleep by Paul and another officer bursting into my cabin with a mysterious package from P & O. They seemed to know what it was, and I opened it to find new epaulettes bearing two stripes, and a letter from Personnel confirming my promotion and pay rise! This was all a nice surprise and once the excitement had died down I speculated on how it had come about. Was it planned once I agreed to join *Dwarka*, or triggered by a certain date? Or was the ship not legal without two full R/Os on board? They were questions never to be asked aloud, so I simply held a pre-lunch "shout" inside and then outside my cabin to celebrate, handing out most of my stash of beer intended for the duration in port. A larger-scale event was still expected for when we sailed, to be followed by another one for my 21st birthday a few days after that. The extra salary was going to be needed.

A tailor named Mr Gerimal used to visit the ship looking for business and I handed him my uniform jacket to sew on the new epaulettes. At the same time, since it was the 1970s, I ordered some cheesecloth shirts. Later I would order more items from him in an attempt to modernise my uniform; more Red Sea/tropical shirts, made to measure and with new two-striped soft epaulettes of their own, and uniform trousers with trendy 26 inch flares! I don't think I kept those for too long. We now had twelve days in port, a decadent end to my first round trip on *Dwarka*.

11 Dwarka – Bus Route

The previous chapter was based upon one round trip, but I completed six more. To avoid repetition this chapter relates some specific moments and subjects from the next five months.

South Pacific

Hughie hated *South Pacific*. Paul owned a cassette of the soundtrack, which looked incongruous in his music collection, although I can empathise as I have a major weakness for *Oklahoma!* Before each departure from Bombay a full test of the PA system had to be carried out in addition to the lifeboat drill. The test was normally half an hour of the Purser speaking while officers walked the decks, but before our next departure Paul and I prepared a little surprise. We ran a tape which began with the song *A Wonderful Guy* from Hughie's least-favourite musical. It was over before he could complain, and the tape progressed to *Y Viva Espana*, and other catchy pop tunes. As "Espana" played we walked the decks as all the newly-embarked passengers took to their feet, smiling, dancing and swinging their arms. We must have created a holiday mood, and everyone said the tape was a good idea.

Paul had had to borrow his *South Pacific* tape back from Bobby, the Security Officer on board. His role, created after some violent incidents in the 1950s and 60s, was to maintain order as passengers joined and left, and to look out for any offensive weapons being carried. Bobby was an old-school former police officer who seemed to belong to an earlier time, exemplified by his frequent helpings of gin and tonic preceded by 'I'll have another one for the Empire'. A long time on *Dwarka* had taken a toll and this mainly manifested itself in an obsession with Paul's tape. He played it over and over, in the bar and his cabin with the door open, the songs clearing the public spaces and reverberating loudly down the passageways. In particular he played the song *I'm Gonna Wash That Man Right Outa My Hair* over and over again, tormenting anyone within earshot. It reminded us of an episode of the TV series *Colditz*, in which a man seeking to escape pretended to be losing his sanity, hoping for compassionate repatriation. As he appeared to deteriorate he tormented and disturbed his fellow inmates by playing the same record day and night, and when he eventually "succeeded" it turned out that he had to be institutionalised once back in Britain.

One day things came to a head. Bobby tried to play the tape in the bar at lunch time, and Hughie stood in his way, projecting some hostility and directing him elsewhere. The tape went unplayed but over lunch Hughie was told that *South Pacific* was the reason some Indian officers never used the bar. When he returned to the bar afterwards, Bobby was already there and playing the notorious song again! Hughie ejected it from the player, stepped outside and threw it overboard into the water. He instantly became the most popular man on board, except with Paul who rued the loss of his tape. Hughie promised him money for it and there were many offers of contributions.

I was yet to sail as a solo R/O at the time. Had I done so I might have recognised the level of isolation which can be felt by someone working in a single-person role. Loneliness and alienation are recognised issues within the seafaring community despite the apparent camaraderie on board, and they can manifest themselves in strange ways. That also goes for the feelings of powerlessness and frustration which can fester at sea while contemplating things which need to be said or done at home. There were certainly times when I felt all these things, particularly on my later ships. Bobby often sat with us, especially when we took drinks and deckchairs out onto the upper decks, and while we did converse with him we may have attributed some silences to the generation gap rather than to what may have been more serious signals.

Bobby may have been the last of his kind in the company. When he left the ship, hopefully to a better outcome than the man from *Colditz*, one of the Pursers, Norman, took over his role.

Captain Hankin

Grenville Arthur Hankin was perhaps the most famous captain I sailed with, synonymous with *Dwarka* and the BI shipping line. He was born in a hill station near Madras (now Chennai), with the sea and company in his blood as the son of a BI Master. Although based in Hampshire he returned repeatedly to *Dwarka* until both man and ship retired. He is remembered as something of a one-man institution, but such a term can be a loaded one. He saw himself as safeguarding the ship in a way beyond anyone else's capabilities. He was very well-spoken and could project a suitably dignified manner. He had a good sense of humour at times when he relaxed. On the other hand he frequently dominated the bar, staging arguments and trying far too hard to be the centre of attention. Worse, on nights like that he took control of the cassette deck and played his own music which was very different to ours. We all sometimes made musical choices which sparked disagreement but I never saw any other Captain even try to do this. During one evening his music consisted of chewed-up tapes of Scottish dancing and bagpipes, driving us elsewhere before he fell asleep overnight in a deck chair just outside the bar.

At 11 pm one night a deck cadet came into the bar to tell me the auto alarm had gone off, signifying a possible distress message. The Captain's response to this potentially urgent situation was to tell him off for being improperly dressed in the bar! Yet he drank in the bar while wearing a long white Arabian robe along with headdress and sandals, a confusing sight and one which seemed to sum up the contradictions in his sometimes chaotic lifestyle. When I first saw him in this garb I asked if he spoke Arabic too. He replied that he had worn it once ashore in Doha and been able to haggle 25 per cent off in the market.

Curious new rules were introduced, such as having to ask his permission before showing a film. This was a significant issue to people accustomed to showing films frequently and at times to fit in with their own work routines. I was sent to ask his permission one day as he tried to sleep and to pretend I wasn't there.

'Excuse me Sir, I was going to show a film this afternoon but I understand I need your permission.'

'That's right.'

'Well, may I show a film?'

'You showed one this morning.'

'I didn't see any film this morning.'

'All right.'

Later, film shows were banned outright except while in port in Bombay. I never saw or heard of any such restrictions on other ships. It also became necessary to have to ask to see the company personnel lists as he did not want them readily available. Again this was a unique situation. The bar became less well-used and events in cabins proliferated, until the Captain realised his audience and welcome had diminished and chose to spend more time in his own cabin. He had his own entertainment anyway. On one late night watch Kiran beckoned me out of the radio room with 'When did you last see *Starsky and Hutch*?' He led the way across the deck and we stood and watched through the Captain's window as he stared at the programme on Bahrain TV, unaware of our presence in the darkness behind him.

He featured prominently in a BBC TV *World About Us* programme, made around 1979 and titled *RMS Dwarka: An Arabian Voyage*. This can be viewed, albeit in less than perfect condition, on *YouTube*. It gives the impression of a very well-ordered ship being run in a hushed and professional manner, only some of which I recognised. Dining table chatter about the schedule was surely just for the cameras, as during my time and from subsequent reports the relationship between captain and senior officers fell to well below normal speaking terms. Similarly I was amused to watch the officers on the bridge wearing their uniform caps as the ship sailed into Bombay. I never saw them worn, even when we were lined up and presented to the company chairman, Lord Inchcape, during his visit to the ship. I carried my cap around for four years before leaving it on a plane and never needing to replace it. My one photo of Captain Hankin at work on the bridge shows him at the radar in his vest. Still, the programme makers got the images they assumed they would see and which they set out to capture. The film also shows a horticultural Chief Officer (not Hughie) with his plants, and also Norman, very distinctive with his handlebar moustache, standing at the top of the gangway. In addition there was a passing mention of an engineer who joined the ship during my time and who had served on board for his first trip back in 1954. Perhaps Captain Hankin was not alone in his level of connection with the ship.

I suppose he was a "character", and thus fairly memorable, if for mixed reasons. By contrast I found when writing all this that I remembered almost nothing of his predecessor on board, or of some other captains I was to sail with later on.

I read that upon retirement in England he took up amateur radio, and that after passing the exam he became closely involved with the Radio Amateurs' Emergency Network (RAEN), a voluntary organisation supporting the emergency services. I wonder if one of my fellow R/Os might have influenced him.

Unplanned Leave

Remembering Captain Hankin brings me to an embarrassing incident in which he played a major part. As I mentioned above there was often confusion over sailing times, leading to mishaps or narrow escapes. This may come across as my getting an excuse in early, but the context is important. In Dubai the loading of scrap and passengers was said to require 24 hours but we sailed abruptly after 12. In Karachi an Arab passenger from First Class stepped ashore and returned to find the gangway being raised; he was just able to scramble on board. Another passenger then belatedly appeared on the wharf but the gangway was not lowered for him and he was left behind. A stowaway was then found; he had fallen asleep in Karachi and woken up to find the ship had sailed, taking him on to Bombay. There, Paul went for a medical appointment and had to rush back five minutes before sailing time, only to find it had been delayed by three hours.

The meeting with *Strathmore* in Karachi led to a chaotic situation. We were due to sail at 5 pm but at 2 pm Hughie let it be known that we were sailing in an hour. Paul and one of the Third Mates were over on *Strathmore*. Hughie sent another officer, Dan, over to fetch them and no-one returned. At 2.30 I was sent over; I found them all in the bar and Dan had not told them of the new sailing time. I was given a beer too, drank it quickly and we all returned to the ship with ten minutes to spare, only to find that we were sailing at 5 pm after all. The new sailing time was a ruse intended to stop people getting drunk before we sailed.

As we left *Strathmore*'s bar I noticed a man standing on a chair trying to set up something. It prompted me to ask Paul who their Sparky was, and he replied that it was Joe, the man on the chair. I knew Joe, or at least felt I did, as I had been in contact with him at times and also heard him mentioned as he had been Roger's first boss. I realised I had missed an opportunity to meet him in person, and when, several weeks later, we were in Dubai and once again beside *Strathmore*, I decided to visit.

Hughie confirmed the sailing time and wrote it onto a board at the gangway. He planned to visit with me after lunch. When the time came the Captain had called him into his cabin for drinks instead; they were still on speaking terms at the time. I went over and met Joe for a chat and two beers, followed by a look at the radio room. Just as I was about to return to *Dwarka*, we passed through the bridge and Joe stopped. 'Is that your ship there?' he asked. It was, and it was sailing, early. In fact it was already clear of the wharf and beginning to move forward.

I called *Dwarka* on the VHF for a full five minutes, but received no reply. Then I heard Captain Hankin calling the local agents to say they had sailed without me. I interrupted with where I was and that I had been calling. Without a word he passed the handset to Don, who had newly rejoined the ship after his leave, to act as an intermediary. I suggested I could come over to *Dwarka* by boat, since the pilot still had to be brought back to shore after sailing and the agent's launch was also available nearby. I heard the Captain said 'No way', and he asked the agents to fly me to Doha. He then changed his mind and said to make it Bahrain.

I was completely crestfallen, hardly believing this was possible. There were certainly warning signs, but they could be read in different ways. The fact that the Captain and Mate were drinking together just before their sudden decision to sail was another factor. We watched the ship clear the breakwaters and the pilot boat go out to meet it; I knew I could have been on it and that the incident would then have been forgotten. Instead, Joe loaned me some local currency and I walked to the dock gates to surprise

Immigration with my predicament. I played dominoes with them for an hour and a half before someone from the local agents arrived to take me to a hotel. The fact that I was carrying my seaman's card helped.

It was a mixed day for the superstitious. On the one hand it was Friday the 13th. Then again, I picked up a local newspaper that evening and read my horoscope for the day. It said 'Very good day for paying calls, both during and after business hours. Look in on friends or neighbours.' Amazing psychic skills...

I got a nice hotel room, enjoyed a good meal and watched a film. It was not a bad place to be stranded. The following morning someone from the agents phoned and told me to check out. A second agent arrived at the hotel front desk and told me to stay in the hotel for the rest of the day. The first agent phoned 15 minutes later and told me to check out after all.

'When is my flight?' I asked.

'We haven't booked it yet. We just need you to check out to keep the costs down.'

'Shall I come to your office then?'

'You're not coming here.'

'Okay, so what shall I do for food and how do you plan to contact me after I've checked out?'

This led to a pause. 'Okay, you had better stay on at the hotel. I'll bring you an air ticket at 4 pm.'

I passed the whole day in and near the hotel, checking at times with reception for any more calls from the agents. I socialised with a Chief Engineer and Cook who were about to join a Shell tanker, and walked around the nearby souk and gold market. I would return to buy gold a few weeks later. The agent never arrived, and I had time for dinner in the evening. While watching TV afterwards I was abruptly called to reception as the agents had sent a taxi bearing a flight ticket for me. I caught a late-night Gulf Air flight, more than 30 hours after *Dwarka* had sailed. The flight took 40 minutes to Doha, and after a short wait on the tarmac made a 15 minute short hop onward to Bahrain. It occurred to me that had I been put on that flight the previous evening, or even one that morning, I could have rejoined the ship in Doha. It felt as if the mistakes were piling up.

After a night in a more basic, yet more expensive, hotel in Bahrain, I ate a hurried breakfast and was driven to the port. I stood on the wharf as *Dwarka* berthed, hearing some loud and obvious comments from my colleagues on board. I could only reply with 'My escape attempt has failed!' The Captain said he would see me later; in the meantime I responded to invitations and offers of beer and began telling my story around the ship.

I was expecting to see my name go into the ship's log, a traditional disciplinary measure. It used to be said that the threat of being "logged" was enough to bring any errant sailor into line, although in practice it mainly recorded when someone had been late appearing on deck for work. Even this stood as a permanent and less than desirable record somewhere, even if many oversleeping or overnighting sailors claimed defiantly afterwards that it had been 'worth it'. I had been away for two nights, and even if the circumstances felt unlucky I felt I had to look at myself too and recognise that the headline would not look good. I could accept that in theory people made at least some of their own luck and that I didn't really need to visit the neighbouring ship that day; however several colleagues knew I was there and I still felt the incident simply should not have happened. I was prepared to defend myself on this basis.

When I finally sat with the Captain he was more subdued than I expected, and I did not grace the ship's log. We quietly went over the events, after which he said he had to send a report to the company and that they may expect me to pay the expenses involved. I said I didn't think I should be liable as it had all been so unnecessary, and without descending into argument we simply left it that we would 'wait and see.'

I received a letter from Personnel saying they had been advised that I was not on board when the ship sailed despite the sailing time being posted. I was reprimanded and told that the charges would be to my account. The bill looked expensive at first glance, especially given the agents' charges for 'attendance', but I tried to think of it as just a weekend break with flights included. I suspected Personnel had been led by omission into drawing some conclusions of their own about the circumstances. This prompted me to write my own letter, stating that although the sailing time was posted the ship had sailed before that time and 'this was a contributory factor in my missing the ship.' I also pointed out the measures I had suggested from the bridge of *Strathmore*. I was completely factual yet did not explicitly blame any individuals. Company letters had to be countersigned by the Captain and I took it to him. He stared at it for a long time. Eventually he nodded, murmured and signed it. He probably realised that I could have written much more, and that I had worded the circumstances quite carefully. The letter went to the company and there was no further correspondence on the subject; nor did they ever charge me the cost of my unplanned leave.

Meanwhile the sailing procedures on board actually seemed to improve afterwards, so it appeared that some lessons were learned. An additional measure was that for the next two or three ports it became clear that Hughie was watching my every move, ready to inform the Captain if I stepped ashore! I stayed on board.

Survival Strategies

Half way through my time on board, Paul left for the UK and my predecessor, Don, returned. He said he had only done three and a half months on *Dwarka* before and that he had not wanted to leave so early. His rosy recollections of it soon dissipated as he faced the realities of life back on board. Even so, he made the best of things.

He was also fairly close to my own age and we worked well together and found much to talk about. We were both new and enthusiastic photographers and often compared gear and pictures. We divided up the watch-keeping hours more evenly and formed a more effective team. We also shared a slightly anarchic outlook which occupied our minds on watch and helped us to deal with the repetitive nature of the ship's route and some deteriorating conditions on board. After some conversations about things we used to write in earlier times, I wrote a long poem on the subject of what might happen on *Dwarka* if all drinks were suddenly made free. This name-checked most officers on board, using in-jokes and observations to imagine how they might each go about consuming the unlimited alcohol. I name-checked myself too, as going onto *Strathmore* to bring back more beer stocks. The poem ended with the ship zigzagging drunkenly out of the Gulf and disappearing into the wide ocean in search of more supplies to keep the merriment going. Then:

The Dwarks were never seen again
Though legends of them still remain.
Some say they found a paradise
With Jellybeans and lots of ice.

Over the ocean, ghostly songs
Still haunt today's nautical throngs.
Sailors fear the dreaded cry:
'THE GOOD SHIP DWARKA WILL NEVER DIE!'

The poem was passed around and pinned onto notice boards, and Don responded with one about the ship's air conditioning units which referenced a dispute between deck and engineer officers over the quality of their respective units. In an example of real life imitating "art", the bar was promptly made free of charge to celebrate the Queen's Silver Jubilee, and we each provided a little entertainment by reading out our poems to all present.

We subsequently went a stage further, writing and recording a "play" in which conditions on the Star Ship *Enterprise* matched those on *Dwarka*, and appropriately titled *Bar Trek*. Its style borrowed much from *The Goon Show* and referenced people and events on board, taking things just a little further. Others were happy to contribute, adding their own impressions of senior officers; for example the Captain's hissing laugh was ripe for parody. My recollections are fragmentary now but one sketch, set in the dining saloon, went like this:

CAPTAIN	Steward! Bring me some cheese.
STEWARD	In that case I shall have to boldly go where no man has gone before. The handling room!
ALL	(*Loud and shocked*) NOT the handling room!!!
	Steward walks away. Loud scream as he is devoured by cockroach.
DON	Damn, that giant cockroach has got another one!
CHIEF ENG	Do you realise, Captain, that's the third steward we've lost this week?
CAPTAIN	I'm going ashore to buy some cheese.

Such workplace humour was not unique to *Dwarka*, just as they were, and are, common in other workplaces, as emotional outlets bearing hints of truth. I remember some documented 'instructions' for families as they welcomed their loved ones home from a trip. These included something like 'Do not be surprised if he sets off to see friends, carrying beers and dressed only in shorts and flip flops! This is normal behaviour for him.' It was certainly recognisable on this ship, although we developed some upgrades on the dress code.

One of our innovations was to introduce a uniform for the many cabin and deck parties on board. This was a black boiler suit, which eked out our hot weather gear and almost fitted in with the dirty boiler suits worn by deck and engineer officers as they clutched a beer on deck after their shifts. Some of them ordered the same black ones as ours anyway and we arranged for Mr Gerimal to add lists of the ships we had each worked on, and some embroidered badges. One such badge showed the ship's name surrounded by the lettering: 'I will go to heaven – I have done my time in hell.' Events on board prompted additional badges, such as 'Dwarka Gold Rush.' This stemmed from a customs raid on one arrival in Bombay due to some passengers being suspected of gold smuggling. Soon afterwards we learned of a story circulating around the crew, describing how the customs had chased a terrified individual through the decks and then dragged them away. We were amused to learn that this grew from one crewman seeing a group of us in our black boiler suits and dark glasses on our way to someone's cabin for a party. On another occasion we wore the boiler suits to accompany Norman around the decks on his security round and appeared to strike fear into those passengers who happened to be awake. We later had some bomber jackets made in the same style as the boiler suits, as a slightly varied uniform for visiting other ships.

Despite my misadventure in Dubai ship visits remained a welcome diversion, particularly in Bombay when there was sufficient time in port to do them justice and avoid any more career-damaging surprises. During one stay we were joined by two P & O ships for exchange visits and a third event, a darts match against a competitor's ship.

On another stay we watched two unusual Russian ships arrive nearby which proved to be ocean survey vessels, in the area to study the imminent monsoon. Four of us decided to visit one of them and found that the Russians were happy to welcome us aboard and show us around, although the radio room was off limits. We were taken to the Electrician's cabin and given several glasses of Bulgarian wine, then gifted a bottle of Russian vodka to take away. We then moved to their First Mate's cabin for a chicken meal, served with Russian cherry brandy and yet more Bulgarian wine. Most officers were happy to practice their English, albeit carefully as even everyone's inebriated chatter and laughter seemed to be monitored by another crewman in plain clothes, who we took to be the fabled "commissar". We had heard of these people, planted to ensure that Party lines of thought, speech and action were followed. There was one awkward moment involving someone sitting in on the occasion and seemingly enjoying the company, and the drink, while maintaining that he spoke no English. This was understandable and we thought nothing of it until he was prompted by some football discussion to offer a short opinion. He received a sharp stare from the commissar and lapsed into silence again. For good measure, at some point in the evening I was given a propaganda book telling the history of the USSR in its own way. We reciprocated the following evening, hosting them in my cabin since it had the best air conditioning unit. They brought Russian caviar on board which we ate with them, and we filled them with lager and Scotch whisky and gave them books. I remember giving away, and signing, an *Observer's Book of Cars*, to a Russian officer who had been very excited by its range of vehicles and who expressed his love of Triumph motors. We felt we had "done our bit" for international relations regardless of the state of the wider world.

Things became more unpleasant on board as the temperature and humidity escalated. The insect life became rampant, and my cabin started to remind me of Steve McQueen's solitary confinement cell in *Papillon*. I woke one morning to find myself looking straight into the eyes of the biggest cockroach I had ever seen. After springing to my feet and swatting it I fumigated my cabin and killed another fifteen. After taking up residence again I put on some plimsolls over bare feet and felt another cockroach squirming around my toes, which must have been just as unpleasant for the creature. After despatching it I felt at breaking point myself. Others lived with the same conditions which added to the general angst around the ship. It hardly helped when we sat outside to try to keep relatively cool, as we found that at least some cockroaches could also fly! This led to a constant degree of vigilance even as we tried to relax and chat, but the things were doubly hard to see coming at night. Their resilience was quite sinister too. Someone jumped on a large one with a loud crunch. A while later it drew our attention as it began to move, and a white inner creature wriggled out of its shell and crawled away. It was as if invaders from other worlds had really arrived, and that they were invincible.

The monsoon season arrived in Bombay, with spells of heavy rain and thunderstorms confining people to the ship more. They began to wilt in the conditions, constantly changing shirts and struggling to remain even moderately dry. Air conditioning units broke down more frequently and repair times became longer, with numerous questions, entreaties and threats being made. Several officers became due to go home with no sign of replacements, leading to depression and tantrums as they faced yet another round trip. The company paid an extra 20 per cent of salary for extra time worked beyond the scheduled five months, but this meant little to anyone more than ready to leave.

Two of the Mates arranged watch cover so they could go ashore together in Karachi. Hughie stopped them as they were about to leave and forced them to return to their normal watches, saying there would be 'no swapping and changing in the middle of the Gulf.'

'We're not in the Gulf,' one of the Mates replied.

Hughie was unmoved. 'You're not going ashore. You're on the 8 to 12 for a reason.' This reason remained unspecified. The Chief Engineer heard this exchange and spoke to the Captain, who summoned Hughie for a less than convivial chat. Thereafter Hughie took all his meals in his cabin, a serious situation between Master and deputy. As the situation festered, he publicly told the Captain that the ship had once been a clean and tidy one, blaming him for the perceived decline. Everyone within earshot thought this highly unfair, as did the Captain who asked the company to remove him from the ship. He was unsuccessful as no alternative ship was available and Hughie was on a long overseas contract. Both Captain and Mate were bound into a grim arrangement, like Steptoe and Son.

Don and I were largely unaffected by this and could only observe, and comment in our usual way. One evening I took over in the radio room and found that he had written one more ode:

Remember, remember, the fifth of November,
Gunpowder, treason and plot.
But it's harder, much harder, here on the Dwarka,
With politics and fireworks – the lot.

Whatever else could be said about the ship, it was never boring.

Bombay

I became progressively more confident in navigating around Bombay and decided to branch out from the familiar and visit some of its more important sights. Many of these were clustered near to the Breach Candy so I was already familiar with the route. I took a taxi to Malabar Hill, a high point overlooking the city and Back Bay, to visit the Hanging Gardens. This pleasant green space was created in 1881 to cover the city's main reservoir, and features terraced lawns and hedges sculpted into animal shapes. The adjacent Kamala Nehru Park included a giant Old Woman's Shoe, a feature which children could play inside. I was approached by a guide offering to show me the nearby religious locations for a fee of about three pounds, and since this made access to them seem less daunting I agreed. He seemed to know his stuff and I was led to the following:

Babu Amichand Panalal Adishwarji Jain Temple. An impressive white marble building built in 1904 and dedicated to the founder of Jainism, with multiple carvings and a large hall for prayer. This had a very impressive zodiac-style ceiling decoration with representations of, among other things, elephants, mythical beasts, storytelling scenes and the sun, moon and some of the planets.

Mahalakshmi Temple. Built around 1785, a famous temple with a back story. Bombay originally consisted of seven islands which were gradually linked through a series of reclamation projects. After failed attempts to build one sea wall, the chief engineer dreamt of a statue of a goddess in the sea. He organised a search and found the statue. A temple was built for it nearby and the sea wall was completed without further problems. The temple contains colourful images of a trio of Hindu goddesses, and is surrounded by stalls selling flower offerings.

Tower of Silence. A roofless circular structure surrounding a pit where Parsi (Zoroastrian) bodies are laid out to be consumed by birds, usually vultures. This reflects a tradition in which dead bodies are considered unclean and liable to pollute the elements, making cremation or burial unacceptable. Vultures circled overhead, and my guide explained that bodies could be picked clean in as little as two hours, after which the bones would dry out and disintegrate in the sun. He added that on days when there were no dead, mutton was left out for the birds. More recently the opposite problem has arisen, as increased property development in this highly expensive area has greatly reduced the vulture population, leading to a backlog. Solutions being trialled include a vulture breeding programme and the installation within towers of a device called a solar concentrator.

I also saw the **Haji Ali Dargah**, a mosque, located at the end of a narrow causeway only revealed to allow access at low tide.

I took a taxi back into central Bombay, stopping to view the **Mahalaxmi Dhobi Ghat**, an open-air laundry believed to be the world's largest. Here around 200 families live and work, collecting clothes and linen from homes and hotels to beat, scrub and dry them in concrete pens. After sensing the spiritual it was a reminder of the intensity and relentlessness of life in the city. The taxi stopped on a bridge overlooking the *dhobi* while I took a photo. I have since seen TV travel programmes visiting the same spot. Soon after visiting the *dhobi* my taxi got a puncture and I paid the driver and walked the rest of the way.

Mahalaxmi Dhobi Ghat

On another visit to the city I took a boat to **Elephanta Island**, as named by the Portuguese, and also known as Gharapuri. The island is home to cave temples dedicated to the Hindu god Shiva and celebrated for their sculptures carved out of the rock.

At other times I simply walked the streets, feeling increasingly at home and perhaps beginning to look like someone who had been there for a long time as I grew my hair and my first beard during my later months on the ship. I watched cricket on the *maidans* when the weather permitted it, sometimes even during breaks in the summer monsoon rains which may have produced surfaces particularly friendly for spin bowlers. Street food and drink became familiar. I liked to buy sugar cane juice, pressed by hand on demand by street vendors and providing some welcome refreshment for one rupee. Some people considered this unhygienic but I never had any health issues afterwards. I was challenged to find fresh milk as some colleagues began to crave it after months of limited consumption of UHT. After visiting some large stores and dairy shops I learned that milk was quite scarce at the time, with even rich families having supplies rationed and a black market meeting some demand. Then in a chance meeting and chat with a street-savvy western tourist I was told about the Parsi Dairy, which I duly found and where they sold me six pints, and some Indian sweets. My find earned me some gratitude on board, and requests for more milk deliveries on subsequent visits to Bombay.

I also continued to frequent the hotels and Breach Candy with my colleagues, and we even sought an introduction from the agents to the highly prestigious Bombay Gymkhana to play tennis there. It would also have been good to visit for its place in Indian cricket history, since among other moments the first Test match in India was played there, in 1933. Gaining access was apparently possible but required a little time, which we did not have before leaving again on my final round trip. I settled for the view from the nearby *maidan*.

English Passengers

Western passengers were rare on *Dwarka*. Once in Dubai we learned that a British woman was due to travel with us to Karachi. We saw her step out of a car, stare at the ship, and drive off, never to be seen again. A family from London were more daring. Nick and Diane joined in Bahrain with their two young daughters and sailed on board to Bombay. While we toured the Gulf for our next round trip, they visited Delhi and Agra and then moved on to Kashmir for ten days. They rejoined *Dwarka* on schedule and sailed back to Bahrain, waving from the rail as I waited on the wharf after my flight from Dubai.

Once Nick and Diane had settled back into their expat lives it was arranged that Don and I would visit them during a stay in Bahrain. They drove us to their house in Awali, a modern compound of homes and facilities for employees of Bapco, the Bahrain Petroleum Company. We talked, went for lunch at the nearby Bapco Club, saw some of the sights (and camels) of Bahrain and visited the Sheikh's private beach, onto which access was permitted to non-Bahrainis. The Sheikh's yacht was visible nearby and the Sheikh himself could be seen circulating on the beach. Back at the house we watched slides of their Indian holiday and contemplated future travels.

I would encounter them again on my next trip.

Distress

Despite the chaos, decadence, discoveries and mishaps, we still had jobs to do and worked quite hard when necessary. Messages sometimes took long times to clear as local stations and operators varied considerably from one day to the next. Some, such as Bombay, did not send a call sign tape and all we could do was keep sending their call sign on their receiving frequency and wait for an operator to break the silence with a "DE".

Even after making contact, radio stations were highly unpredictable. Don was sending a message to one station when the operator stopped him, said he was going off watch and to try another time. Another station could only receive Morse at around 8 words per minute instead of the usual 20 and I had to concentrate on sending so slowly. Sometimes even that was not enough to ensure success. In one port a relieved agent came on board brandishing a telegram which originally gave our date and time of arrival. The message in the agent's hands read 'ETA NOW WEQTP NO PFM', which (obviously) made no sense. We had also sent them three other messages which never arrived at all, and the agents had been concerned over receiving no ETA. We had been thought lost at sea, but we were only lost in translation.

Sometimes we could receive weather forecasts, but at other times days passed without local coast stations sending one out on schedule. Most forecasts we received could have been guessed just by looking out of the window. We suspected that some forecasts were just repeating our OBS messages back to us, and when it was decided for a while that the ship would not compile these messages because we were "coasting", it was significant that the availability of forecasts fell away.

There was no prediction of the windy conditions and heavy swell we sailed through on one passage out of the Gulf and on to Karachi. Messages began to proliferate requesting ships to look out for a Cypriot ship called *Eurobulker*, which had disappeared while carrying a cargo of cement. Reminders were sent out for over two weeks with no further information coming to light. It is now recorded as a wreck off the Omani coast, with the cause given, slightly curiously, as a 'hurricane', not appropriate to that part of the world.

We were asked to try to contact a barge, managed by Mackinnons, which had left Bahrain five days earlier bound for Bombay. Their passage was to take eleven days and the barge only had an R/T (radiotelephony) set on board. If we made contact we were to advise Mackinnons of 'their well-being and ETA'. We tried to call them on 2182 kHz for a few days without success, before concluding that they must have arrived safely, if secretively.

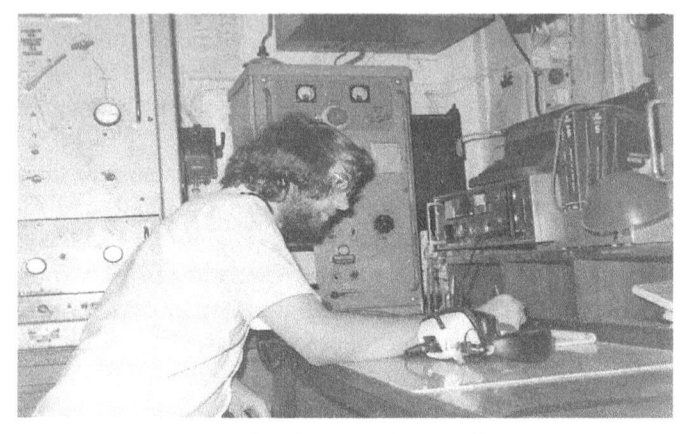

Concentration in *Dwarka*'s radio room

Maintenance tasks on *Dwarka* were quite intensive. We had to renew or repair at least one wire aerial on every round trip. There were instances of our splicing aerials and replacing insulators out on the upper decks by night before we could send any new messages. We fixed numerous hardware faults on the older equipment and helped isolate several electrical shorts and breaks around the bridge deck. Having the two of us working together on these things must have made a big difference.

The lifeboats were the subject of constant scrutiny, with repeated surveys and then claims soon afterwards that the survey which had been passed three weeks earlier was now only a 'deferred judgement' to be assessed yet again. Boat drills were sometimes chaotic. On one arrival in Bombay the Captain asked for the ship to be berthed facing the opposite way to its normal direction, to enable the boats on the less-tested side to be launched. This was done, but a boat drill was held without swinging out the boats so they were never tested after all. A fuller drill was held next time in Bombay, back on the usual boats. A wire aerial and mast had to be lowered before my lifeboat could be winched into the water; this was normally carried out by trained crew as part of the drill but on this occasion it was not done and we swayed in the air expectantly. Finally the Captain ordered that the boat's engine be started instead, and it ran out of fuel after a few seconds as we continued to hang above the decks. Once out of the boat afterwards we had to install a new searchlight on it and to troubleshoot when it failed to work. Finding the fault was easy: this expensive item had arrived without a bulb. Once this was fitted, the emergency power failed, and we also had to hastily source more tools for the lifeboat kit after finding they had been stolen from the boat. How we might have abandoned ship in a real distress situation hardly bears thinking about.

Exit

My appointed five months on board passed, with no sign of a relief. I became entitled to more pay but it hardly compensated for the certainty of yet another round trip. I scared Don by telling him I had received a message naming my relief as Burbling Bob, an older R/O with a reputation for drunkenness and with whom he had sailed before. 'Oh no!' he erupted, before recognising the prank. Actually I thought Bob, who I never met, might just have liked the ship and fitted in well.

There was more commotion on board as the ship was subjected to another customs raid. This time wristwatches were being trafficked rather than gold, and a large consignment was found behind a pipe in the galley. This spurred them into intensive searches of every cabin. They burst into mine while I was asleep after working overnight; I got up and sat on the edge of my bed, not yet able to say more than the bare minimum but allowing them to search. One of their officers took an envelope from my desk drawer, heard a jingle and loudly proclaimed 'A watch!' His colleagues gathered round and they were all visibly disappointed to find it contained 30 pence in loose change. Somehow this made me a suspect and they repeatedly complained about my English money and two cameras before finding I had already declared them in writing. Finally they left my cabin and told Hughie I had been 'uncooperative'.

My air conditioning unit just failed to go the distance, waking me with a loud bang and falling into silence. There were various attempts to fix it over my final few days, and successes proved very temporary leading to some uncomfortable final sleeps on board.

The company finally persuaded someone to take over from me and upon the next arrival in Bombay I left, laden with baggage, souvenirs and presents, for the traditional hiatus at the BI Club. Once inside the door, the agents noted all the stairs, stepped outside and returned with a very old man who was to carry all my bags. He looked at least the same age as my grandfather and like someone who had already endured more than enough suffering. He made heroic efforts to carry and drag each item upstairs while everyone simply stood and watched. It all seemed a normal sight to the agents and staff but despite everything I had seen over the previous few months I felt uncomfortable. When the show was over I passed him a ten rupee note, which I knew was far more than expected, however little it might sound (about 70 pence at the time). He seemed shocked and loudly gratified all at once, and as the agents tried to usher him towards the door he fought them off to stand upright and offer me a full military-looking salute.

One of the agents reminded me that I had given too much, and I said I knew but didn't care.

My flight departed at 2 am and soon became as chaotic as the ship had been. As the plane left the runway a loud bang startled everyone and heads turned towards the left side. It transpired that the problem was with one of the doors, said to have been not properly closed, and over the next hour the cabin crew returned time and again to nervously check it and mutter about whistling noises. The first stop was Delhi and upon landing we were told the plane needed a new door. After three or four hours on the tarmac the requirement had been revised to a new plane and we were all taken to the Ashoka (Ashok), a five-star hotel in New Delhi. People crowded into the public spaces and the limited available rooms and slept where they could, having already been up all night. The doors of the hotel's vacant rooms were kept open and if someone happened to walk past and see a vacant couch, chair or bed they could walk straight in, take possession of that item of furniture, ignore anyone else dossing in the room and try to sleep for a while. This was all too strange for me, even after life on *Dwarka*, and since I was unable to sleep I joined other groups strolling around the hotel's pleasant grounds instead. The day passed slowly before we were herded back to the airport in the evening. The purgatory continued: eight hours of mostly heavy turbulence followed by five aborted landing attempts before finally touching down in Rome in torrential rain. Exhaustion overcame me and when I woke the plane was half way to its next stop, Frankfurt, and the night had become clear. Arriving at Heathrow after a second full night in transit I knew it was early morning but had no idea what day it was any more. I was also confused by newspaper headlines stating 'The King is Dead' and wondered how many sovereigns I had lost track of on *Dwarka* until I learned of the death of Elvis Presley.

I would encounter *Dwarka* again: by sight and radio from my next ship and, some three years later, visiting it in port in Bombay.

Sadly, despite my poetry the ship finally did die. The TV documentary showed its sister ship leaving for the scrapyard in 1979. *Dwarka* herself kept going until May 1982, even appearing in a cameo role in the film *Gandhi*, before its inevitable sale and final voyage to the breaking yard. It was not quite the last ship in BI colours as *Uganda*, a few years younger, returned from Falklands service to resume commercial cruising until January 1983, before being chartered for another two years as a troopship at the end of its life.

12   Strathdirk

m.v. Strathdirk General Cargo Liner

Built: 1976, Sunderland

Tonnage: 9,230 (gross), 6,103 (net), 15,088 (deadweight)

Dimensions: Length 462'7" (141.00m), beam 67'2" (20.48m), depth 38'6" (11.74m), draught 29'0" (8.86m)

Origin of name: Small Scottish dagger (not a place name!)

I finally got my own ship, or at least my own radio room! The ship was a fairly new one, the first of two "SD-14" ships I would sail on. It was a revelation after *Dwarka*, although the Redifon equipment in the radio room was unfamiliar to me so I needed to do lots of reading and experimenting in the short time before the ship sailed from London's Royal Albert Dock.

My predecessor had only just learned he was leaving, and he sportingly moved to the pilot's cabin for a final night on board, allowing me to move straight into mine. The R/O's cabin was located at the foot of the stairs leading to the bridge and radio room. It is said that stairs on ships should be called "ladders" as they tend to be narrow and steep, except on passenger ships. My experience was that on modern cargo ships the stairs were just that, as usable as passenger stairs and a better description than ladders. I don't recall anyone using the latter term. Anyway, in the event of an overnight emergency I could be in my domain in seconds.

My cabin was an upgrade compared to my last two ships and I once again had the luxury of a double bed (even if it was still known as a bunk), couch/day bed, desk, wardrobe and en suite shower room. The Chief Engineer's cabin was next to mine, and the Captain's next to his. It felt like I had gone up in the world, but also become more visible in the event of high-level scrutiny.

Some things were depressingly familiar. Marconi were due on board to work on the echo sounder but had not arrived, so I phoned Mr Merry to check the arrangements. I tried to sound polite and cheerful, but as I introduced myself as the Sparks he interrupted with 'You're not a Sparks, you're a Radio Officer!' His deputy then came on board bringing the same attitude with him, although I was able to surprise him by starting up all the equipment successfully. He still delighted in asking me some obscure questions about the equipment and even about the purpose of a stray rope he happened to have noticed behind the accommodation! Someone clearly had nothing better to go and do.

I met the Captain and realised I was in for another tough voyage. Captain Butcher was a large, bearded man who I remember as looking rather like Bluto in the Popeye cartoons; these characteristics were supplemented by a loud voice and short temper. If only I liked spinach.

Marconi duly arrived and replaced a part on the echo sounder but this led to a series of other faults which took the entire day to resolve. Everything related to radio and navigational kit was, for now, fixed but many more faults lay ahead.

The ship had already coasted and mostly loaded, so after a few days it sailed, direct to Port Said for Suez Canal transit and on to the Gulf. It was expected to return to the UK after about ten weeks. My first watch went to plan, with my receiving a weather forecast and gale warning and sending my first messages as we passed through the Channel. Then as I was about to send the Captain's next message a fuse blew within the main transmitter. The Captain walked in as I was opening the power supply and asked what was happening. When I told him he roared

'Don't tell me your troubles, boy, fix it!' The door slammed on his way out.

Once this little crisis was over he complained about the radar display; it was a Radiolocator which I was familiar with and it looked fine to me, and the other deck officers agreed. However he complained repeatedly over the next few days and I had to make a show of adjusting video outputs and tuning the set several times to prove it was as sensitive as possible. He eventually pronounced it 'slightly better' but this seemed more of a face-saving gesture.

I was told to test the auto alarm at noon each day, just as the ship's other alarms were being tested, as he liked a loud din on the bridge at that time. It hardly seemed to matter that we might be unable to tell which bells were which. He demanded a time signal in order to check the bridge clock. The clock was relatively new quartz technology and had lost seven seconds in eighteen months, but verifying clocks with radio time signals was still a statutory requirement and easily performed. When I connected the time broadcast through to the bridge he roared 'It's no use now lad, we're too busy!' The weather forecasts I received were deemed inadequate as he demanded ever wider coverage, and even my placing a typed forecast in the usual place on the edge of the chart table provoked another outburst.

This kind of treatment was a bad position for an R/O, a one-person department and reporting direct to the Captain rather than via a senior officer. Fortunately the general mood on board was good, and the other officers were friendly and sympathetic to my plight. We were also carrying two wives and two children whose games and schooling needs invariably brought people together. I learned that Captain Butcher's temper was particularly notorious within the company, as if I hadn't already guessed. He did appear to have some redeeming features in that his domineering presence on the bridge actually also brought some deep knowledge and occasional willingness to teach his captive audience. One officer told me that this Captain had taught him how to fully use one of the then-new electronic calculators, and how this had improved his navigational work.

My days were fairly busy with communications work and they passed quickly as the ship entered the Mediterranean. Solo working meant I could no longer tell anyone very much about my working days as they would have meant little to others on board. From now on I would be, like most Sparkies, the maritime equivalent of a football goalie: competence or success taken for granted, and mistakes or disasters always noticed. I had to find motivation from within, and ensure I remained ahead of events whenever possible. The deadline was approaching for ordering Christmas gifts from the small Kays catalogue we carried, and I put up a notice urging people to place any orders before the crucial date.

As we passed Malta the main transmitter failed again and I spent hours working on this as the messages piled up on my desk. In the evening the Captain came and sat in the radio room, asking me to show him on the diagrams what I had attempted so far and what my thinking was. He did not particularly understand the diagrams, but in his own words he had 'forced me to think', or at least to an even greater extent. Next morning I found the fault, a blown rectifier diode, which earned me a pat on the back from the Captain.

The good feelings were short-lived as the transmitter soon developed yet another fault. This may have been brand new equipment but possibly built on a Friday. After more time fault-finding I believed a transformer to be faulty, for which the ship carried no spare. I sent a request to our infamous superintendent and waited to see how well he performed his own role. In the meantime I began asking nearby ships to relay my long-distance messages for me, including a German cargo ship, P & O bulk carrier and a Japanese tanker. The emergency transmitter was only for shorter-range use and even then I was sometimes told by local stations that my signal was too faint.

Radio room, *Strathdirk*

I expected a package or Redifon technician on board during the Suez Canal transit, but nothing and no-one arrived. We passed through the canal uneventfully, following most of the convoy as we were 19th out of 22 ships. Another P & O cargo ship, *Strathaslak*, was ahead of us in the convoy and the Captain beat me to asking his counterpart for the obvious favour, for their R/O to relay messages for me. The R/O, Willie, was happy to do this and at first I was able to help in return as I had a weather forecast he had missed while sending messages. At first there were mainly the usual company messages and weather observations, but as we sailed down the Red Sea on the day of the catalogue deadline I suddenly had no fewer than fourteen orders to send. Willie kindly sent them along with his own batch of similar orders and said he felt like Father Christmas himself. I felt I owed him numerous beers. That night I was rebuked by the Captain for having put up the notice, although I defended my having done so.

My responsibilities on board grew in small ways, usually stemming from the general presumption that Sparkies were not particularly busy. I took on the running of the officers' bar, ordering the daily stock and sifting through signed paper scraps to calculate people's bar bills; it was easy to tell which ones had been signed later at night, and not always so easy to decipher the scrawls into names or drinks! The bar normally ran at a small profit which was used to finance special occasions and donations to the RNLI. I had to take minutes at the ship's management meeting, which theoretically got me more involved although the Captain dominated the meetings while most officers present were cowed into silence. When the subject of Maintenance arose there was a pause, and I said 'Perhaps I should mention the main transmitter.' The Captain immediately silenced me and, after a few awkward seconds, started to talk about the transmitter himself! I reverted to simply taking notes. An Accident Prevention Committee was formed and I was nominated as secretary. The Mate ran the meeting; there was nothing at all for me to write down and I offered my resignation afterwards. Meanwhile I was also producing a news sheet again, now branded *The Daily Dirk*.

There was much banter between the deck and engineer officers over their respective performance. The engine room had its own readouts which estimated the ship's speed based on engine revs, and this was often compared with the actual position as determined by sightings and affected by ocean currents. The engineers claimed that the engines had arrived in Muttrah two days earlier and were now waiting for the rest of the ship to catch them up.

This was all part of the eternal debate between the deck and engineer officers over who was more skilled and whose jobs were best. Engineers pointed out that they could probably take over the bridge and estimate the ship's position, set a course and steer but no-one else could make the engines run. The Mates considered their jobs best as there was always something different happening outside or on the bridge. I could see some merit in each statement although my experiences with captains so far also suggested that the more outwardly-glamorous positions could take some kind of long-term toll.

We arrived at Muttrah's anchorage and learned that we were to stay there for three days due to public holidays. The next day was a Sunday and all the officers congregated in the bar for a drink before a sirloin steak lunch. At noon the phone rang with a call from the bridge advising that we were going into port in an hour; the engineers all had to change and go below, missing their lunch. I was also looking forward to some quieter time at anchor, but I got my lunch anyway.

Once alongside, the Chief Engineer received a letter from Redifon advising that they were coming aboard in Suez! We could only smile ruefully and shake our heads. It was decided that we should wait and see what happened in Dubai, a better-connected location. Meanwhile one of the two VHF sets had failed, and the Captain was complaining about the second one. I called the local radio station on it and they said they could hear me perfectly. The Captain then burst into the radio room to tell me he had seen the crew putting up their own aerials, and that there must be a problem with the communal aerial. He was right about this one; I found a fault in their end cabin and was rewarded with a drink in the crew bar.

A relic of old BI appeared as *Daman* came into the port. I told people I had worked on its sister ship, and they could not believe the company still had such a ship! The Captain and R/O from an old Greek ship came on board and I showed them around. They were very impressed with the radio room, proving how deceptive appearances can be; they were also keen to copy some frequencies from my Admiralty List of Signals as their only similar book was from 1968!

Daman, *Dwarka*'s sister ship, docking in Muttrah

I finally saw something of the town, followed by a day out in the interior of Oman. We were invited by the building contractors Wimpey to a country club within a project they were building in the city of Nizwa, 87 miles from Muscat but 120 miles and three hours by poor roads at the time. Once there we swam in the pool, played them at darts and enjoyed a steak meal. Heavy rain arrived in the evening and our return journey was hampered by flash flooding across the rugged terrain. I understand the route has a much better road now.

Just after sailing, the engines stopped and we wallowed for two hours while repairs were carried out. I was looking out for *Dwarka* as I heard them sending messages within the Gulf. Somehow it was always interesting to note that it was still out there, and not only because I still knew some people on board.

The port situation in Dubai had improved dramatically and we docked straight away. Uncannily, *Strathmore* then came into port! One of our engineers visited, returned and said I was well-remembered over there. There was only really one reason for this and I again found myself telling the story of what happened six months earlier.

News arrived that we were not returning directly to the UK. After unloading in the Gulf we would ballast (basically sail empty) to East Africa and load cargo for the USA. A short and routine trip was turning into a bigger adventure. It was assumed to be a one-off and that the ship would return to the Gulf with American cargo and then to the UK afterwards, and we were each asked how long we were prepared to remain on board. The options were to leave after five months, which was presumed to be somewhere in the USA, or to stay until 'the end', an assumed date when the ship might resume its previous route. The antagonism I had faced from the Captain had largely abated at the time and I was enjoying everything else about the ship, so I opted for the latter.

More company ships arrived. *Stratharos* and *Strathnevis* anchored outside the port just before being sold, and we sent boats to collect any useful spares. Ships were disappearing from the company lists before I had a chance to even see them. Willie's ship *Strathaslak* would follow soon afterwards. Each ship was of a similar age, dating from the early 1960s, and this trip was the only time I encountered them. All had had previous names within the fleet and they would gain new names and see further service under new owners despite becoming uneconomic under a British flag. *Strathardle* arrived alongside, one of the company's more impressive cargo liners known as Super Straths. Theirs was a short visit to collect empty containers, but being more than familiar with visiting company ships in Dubai I went to meet the R/O. The radio equipment looked rather dated, the ship being the same age as *Tekoa*, although I knew some of my new equipment had hardly distinguished itself so far. The accommodation was spacious and the bar distinctive: a collection of some 2,000 matchboxes from around the world lined the walls.

The Captain remembered his concerns regarding the radar and sent for a Marconi technician, who also assured him it was in perfect order. He accepted this for a few minutes, then asked me if I could do anything to improve it. I increased the internal gain and brilliance pre-sets a bit more, beyond what would have passed muster in an exam, and he at least noticed the difference and became placated for a while.

Two more technicians arrived bearing the transformer I had requested. To my great relief it solved the problem. Being wrong on this high-profile fault was unthinkable. They took away the faulty VHF and returned it the next day as unserviceable. The captain's wrath was turned upon them and they promised more attention at a later port.

Before then, a full social life beckoned with events on three successive nights. Divers from an underwater surveying company came on board for a darts match, followed by a lively sing-song as one of them had also brought a guitar. Personal connections led to an invitation from expats to a barbecue, which was pleasant and sociable except for the Captain falling asleep at midnight and turning many heads with his loud snores! Next, the divers sent cars to take us to their social venue for hospitality and a return darts match.

The next day saw some sore heads and drooping eyelids, along with hopes being expressed that the sailing would be delayed. Those unable to attend the previous night out due to work shifts had ultimately visited another ship instead and now nursed hangovers of their own. However we had to sail by mid-morning to make space for the incoming *Dwarka*!

We passed the breakwater and our pilot transferred over to *Dwarka*. I called them on the VHF and asked Captain Hankin to put Don in touch after they had berthed. I don't think the Captain recognised my voice but Don did call back for a long chat, beginning with 'What are you doing here?' from him and 'What are you still doing on there?' from me in return. He had been on board for a surprisingly long time. Conditions there were still worsening; he said there was no working air conditioning with the exception of units for the cabins of the "big four" ranks. He was due to leave next time in Bombay, and surely, as per our boiler suit patches, he had earned a place in heaven!

A short stay in Kuwait saw me challenged by the Captain's latest concern. He wished to know if the ship had a Marconi Autoguard, a link between an auto alarm and the ship's direction finder (D/F) through which the D/F would automatically take a bearing of a distress message. After some research and tracing of undocumented cables I had to say that the Marconi D/F was fitted with Autoguard but the Redifon auto alarm had no external connection to it. Mixing manufacturers had resulted in losing a potentially useful feature, but it was a good learning exercise.

We moved on to Bahrain and I phoned Nick and Diane from the British Club. They were going to an interesting-sounding talk that evening and arranged to collect and take me along. The talk was by the Norwegian explorer Thor Heyerdahl, famous for his ocean voyages on small boats, notably *Kon-Tiki* and *Ra,* made from native materials and intended to prove the long-distance sailing capabilities of ancient peoples. He had started out in Iraq and built another reed boat, *Tigris*, which had now reached Bahrain. In fact once back on the ship I realised I could see it moored in the distance.

Heyerdahl spoke of his objective of proving the extent of trade links between Mesopotamia and other civilisations. There was an additional talk by the British archaeologist Geoffrey Bibby, whose excavations in Bahrain led to the conclusion that it formed part of the legendary land of Dilmun. It was thus a real-life location for the ancient heroic tales within the Epic of Gilgamesh, considered the oldest known work of fiction and recorded on clay tablets some 4,000 years ago.

Bringing Nick and Diane onto the ship took two days to arrange with the port, and in the meantime they took me to see some of Bahrain's archaeological sites, including buried temples and Bahrain's famous ancient burial mounds. The mounds form a UNESCO World Heritage Site and there are hundreds of thousands of them, although some are now endangered by creeping urbanisation. We also went to the fort, built by the Portuguese in the 16th Century, and Heyerdahl and Bibby promptly arrived with a crew and began filming. We felt we were at the centre of Bahrain's events. Eventually I was able to play host in return and they were amazed by the contrast between my new ship and what they had lived with on *Dwarka*. Christmas decorations had just been put up, the tree and artificial snow forming incongruous sights compared to the heat outside, and over dinner Nick and Diane told me of their plans to drive home to England in their Japanese mini-Jeep, which they later accomplished.

While in Bahrain we were docked close to a US Navy ship and some of their crew paid a visit. I showed them the radio room and then left the cadets to entertain them in the bar. This yielded several phone numbers which the cadets hoped would prove useful in the USA. *Strathaslak* also arrived, and I was at last able to greet Willie in person.

My first visit to Abu Dhabi followed, and after buying Christmas presents for the wives and kids on board I received a gift box myself that evening. It was from the local agents and contained a new VHF unit. When I began installing it next morning the Captain told me off for not informing him of it the previous night. He had been ashore at the time. The truce was over.

After a delay due to dense fog we sailed again and paused at the Dubai anchorage to unload some overcarried cargo onto a barge. We then left the Gulf and began our voyage down to Dar es Salaam. We were told to sail slowly as no berth was available until New Year's Eve, ten days later. However the engines were already running at close to minimum revs, so it was accepted that we would arrive early and anchor outside the port.

There was time for me to provide a little instruction, as one of the cadets had some learning objectives. I taught him Morse code and how to tune the main transmitter, and signed his paperwork. I must have been starting to project a little seniority, which also enabled me to smile wryly at the unworldliness of others. At some point the Captain had referred to our spending Christmas on 'the oggin', a slang term for the sea. Soon afterwards I found a junior officer looking intently within an atlas and discovered that he was trying to find the place the Captain had mentioned! Oggin was nowhere in the atlas, although it would have been fun to see a map featuring it.

Christmas Day saw lavish catering throughout. The Captain had boasted that we would enjoy kippers and champagne for breakfast, and kippers were indeed served but without the champagne. He may have intended to provide white wine since some had appeared where the bar led into the saloon, but an overnight watch had found and consumed all five bottles by breakfast time. Still, the day was a relaxed one centred on the bar with lots of presents for the children and good humour all round.

Christmas lunch was a superb buffet set out in the crew mess, with two turkeys, a giant ham, salads, cheeses, sausage rolls, mince pies and Christmas cake. A barbecue stood outside on deck with sausages and fillet steaks. I still had watches to complete, as did everyone else, but people came and went throughout the day, catering at will and enjoying the calm weather. One officer who was confronted with an unseasonal request for the status of an outstanding task simply pointed at the ship's motion over the sea and said 'The thing's still running, isn't it?' His answer seemed to be accepted.

Boxing Day saw a brutal Crossing the Line ceremony. This was normally just drinks in the bar and optional references to King Neptune, but temporarily-evil minds fuelled by Christmas refreshment had devised this one. The three "first-timers" were tied to the side of a cargo hatch, covered in engine grease, subjected to haircuts with hedge trimmers and then hosed down. They were still expected to buy drinks afterwards.

The hose down for the Crossing the Line victims

We arrived at Dar es Salaam with three days to spare and anchored outside the port. This offered a view through a narrow approach into its wide harbour full of traditional and modern ships, and also of the beach where crowds gathered around the returning fishing boats.

We had to find ways to fill the three days. The Second Mate's wife provided some much-needed haircuts out on deck. Several of us took a lifeboat to a nearby uninhabited island fringed with sand and coral. We beached the boat on a sand spit and passed a carefree day, playing football, enjoying a barbecue, strolling along the water's edge and simply relaxing in the sun. As the sun set we loaded everything back into the boat and left the island as unspoiled as we had found it.

We berthed on schedule, not alongside but against a buoy within the port area, ready to load Zambian copper from barges. The copper was arriving in stages on a 1,160 mile railway line which opened in 1975, providing easier access to the sea for landlocked Zambia and its copper belt.

It was New Year's Eve and midnight brought a chorus of ship's horns, whistles and bells along with a display of lights and red distress flares. People crowded onto the bridge to watch the spectacle and find new ways of joining in. I flashed 'Happy New Year' in Morse towards other ships on an Aldis lamp, and received similar greetings back. The ship's navigational lights were flashed on and off. This all continued for half an hour, during which time the Captain phoned the bridge four times demanding that we 'desist from making so much noise.' I doubt the harbour would have been much quieter without our contribution, and his final call was answered by the Fourth Engineer who told him to 'Bog off!' Incredibly this seemed to work. The Captain enacted some kind of self-defeating revenge the following morning by locking the bridge and refusing access to anyone. Eventually I borrowed the Purser's pass key to go through and start work in the radio room.

I had a few new technical issues to work on, some real and some imagined. The Captain complained about the radar again, insisting the performance monitor must be faulty. I checked this over and over again, and the deck officers insisted it was fine, yet technicians were called in both Dar and Mombasa who told him the same. His own broadcast receiver was faulty and I found a fault, but soon afterwards it developed a new problem. The Direction Finder, something which seemed to be used more on this ship than any other, also went down; I worked on it and ordered a replacement transistor. I was then asked to look at the electronics within and linked to a Kelvin Hughes Transmitting Magnetic Compass (TMC), something entirely new to me. It provided a digital reading more accurate than one taken by sight from magnetic needles, with links to other bridge devices. Working around other faults, I spent three days reading documentation, making tests and narrowing the fault down as there seemed to be no local expertise for this. I was becoming more methodical as I dealt with these situations knowing there was no-one else I could call upon, and my confidence seemed to be growing even while grappling with unknown equipment.

The approach to Dar es Salaam harbour

The Captain may not have noticed the extent of this yet. One morning the Electrician arrived as the Captain had asked him to look at the compass, telling him I was 'too busy.' I had said no such thing. We agreed that it was as much outside the Electrician's areas of knowledge as mine, so he left me to it, commenting that the Captain was trying to stir up trouble. Soon afterwards the Captain himself burst onto the bridge, unleashing a furious tirade which brought up every complaint and argument from throughout the trip. This went on for 45 minutes as I disputed some of his statements but surprised him by accepting others to the effect that I still had much to learn. Among other accusations, I was apparently someone who gave up too easily and was not making enough effort to fix the device, all while I was working on it and surrounded by components and test equipment. Suddenly he ran out of steam. 'Look, I've no doubts over your ability as an R/O. And you did a good job over the Christmas period in difficult circumstances.' With that, he left and I went back to work. I narrowed the fault down to one small area and then had to wait for a technician with spare parts in Mombasa. Even the Captain recognised that this was progress and an acceptable moment to put it back together.

There were opportunities to go ashore, using a highly erratic boat service organised by the agents. It was supposed to be a free service but some boatmen demanded payments to take people to the nearest jetty, dumping them across the bay otherwise. The same happened on the return journey, with the boatman demanding an extra twenty shillings despite having already been chartered by the agent. We walked into the agency office to tell them. The manager roared 'I'm fed up of these people!' and sent someone back to the water with us. Another boatman had taken over who insisted on fifteen minutes' sleep before taking us back on board. The agent asked for us to get the Captain to write a protest letter, which he apparently did, perhaps welcoming the chance to articulate a new grievance, but nothing changed. Despite all this I managed to see some of the city and to spend time in its well-equipped mission. I also walked among the stalls on the beach, avoiding the undoubtedly fresh fish but enjoying delicious slices of fresh pineapple.

After eight days on the buoys we had loaded over 7,000 tons of copper from the barges and prepared to sail for Mombasa. We travelled around the eastern side of Zanzibar as the water between the island and the mainland was too shallow. The ship rolled heavily in the swell despite its new cargo. A nearby ship with a transmitter fault needed its messages from Portishead, and I obliged; I had recently been helped in the same way myself.

Strathdirk at Dar es Salaam, high in the water and ready to load copper

We anchored a long way off Mombasa as the Captain refused to believe the Second Mate's advice that there was an inner anchorage. He demanded a phone call to the ship's agents, and stood over me while I tried to alert the nearby radio station.

'Can't you get them any quicker?' he fumed.

'I'll keep trying until they answer,' I replied. I knew that anything which sounded like an excuse was likely to be provocative.

'Well I want to speak with the agent!'

'I know.' I hailed the station again.

'I want to speak to him!'

'I'm still trying.'

The Captain retreated slightly and paced up and down the bridge until a voice finally answered me, took the details and connected his call. The agents were surprised by our position and pressured the Captain to sail towards the port. He eventually found himself anchoring exactly where his junior officer had suggested, but offered no acknowledgement or apology. A little later we moved again, into the deep-water inlet forming the port, and to a loading buoy similar to those in Dar es Salaam.

Six of us took a boat ashore for what was billed as a night at the mission. It began that way, with drinks and several games of pool in the gently-lit bar area open to the sweet air and the darkness beyond. Music, mostly Donna Summer and Boney M, drifted from the bar's speakers to compete with the insect chatter and the clatter of pool balls. This was all fine and just as expected, but after a while someone who knew the city decided we were also going to the Tamarind Restaurant, one of the city's most highly-rated. I see the restaurant still exists with its reputation undiminished. We sat at an outside table overlooking the water and palm trees, and polished off seafood, steaks and three bottles of wine. Some of us had been unprepared for such a night out and could only just pay our share of the bill, after which we were keen to return to the ship. Others had different ideas and insisted we move on to some of the city's nightlife. Enough money was shared around to fund taxis and get us into a club where we watched the eye-popping entertainment while drinking our Tusker beers very slowly. Eventually we woke up a boatman to take us back to the ship at a very late hour.

Bigger things were planned; a safari day at Tsavo East National Park. This seemed a unique opportunity and we filled three minibuses for the two-hour journey. The Park is one of the world's largest reserves and gained notoriety for its lions when two man-eaters killed numerous workers during the construction of the Kenya-Uganda railway in 1898. We were driven around for most of the day, seeing no lions on our visit but we did view herds of elephants, antelopes, zebras, oryx and many more, either side of a lunch break at the modern Voi Safari Lodge, waited upon as we overlooked the park's wide panorama.

Sport played a big part in our stay. The mission had a swimming pool and badminton court which were well-utilised. Football matches against neighbouring ships were arranged, and I played in three games within a week; half of one match in goal and the remainder in outfield positions. The first was painful for everyone, both physically and because we lost heavily. In the second match we followed a good plan throughout a well-contested game which ended in a 3-3 draw, leaving us all feeling proud afterwards, and after the third, a big win, I felt I could just go on and play all over again. Even then I thought of it as a physical high point which I would probably never achieve again.

There was considerable interest in shopping as bargains were to be had. All big-game hunting had been banned in Kenya and any trophies and ivory had to be sold off at half price before a deadline. In the end I bought souvenir wood carvings but no ivory, as it simply did not appeal to me.

Meanwhile we had moved alongside at the port and the loading of coffee accelerated. We gained some appreciation of the economics driving our voyage; the copper was valued at £3.5 million and we were told the coffee would be of a higher value. As I write, and after some commodity price highs and lows, our copper cargo would be worth some ten times the above. Coffee prices have been highly cyclical but currently appear to be around the same price as then, a depreciation in real terms but still a valuable cargo in itself.

Events in the radio room also moved quickly. The D/F part I had ordered arrived and cleared the problem. The compass was fixed. Technicians worked on the radar performance monitor and pronounced it good; the display still looked the same as before but the Captain was pleased, if only for a while. I even climbed the radar mast myself and checked the scanner. After testing the lifeboat transmitter during a drill I could pronounce everything working. We moved out into the waterway to take on fuel, then sailed for Suez, Valencia and New York.

Two mornings later I was woken at 5 am by heavy rolling and falling objects. The reason became clear as the engines had stopped. A cylinder head had cracked and it took seven hours for the engineers to complete a repair. Once we were under way, strong currents slowed the ship dramatically.

I manned some busy watches in variable conditions. Inevitably the Captain entered another difficult phase. I always delivered messages to him but one morning he irritably told me to just leave it on his desk. He arrived in the radio room ten minutes later, bearing the receipt slip.

'Was that message really so important?' he roared.

'Maybe not, really,' was all I could think of to say.

'Well you've got a telephone there, you don't have to come racing down to my cabin like the charge of the Light Brigade!' I just let him burn himself out and continued to deliver messages as normal afterwards. I was not the only one in the firing line. Although I only saw a fraction of what took place I did see him storming out of communal rooms leaving people muttering 'Head case!' after him. We all knew, here and on other ships, that we were supposed to respect the captain and his authority, but there could be circumstances which were too much for anyone. It was usually best to simply let the difficult moments pass, and then to commiserate with each other.

We sailed up the Somali coast, passing as near as 3.5 miles at one stage, staring into deep darkness by night and training binoculars upon steep orange cliffs from the bridge wing during the day. There were no security concerns in the region at that time. We had five Somali crewmen on board who became quite homesick for a while. Passing into the Red Sea we sailed close to Yemen's volcanic Zubair islands and peered through binoculars at the lighthouse on the 566 foot summit of Centre Peak Island. In 2012 an underwater eruption formed a new island in the group, with the attendant seismic activity apparently destroying the lighthouse.

The engines failed again in the evening, suddenly plunging the accommodation into darkness. The engineers raced for the engine room while I groped through the darkness of the upper decks to the radio room. After a few eerie minutes a generator was restarted and normality began to resume. Arriving at Suez we anchored overnight and joined a morning convoy through the canal. In the Great Bitter Lake I saw and admired one of the company's newest ships, *Stratheden*. It was on its maiden voyage and I called Jim, their R/O, on the VHF for a chat. In the future we would change places; he would sail on *Strathdirk* and I would sail on *Stratheden*, and on two of its sister ships, myself.

We passed between Malta and Sicily, sailing into heavier swells which rolled the ship by up to 27 degrees either side, not the biggest rolls we would encounter but enough to cause some inconvenience on board. Better weather arrived near the Balearics and after anchoring off Valencia we spent a day in port. I took the opportunity to spend a morning ashore seeing the city and stocking up with essentials. The Captain's wife and son joined the ship, heralding a calmer spell on board. We soon saw why; during one of his outbursts she interrupted him with 'Oh shut up, Butch!' upon which he lapsed into an embarrassed silence. We had witnessed real power. The sailing conditions improved for a while too as we passed Gibraltar at over 16 knots on flat seas.

The stores began to run low, and complaints stacked up after a long run of daily appearances for roast veal on the menus, either as a hot course or a cold one. The galley staff dug deep into previously-unknown stocks and found a few alternatives even if the veal was never far away.

Imaginative new starters appeared, such as kromeskies, tasty parcels of minced and seasoned meat, but clearly also a new way of using and disguising leftovers. A major food order was promised for New York.

Half way across the Atlantic we encountered several days of bad weather, the consequence of a deep depression to the north. On one day the ship covered only 112 miles, an average speed of 4.67 knots, while pressing through 30 foot waves. 40 degree rolls each way became normal. I worked while sitting on the radio room deck, my chair wedged into a corner and my books and paraphernalia scattered over the carpet. Walking around the ship meant sliding along bulkheads as much as walking on decks, flipping constantly from one side to the other; passing someone at these moments could call for Twister-style manoeuvres. Soup continued to be served in the saloon, handled adroitly by both stewards and officers accustomed to making adjustments every few seconds. We treated the soup as something of a parlour game, but I'm not so sure the stewards saw it that way as they had to "play" so many more times and to clean up afterwards. Tablecloths were dampened to try to hold the cutlery in place, with mixed results.

The next two days saw the speed gradually increase to between 6 and 10 knots. One night the main generator stopped, halting the engines and cutting the power again. This made the auto alarm bells ring and it took some time to dress and stagger up the stairs to the bridge deck and radio room as the ship swung sharply from side to side. Everyone was thankful the failure did not happen when the storm was at its worst.

Meanwhile Portishead was affected by the same weather system. One evening the radio station was broadcasting the following message: 'Due to bad weather and heavy snowfalls, staff are having trouble reaching the station. Services will be severely restricted until conditions improve.' I was glad I had already been able to send a long and detailed message about engine damage earlier that day.

Leave application forms were circulated. Most of us had previously expressed a willingness to remain on board for a long time but second thoughts had grown since then. It became known that the Captain was still staying for the unspecified long duration and this, along with the difficult crossing, may have swayed most people towards leaving after five months after all. There was only one waverer, as the Second Mate had joined later than the rest of us and could not normally expect a relief so soon. However he still had to complete a form and his intentions changed from one day to the next depending on how well or badly the Captain treated him. We wondered how the head office would view such a mass request to leave, however outwardly uncritical they were towards their captains.

I began to hear American radio stations, fuelling a sense of optimism and anticipation at getting to spend time in New York. I exchanged final messages with the local radio station, Amagansett Radio, located near the eastern tip of Long Island. As we sailed along the island's southern shores the sea became calm and the day bright and clear, though the temperature was touching freezing point. The afternoon progressed until a pink haze ahead became a magnificent red sunset. In the dusk which followed, lights began to fill the horizon and some legendary sights gradually became visible: the World Trade Center, Empire State Building and a relatively small white pillar of light which through binoculars resolved itself into the Statue of Liberty. We sailed past the Manhattan panorama and into Newark; the first crew member leaping ashore to secure the mooring ropes sank into deep snow.

As we tuned the usually troublesome TV into most of the available 56 stations, we began to make plans for trips ashore. Some planning was definitely called for as we were not close to Manhattan or familiar with the transport options, although we soon found the bus service from the nearby airport. Meanwhile one of the cadets began calling the numbers collected from the US warship in Bahrain. Some contacts were still away but one US seaman, Dewey, promptly packed a bag and drove his converted van some 600 miles from his home in Michigan to New York. A spare cabin was found for him and he lived on board for a few days, acting as our driver and guide.

Many of the places we visited were entirely predictable, but almost any first-time visitor would take the opportunity to see them. A ferry from Battery to the Statue of Liberty and a scramble up narrow metal stairs to the figure's crown; the torch was closed for maintenance. The World Trade Center and its 45 second lift ride to the top for its breathtaking views. The Empire State Building for its history, different perspective on Manhattan and to buy a King Kong badge. A very run-down and infested Grand Central Station, years before its renovation. A glimpse of Central Park. The U.N. Building. Times Square.

Much of the city was quite dilapidated by today's standards, a situation which forms a significant backdrop to the memoirs of the musicians whose careers took off at that time, including Patti Smith and Debbie Harry. If only we could have known who to go and see play, and where. We had heard of Studio 54 even if we thought it "not for us", but had not yet heard of CBGB. The state of the streets did not seem unusual to us as they matched the appearance of many British cities then. The most noticeable difference was the weather; the city was in the middle of a cold snap and we waded through thick snow or side-stepped high piles of it, and slid on icy surfaces. Bright windows became abstract paintings behind beads and streams of condensation, clouds of steam rose from vents and as we walked we kept warm with purchases of pretzels from hardy street-corner sellers.

Snow-covered New York, early 1978

Times Square had some bright lights but well short of those which shine today, and was lined with dubious "adult show" venues and similarly seedy shops. These included many photographic and electronics shops offering goods at apparently bargain prices but staffed by fast-talking men who rapidly calculated final sums, adding taxes, unwanted accessories and unwelcome price padding. Two of us bought new cameras there, spotting some irregularities in time to renegotiate but missing others, and feeling we still had good deals overall even if we also left the shops with a slightly sour taste in the mouth.

The first meal out was the most memorable, for slightly bizarre reasons. A burger bar near Times Square promised unlimited free beer or wine with every meal, an irresistible challenge for us. We enjoyed our meal and requested more and more beers. The staff thought this was hilarious and possibly a degree of revenge on "The Man", joining us around the table to share drinks and just occasionally getting up to serve other tables with looks suggesting they hoped the few other customers would soon leave. We stayed until closing time when the staff waved us away merrily.

We thought of visiting the place another time but the city held too many other options. One East Side restaurant we visited, Il Vagabondo, served amazing food and was already justifiably busy but would soon become even more famous for its celebrity customers. It seems to have closed relatively recently after a long innings. After the death of its owner the property comprising restaurant, residential space and garden was placed on the market in 2019 for $8.95 million. We also made a return visit to the World Trade Center, but by night. The observation deck became a cocktail bar and I sipped my first ever pina coladas while looking out upon the shimmering lights.

As might be expected, there was plenty of entertainment around. We watched the original (and new at the time) *Star Wars* film in a huge cinema which filled with deep sound and where the floor and seats vibrated as the battle cruiser passed over, earning our instant devotion. A Broadway musical was also on the wish list, and no less a star than Liza Minnelli was appearing in one. The show was called *The Act*, with music and lyrics by the songwriting duo Kander and Ebb soon after their better-known *Chicago*. It was something of a vehicle for Minnelli's dancing, singing and acting talents, and four of us went one evening, enjoying a superb performance.

After pounding the streets for several days and evenings I paused to recuperate and to catch up on some paperwork. One morning I overheard the Captain grumbling to the Chief Engineer about someone; I was unable to tell if it was me and could think of no reason for it to have been. It wasn't about me, but it meant I was prepared when he phoned the radio room and summoned me to his cabin. Unusually he told me to sit down and then said 'Bad news I'm afraid. Your father's died.' This was completely unexpected and he was actually quite sympathetic, leading me to the agent's office by the dock gates and putting calls through to the company and to my family. It was resolved that I would fly home although it would take four days for my relief to obtain a visa and join the ship.

In the meantime we left Newark and sailed through the East River, standing outside on a brilliantly cloudless day in thick coats and hats as we watched Manhattan slip by from an unusual viewpoint. After anchoring for two days in a scenic setting just off New Haven, Connecticut, we docked and my relief arrived. I was put on a bus to JFK airport for an overnight Pan Am flight, after which I drove a rental car home from Heathrow ready to do what I could.

13   Gulf Runs

m.v. Strathduns General Cargo Liner, identical to Strathdirk

Origin of name: Town in Berwickshire

m.v. Strathewe General Cargo Liner

Built: 1978, Gdansk, Poland

Tonnage: 12,598 (gross), 6,469 (net), 16,905 (deadweight)

Dimensions: Length 557'2" (169.88m), beam 76'2" (23.22m), depth 43'9" (13.31m), draught 32'0" (9.77m)

Origin of name: River in northwest Scotland

By now I had completed three years and inevitably some repetition began to set in. This began with *Strathduns* and its voyage to and from the Gulf, the company's busiest cargo route. I joined Strathewe the following year after a trip on a different route (next chapter) but I have combined these two ships rather than repeat too much from similar voyages.

It began with the usual confusion. Someone new in Personnel phoned me with an approximate joining date and telling me to await joining instructions. When the "approximate" date arrived I called him back to learn that the ship had arrived in Avonmouth that day. I reached it on the following day and thankfully found things in good order since the previous R/O had already left. Before heading for the Gulf I was in for what became a very long coastal trip:

two months, sailing to Dundee, Antwerp, Rotterdam, Hamburg, Antwerp again, Newport and Liverpool.

Another familiar situation was yet another difficult captain; difficult not for its own sake but because he seemed to be on the brink of a breakdown. Everything terrified him; each small manoeuvre during sailing and docking led to loud and terrified cries directed at his officers and the pilot. Weather forecasts mentioning small possibilities of rain or fog led to equally loud exclamations of 'Oh no!' and recriminations as if I had personally cast some evil spell to bring the adverse weather upon the ship. I endured the traditional fate of the messenger. Most captains I had seen adopted at least a degree of hands-off management towards the bridge, but this one passed whole days staring wordlessly ahead through the "clearglass" screen, a spinning pane within the front bridge windows which provided a view unimpeded by rain or sea spray. Like my previous captain he complained constantly about the VHF, convinced it was faulty within seconds of speaking, even if the other party was simply taking a breath before replying. Other officers used it without drama and radio stations invariably responded. There were two visits from shore technicians to investigate the alleged intermittent fault, and each pronounced it in good order. Fortunately this captain was only coasting on the ship, although it was a long "coast" and felt even longer at times.

When not fielding unnecessary engineer visits I inherited a large amount of paperwork. A large batch of Admiralty corrections lay in wait when I joined, and I allocated a certain amount of time to work through this tedious job each day. Just as I thought I had finished, another package caught up with the ship: a special supplement and 17 more weekly instalments of corrections! My predecessor must have had an easier trip. For my part I was developing more attention to detail and perhaps also a higher boredom threshold.

Another arrival was a package from a company called Skyfotos. They photographed ships from the air and sent proof pictures and order forms to be displayed on board by the R/O. These arrived on a few of my ships and people were always interested to look at them, at least for a matter of seconds, but I don't recall anyone ever placing an order. There were potentially trips when the last thing anyone wanted as a souvenir was a picture of the ship!

The route to Dundee took the ship through the Hebrides and the Pentland Firth, and we were thankful for the summer weather which confounded the strait's treacherous reputation. The two-week stay in Dundee was my first trip to Scotland, broken with a mid-stay journey home for my sister's wedding. The 24 hour passage to Antwerp was notable for monitoring a Spanish ship which had run aground off East Anglia. I was awoken by the auto alarm's receipt of the distress message at 4 am and once on the bridge with the details we saw it was six hours away while another ship was close to it and ready to assist.

When not cutting out paper corrections, my main role became that of tour guide. The ship had four wives and a small child on board; I led three wives around the shops and sights of Antwerp, providing them with some unintended entertainment when I stood in the middle of a busy road to frame a photo of a church and was told off by a policeman afterwards. At our next port I led all four wives and the child to Rotterdam's city centre shops, and subsequently took myself to see the canals and windmills of Schiedam again. One of the nearby metro stations chimed with my work as it was called Marconiplein, or Marconi Square, named after the great man. Apparently it also has the same nickname as the eponymous company, being known locally as Macaroni Square, and otherwise it seems to be noted for its street art. Visiting these two cities highlighted a real advantage of working on cargo ships rather than much larger vessels. Instead of being marooned many miles downstream within Europe's two largest ports we were able to berth close to each centre and see so much more.

Newport was marked by failure to experience its nightlife and by a main transmitter fault. One nightclub proclaimed 'No membership necessary' and refused us admission because we were not members. The second one claimed to be full, and the third required ties to be worn. We assumed the final club must have been the roughest of them all, with the dress code providing a clue. After what I had seen in nearby Cardiff, I was slightly relieved. We decided these venues must have had too much money and no need of ours, and instead discovered some local restaurants and the ship's own Scrabble boards. The transmitter had some problems with its synthesis of frequencies, solved after multiple visits and some technical escalation within Redifon leading to successful fault-finding within two oscillators. I used to think of faults entirely as nuisances to be fixed and moved on from, but this one was at least relatively interesting. And to think I had been as far as the city's nightclubs in search of entertainment… Once this fault was resolved, the radio equipment on board mostly proved more reliable than the identical items on *Strathdirk*, a welcome change of fortune.

Liverpool saw some changes prior to the deep-sea voyage. The Captain left; my impressions of him appeared to be accurate as the poor man had to be replaced in difficult circumstances during his subsequent, and final, voyage. Meanwhile *Strathduns* got an approachable captain with whom it was possible to hold a conversation and even swap books. This was all new and very welcome to me. However the deck department became a curiously unbalanced one, even if it did not affect me directly. Any references to the Captain as the "Old Man" hardly applied, as two of his subservient officers were older than him and at career dead ends. The new Mate was 62 years old, a number which said that any chance of his own promotion to Master had ended some two decades earlier. He actually seemed much older than his years. Evidence of this, and of his massive interest in ornithology, appeared early. He and his wife lunched with the Captain and agent while discussing the loading of cargo, and he interrupted all the references to cargo hatches with, in a soft Scottish accent, 'Do you know who is taking over the world?' After the Captain barely managed a bewildered mumble, the Mate continued: 'Sparrows! Everywhere you go, there are sparrows!' He continued to expand on this theme as his wife watched him adoringly. The Captain and agent simply stared, open-mouthed and disbelieving. At the next table myself and a few other officers had to try hard to keep our mirth under control.

He was a very nice man, and perpetually cheerful, but seemed to live in a different world. As we approached Port Said after eight days at sea he took over watch duties from the Second Mate and noticed the echo sounder. 'What's that?' he asked. Incredulous, Steve told him. 'How does it work?' he then asked. This was from someone with over forty years at sea behind him. On the Mate's next watch he forgot to ring 'Finished with Engines' on the telegraph linking the bridge to the engine room, annoying the engineers by keeping them waiting after the ship had anchored. As the officer on the 4 to 8 am watch, as well as the matching afternoon one, he was expected to wake officers covering day watches in time for their breakfast. I did not normally need a call but requested one for early on a particular morning in time to catch a station's early weather forecast; he called me too late as he had been watching the dolphins. He called the Third Mate even later one morning with 'Sorry about your breakfast, but I was watching the birdies!'

The Third Mate was also improbably old for the role, at 51 but with any prospects of promotion long behind him as he did not hold the required certificates. He largely kept to himself and Steve, the only deck officer on a normal career path and very sociable too, seemed to be rather isolated professionally.

Meanwhile the Chief Engineer, Gordon, began the trip in his own state of dudgeon. While in Liverpool we were somehow repeatedly exposed to the single *Jilted John* on TV programmes. One night while watching *Top of the Pops* everyone spontaneously joined in with the loudest line, and Gordon stood up and walked out without a word. Fortunately he moved on from this; perhaps someone explained the song and that it was not directed at him.

We eventually sailed for the Gulf, leaving Liverpool's Gladstone Dock on a Sunday afternoon and heading southwards in calm, bright weather. The sun even shone over our passage across the Bay of Biscay, after which we enjoyed some clear views of the Spanish and Portuguese coasts. A haze descended for a while as we entered the Mediterranean, and the Rock of Gibraltar passed unseen eight miles away as I tried to find a fault on one of the VHF units on the bridge.

There were two tense situations as we passed Algeria. Algiers radio sent an urgent message advising of a man lost overboard from a Russian ship, in a location about two hours ahead of us. A while later we passed a Russian ship leaving the area; we called them on the VHF, assuming it was the same ship, but received no reply. We kept a look out for the unfortunate man but saw nothing, and he was never recovered. Then a ship leaving Algiers cut across our course, forcing a gas carrier ship beside us to divert across our bow just as two oncoming ships also approached. We avoided collisions by being the sole ship to slow down and take the correct evasive actions.

We spent two nights anchored off Port Said waiting for our turn to join a convoy through the Suez Canal, and once in the Red Sea the temperatures soared to well over 100 degrees Fahrenheit. My main receiver broke down and I struggled to receive information on the inferior reserve unit for a while until I could find the fault. Leaving the Red Sea, we passed the port of Aden at a distance of five miles, observing its early-evening lights and the silhouettes of mountains beyond.

Suez Canal transit

The Gulf brought some ports which were new to me, but which were unwelcome to those familiar with them. The first was in Saudi Arabia. Some Gulf states, while "dry" themselves to varying degrees, still permitted alcohol consumption aboard ships. Saudi was an exception; customs would board on arrival, even at offshore locations, and seal the alcohol stores as well as searching cabins for alcohol and any printed matter they might find offensive. We anchored off Ras Tanura, better known as an oil tanker port, before moving to a separate anchorage to unload cargo onto giant barges. Our only view of Saudi was a low, sandy coastline three miles away, interrupted only by a few power lines and a row of oil tanks. The port of Dammam was nearby but not visible; I would go there on later ships but, although it was possible to berth alongside the dock, an armed guard was posted to prevent anyone leaving the ship. It was so nice to be made welcome.

Sailing from Saudi led to a predictable rush to compensate for privations suffered, and people flocked into each bar as soon as fresh beer stocks could be carried up from the liberated stores. Uniforms, boiler suits, shorts and nightwear mingled excitedly as everyone grabbed and polished off the warm cans.

The other unwelcome ports were Basrah (Iraq) and Khorramshahr (Iran). Both lie along the Shatt al Arab waterway, which connects the rivers Tigris and Euphrates to the Gulf. It was notorious at the time for its difficult anchorages both outside and within the channel, and for the long time ships sometimes had to wait for entry into its busy ports. It also had a history of being claimed by both countries, and at the time of our visit the waterway had become controlled by Iran.

We spent a week anchored off Abu Fulus, near the mouth of the waterway, swinging with the tides and unable to see the low-lying land. The passage upstream was punctuated by stops at anchorages until tidal conditions were favourable. By the 1970s the flow of fresh water from the two legendary rivers had been reduced by some two thirds from its peak levels due to dams and agriculture in their upper reaches. Deposits of silt, carried down the rivers to accumulate over millennia, also affected the water flow as well as helping to explain the landscape. These factors increased the dependency upon tidal water for larger ships to be able to advance.

There was some admiration for the backdrop of date palms lining the waterway, forming the world's largest such forest. However this was tempered by what appeared to be a hand-to-mouth existence for the people living in shacks at the water's edge, who would row out in small boats looking for scrap wood and other materials. Many of the palms were subsequently destroyed by military action and deliberate environmental destruction in the 1980s and 90s, and the people largely displaced.

Homes on the bank of the Shatt al Arab

Basrah, now normally written without the "h", is one of Iraq's largest cities and had a population of 1.5 million at the time of our visit. Since then it has been at the centre of successive conflicts and upheavals leading to some depopulation. The port consisted of wharves beside the river, flanked by traditional boatyards and moored dhows on either side. The latter hinted at the region's past when the Persian Gulf may have extended further north allowing direct access to the sea, and also being one of Sinbad the Sailor's departure points during his fictional seven voyages. He and any real-life contemporaries may not have had to face sailing down the Shatt, a major benefit. There were very few other hints of the area's significance in history, either as the cradle of civilisation or the culmination of Roman Emperor Trajan's conquest of much of the Middle East, the latter reaching the Gulf in around 116 CE. An excursion to the "Garden of Eden" was offered, which sounded dubious. The few to sign up were taken to a weed-strewn concrete enclosure just outside the city, which provoked considerable disgust; I was glad to have opted out. There was little additional charm available, and our trips ashore were limited to occasional visits to functional waterside restaurants which proved quite pleasant and relaxed. We had harboured preconceptions of being unwelcome visitors in Iraq and sure of a better reception in Iran; in practice the situations we encountered were different. Iraqis seemed pleased to meet and welcome us, and not only when we were spending money.

Boats and boatyard on the Shatt al Arab

Two weeks passed and, cargo unloaded, we moved downstream to our final port, Khorramshahr. The port was similar to that of Basrah, although supplemented by a busy mission run by Swedes. There was little sign of an active oil industry as this was centred on nearby Abadan, with Khorramshahr being a conventional cargo port. There was a feeling of tension in the city; the revolution was three months away. In the souk, people were sullen and uncommunicative, and few goods were on display. I went for a walk from the mission and along the Karun river, a tributary of the waterway. When I paused to take a picture of a building, a guard sprang upright and pointed a rifle at me. I turned and ran for what seemed a long time. When I stopped again it appeared that the only way back was by the same route, so I kept walking. A bridge ahead eventually offered routes back to the port. In the years which followed, I was to remember the exact location as I watched news reports from the area during the 1980-88 Iran-Iraq war. For a while the bridge formed the front line during the Battle of Khorramshahr; this took place between September and December 1980, leading to it being known as the 'City of Blood' before eventually falling. Iran regained control of the city in 1982.

As I reached the port gates I was stopped by four policemen who took a great interest in my camera. This seemed a really bad sign until one of them asked 'Will you take a picture of us…?' They posed for the camera, thanked me afterwards although they would never see the resulting picture, and I raced onto the ship unsure whether to vomit or laugh as I reviewed my walk around the city.

We spent 20 days in port there, unloading slowly and sporadically. I wrote several letters and eventually made a further trip ashore to post them at the mission. As I did so, a voice said 'They will never get there!' I turned and faced Raj, one of my Bristol classmates who happened to be on another ship in the port, and we talked for some time about our careers since college.

I was far from alone in being pleased to sail. Soon, ships would arrive in the area and be held there for months without being able to unload cargo or replenish supplies. We made it a few miles downstream before both engine room coolers broke down and we had to anchor near Abadan. After a morning of intensive work down below one of them was repaired and we progressed downstream. However we had missed the tide and had to anchor again overnight before leaving the waterway behind.

We sailed down the Gulf for a day and a half and anchored five miles off Dubai, to collect an engine part and unload a few boxes of overcarried cargo. Two hours later we were steaming towards the Strait of Hormuz and then out of the Gulf. Many years later, when Dubai had become a recognised leisure destination, I was asked if I had been there, and then how many times. I got to 'either 24 or 25, give or take', and this may have been one of the "visits" I was unsure whether to count.

I was beginning to notice the differences in communication styles between captains and various offices. Some captains sent each upcoming port authority interminable details covering all aspects of the ship, its numerous statistics and history, 'just in case they want it' and regardless of the word charges involved. Others applied some experience and sent a standard minimum, which was usually all that was needed. Messages to head office could reflect the captain's relationship with the company, or at least indicate what kind of day he was having. Messages to the company's telegraphic address requiring immediate attention, especially outside office hours, could begin with 'URURGENT', and captains would present them for sending with comments like 'Let's wake them up today!' The replies could also be provocative sometimes; some messages commenced with a notorious 'Fail to understand...' One captain famously replied with 'Fail to understand why you fail to understand.' The R/O was the unfortunate middle person in all these exchanges.

Our destination back in the UK was Hull, but while crossing the Bay of Biscay I was called by Land's End Radio with an urgent message. Fortunately it was newly-issued rather than one which had languished at Portishead for days waiting for me to make contact. It would have been even worse to have never received it. We were diverted to Falmouth, to relieve anyone wishing to take leave before the ship sailed to Baltimore and other ports on the US coast to load cargo for the Gulf. This was my chance to see more of America, to complete the coastal run I had missed earlier in the year. On the other hand, I had been away for some time and was needed at home more now. I opted to take the leave. My next visit to America would be two years away.

There was a long day in Falmouth while waiting for reliefs to arrive. In practical terms it began to appear a strange port to send us to; perhaps Southampton might have been more convenient for most people, with the additional fuel cost balanced by needing less time in port. Nevertheless the Personnel Manager arrived and sat in the bar as the officers relaxed after lunch. The Mate was sitting nearby and the Personnel Manager chatted with him before casually asking if he had completed a particular firefighting course. 'No,' the Mate replied cheerfully. A string of other courses were then mentioned, with the Mate giving the same reply each time. The Personnel Manager's face gradually darkened as he heard these responses, until he said 'Come and see me in London while you're on leave.' The Mate's demeanour faltered as he began to realise he may have just triggered his own retirement. I gradually put more distance between myself and our conversational visitor, to ensure no awkward questions were directed towards me.

I joined *Strathewe* ten months later, after a last-minute request to hurry to Liverpool and join a ship about to sail. I had already had to effectively decline one similar request. One day while still on leave I received a phone call from a junior in Personnel asking me to make my way to Heathrow that afternoon and fly to the USA. I asked if it could all be done on the next day to give me time to pack and travel. His response was 'It's only Heathrow!' He had assumed that I, and perhaps everyone, lived in London. When I told him where I lived he responded with 'Oh God!' and went away to find someone else.

Back at college, to impress upon us the value of fault-finding, we were repeatedly warned of a scenario in which we might join a ship which could only sail once we had fixed the main transmitter. Now I faced exactly this, and after joining I found myself working on the transmitter late into the evening. Once I had it working, the sailing was delayed and the moment lost some of its drama.

This was one of P & O's latest general cargo ships, and thus among the last to be built for the company. Six joined the fleet, and I sailed on three of them. They were finished to a high specification, with spacious accommodation and good equipment. The one disconcerting factor for me was the realisation that the main transmitter's large and unusual valves included a ring of Beryllium, a metal used for its heat conduction. At college we had been warned of the highly dangerous effect of the metal's particles upon the lungs, and now I had to hope it had been fashioned and installed in a way which made it safe for me in my seat beside the transmitter. I was certainly very careful when I had to replace one of the valves.

The radio room included a new sight in the form of a fax machine for receiving weather maps. This was new technology in my environment, with the data-carrying signals sporadic and easily compromised, but at times when all circumstances were favourable I was able to hand over impressive-looking weather maps without having to receive long code messages to be deciphered first. I still had to tune into and type out actual plain language weather forecasts in the traditional manner too; the weather map was just an extra piece of information. Any time saved soon disappeared, as the provision of Polish typewriters in the radio room and elsewhere caused considerable stress with their reversal of the Y and Z keys. Tippex consumption soared and bins became filled with screwed up paper balls.

The most conspicuous feature on deck was a V-shaped derrick which could lift up to 300 tons, a perfect example of how a cargo ship could handle unusual items and locations. The afterdeck featured a raised structure supporting a small outdoor swimming pool which could be filled with sea water for those leisurely days outside in warmer climes.

The bar opened out into a large lounge area which provided ample space for film and quiz nights while still leaving room for darts, board games and children's toys. Large Japanese dolls in glass cases were fixed to bulkhead corners, reminders of the ship having followed routes between the Gulf and Japan previously. With the exception of my very last trip, my voyages on these ships always carried some wives or families. This usually brought about more measured behaviour in the bars and more varied conversations. That is not to suggest there were no mad moments on board at all, especially as evenings developed, but in general it was as if I was progressing from residing in student hostels to bigger and better hotels.

The working environment was good too, under benign captains. Tom Kelso was Scottish, an old-school BI man who looked and sounded like many people's ideas of a veteran captain. We had sailed together before and taken a while to adjust to each other and overcome our first impressions, but over time we formed a good working relationship. He had clear ideas on what he wanted from his officers while remaining civil and, in my experience, crossing no behavioural lines. He was also someone who clearly took an interest in many other things in life. John Milburn ("Jim") Burn commanded the next two trips. He was a softly-spoken man from the North East with an easy manner, a sociable nature and a good sense of humour. I think we would all have sailed anywhere with him.

Another senior officer was Alan, the Mate, who was apparently next in line to be promoted to Captain. He was already in his forties and probably even more concerned than we all were over the shrinking fleet and what the future held. He was an open and friendly man who was clearly highly educated and informed; he surprised us by stating that he and his family had no TV set at home. His range of conversational subjects and his performance in quizzes demonstrated the power of switching off the box, at least sometimes, and reading instead.

I spent nine months on board, with one short break. During this time the ship made three voyages to the Gulf and back, the final one also taking in Bombay. The incentive for staying, for myself and several others, was the generally-held hope and persistent belief that once in the Gulf the ship would be switched onto the Japan route. This had happened before, hence the dolls in the bar, but our hopes were not realised.

There were some variations in an otherwise repetitive route, and each voyage had the benefit of being quite short. The first was three months, terminating in London's West India Docks, now at the heart of Canary Wharf. I could have flown home from Hamburg, one of the return ports, for a short break but took no leave. Instead I was able to bring family on board in London and then take a trip home for a brief stay. The second voyage was even shorter, returning to the same London dock after only two months. The ship may have been one of the last to dock there. Twenty-five years later I would work nearby and walk these same docks beside apartments and glass offices. I took a short break from the ship this time and another R/O stepped in for its stay in London and journey around the coast to Liverpool. I was never asked to do anything like that; my coasting times were always linked to "deep sea" voyages. I rejoined expecting to sail soon but the dockers stopped work in sympathy with a steel strike and delayed our departure by two weeks. Gladstone Docks and the Bootle area were not the destinations of many people's travel dreams, but although the ship was trapped we were all able to travel to and from home, keep our cars beside the ship and drive into the city centre for nights out. It is a place I associate with *Going Underground* by The Jam, which became an instant and massive hit at that time. It was certainly an upgrade on *Jilted John*.

Awareness of songs like these demonstrated that punk and its successor, New Wave, were beginning to be recognised in some way, even tentatively on ships where tastes were conservative and knowledge of new music limited. It was mostly just background stuff though. Any adoption of the punk aesthetic was usually met by ridicule, and on this ship many were bewildered by two cadets claiming to be punks. Given the constraints of their work and uniforms there were limits to how unacceptable they could make themselves appear, so instead they simply "talked the talk" a little while adopting the names of Elvis and Suggs. The real (and hardly outrageous) performers with these names were barely known on board so the cadets were able to pretend that their own use of the names portrayed them as representing anarchy in our small portion of the UK. People mostly just rolled their eyes, and an attempt by one of them to equate himself with Sid Vicious ended up being spelled as 'viscous', which summed up the comical situation quite well. The cadets were lucky. A junior crewman also identified himself as a punk and during a rowdy social evening in the crew bar he was tied to a chair while his shipmates shredded his jeans and attempted to give him a Mohican haircut. This got out of control and in the end he lost all his hair and both eyebrows.

The playing of bar music had moved on a little since my days on *Tekoa*. Crooners were no longer dominant and the playing of "safe" pop was generally acceptable. Abba, and Fleetwood Mac's *Rumours,* were even tolerated when senior officers were present, as was Tracy Huang, a singer from Taiwan whose cassettes of pop cover versions were widely available in the Gulf. When people were feeling reflective late in the evening, Chris de Burgh's early albums were likely to be produced. Here we were actually ahead of the curve since he had a cult following for several years before finding mainstream success and beginning to divide opinion. I was able to describe seeing him as early as 1975 when he opened on Supertramp's *Crime of the Century* tour and even his biography in the tour programme described him as unknown. He must have hoped for better publicity. Meat Loaf's *Bat out of Hell* was another growing word-of-mouth success, still far from universally known two or three years after its release but often played on board during louder nights driven by younger officers. It was all as if punk had never happened. By then, "New Romantic" was becoming established, but I don't recall any of us referencing the term. Our knowledge was distinctly patchy, and catching up with tastes back home was sometimes problematic.

The two stays in Liverpool were notable for some cargo for which the ship could have been specially built. The main cargo carried from there was steel, Britain still being a significant producer and exporter then, and other building materials, but additionally a number of large tanks had to be taken to oil facilities in the Gulf. The largest were some 100 feet long and weighing 150 tons, and they were carried lengthways on each foredeck and across it, the latter overhanging each side like massive hotdogs. Somehow British Rail managed to lose one of the large tanks, leading to our having to load it on the next stay in Liverpool and then make an extra stop in the Gulf to deliver it.

The three voyages took in the frequently-visited ports, particularly Muttrah, Dubai and Bahrain, but also some new or less familiar ones. The new ports did not always contribute greatly to anyone's memories, but still added to the places in the atlas we could point to as having visited.

Jeddah, on the Red Sea, is Saudi Arabia's second-largest city and a busy port. It also mirrored the country's Gulf ports in sealing the alcohol stores and placing an armed guard on the gangway. I managed to persuade a guard to allow me to leave the ship and walk nearby so I could at least say I had set foot in Saudi, but some of today's tourism opportunities there would have been nice.

Strathewe with heavy cargo

Salalah, in Oman, is now an important container port. We saw this in its early stages, as containers were stacked around the wide dock areas while we unloaded general cargo using the ship's own cranes. The port was flanked by rocky mountains which we were advised to avoid as they had harboured rebels in the past, and the town was out of sight, so our two stays there were very limited in scope. On one visit we were docked next to a Dutch ship and organised social events, an early manifestation of the P & O Nedlloyd partnership of the future. On our other visit we played endless games of football on a vacant concrete space, starting again whenever we had lost count of the score.

Das Island was the destination for the large tanks. This tiny island belongs to the United Arab Emirates and is fully built over by an oil and gas plant. It had been a familiar sight on previous visits to the region, lying between Dubai and Doha with its burning flare prominent by day and night. I was told that staff there played golf on a course marked out between the pipes and towers. The ship's heavy lifting derricks came into their own here as the tanks were carefully lowered onto large barges while the ship listed in sympathy. The lifting derricks and cargo were the ship's ultimate "train set", massive equipment operated by a small remote control after much preparation.

Unloading large tank off Das Island

Abu Dhabi was a port I had briefly visited before but it became attractive for a new reason on these voyages. The "centre" as we knew it then, almost completely lost in today's expanded street layout, was a square flanked with stalls and shops. One stall in particular sold huge numbers of music cassettes at very low prices (around 45 pence). Bootlegging was obviously a big business somewhere in the world, with this stall being the best outlet we happened to discover. Without condoning the practice, it was an opportunity to buy new music for the ship and for personal use, to investigate music we were otherwise unfamiliar with, and which in some cases we would go on to buy legitimate and longer-lasting copies of. We would step out of a taxi carrying holdalls ready to fill with our new buys and stand at the stall pointing at any which caught our eye, the name of the artist usually being enough to add another tape to the piles building up on the counter. This was not always completely straightforward; securing one particular tape led to this exchange:

'The Police,' I said, pointing at the next cassette case.

The trader almost jumped up into the roof of his stall. 'What, where?'

'No, I want The Police.'

'Why do you want the police?'

'No, this tape, here! The Police.'

'Oh, The Police! Here you are. I don't like the police.'

He was not selling surreptitiously out of a suitcase like bootleg traders in London, but the above suggested he lived with some risks alongside the rewards. Meanwhile for us, filling a holdall with so many tapes counted as a successful trip ashore there. I remember buying 90 of them one evening. As with so many of the ports I visited back then, Abu Dhabi is now known for so much more, but at the time we could only take it as we found it.

All this musical interest on board led to my beginning to list the BBC Top twenty singles in addition to my news sheet. However its value was limited by interference during the weekly World Service broadcast and I usually got some song or band names wrong. For example there was a hit by The Beat called *Too Nice To Talk To*, which I somehow transcribed as '*Still I Support You.*' Similarly the band Musical Youth became 'Musically You'. I hope there were not too many confused record sellers back home when people returned from their trips and tried to buy music.

My news sheet expanded to spoof some of the daily happenings on board. One paragraph read like this: 'The electricians are believed to have set themselves up in business as *dhobi wallahs* following the failure of the last working washing machine. For just a few rupees, you can watch your lovely whites being spun in number one generator, and ironed with a suitable pair of engine room boots.' People sometimes read these as serious news and then had to go over them a second time. Perhaps these pieces also helped to accelerate some repairs. Another item followed numerous earnest discussions on the possible meanings of Pink Floyd's new album, *The Wall*. Eventually I wrote some new verses for the album's hit single, imagining the crew deciding to remain in their bunks rather than "turn to" for work; the hook line was 'Hey! Bosun! Leave those lads alone!'

If some of these things appear frivolous, they also raised spirits a little as well as being a reminder to all that I was doing more than the minimum. All R/Os had to, at times, face suggestions that we were virtually passengers on board, usually made by people with little or no idea of what we did. Sometimes this was light-hearted banter and at other times more serious. I felt that once my role included so many extras – bar management, news sheets, music charts, football pools, football pontoon, daily bingo, film shows, compiling and hosting quizzes, and planning other events – I would at least keep any carping at the jovial end of the scale when the engineers emerged covered in grease from below and saw me looking clean and relaxed.

A similar discussion sometimes centred on which R/Os were considered the better ones. Again this usually stemmed from comments made by people with little or no first-hand knowledge, and when someone named a particular senior R/O as being the standard to aim for, I challenged him.

'How do you know he's so good?'

There was a pause. 'Well…he said he was.'

This summed up the problem. The answer was blatant self-publicity, which I was not particularly keen on, preferring to let my work and contributions speak for themselves, however faintly. Maintaining a regular presence in the bar also helped. I had met the senior R/O in question and been subjected to his speeches and lectures on how things should be done, but I had also relieved him on a ship where he had left a messy radio room with many tasks left undone.

One of the wives on board celebrated her 21st birthday. It was decided that the event would be a hat party and that everyone had to make their own. The lady's husband wore an arrangement of beer cans on his head. Some hats were wonders of creativity; that made by Alan, the Mate, was an entire cardboard house, expertly cut out and assembled with a homely yellow interior and a suspended key. The whole structure was actually built on top of another hat. One of the engineers created a giant stovepipe, which his own lack of height enabled him to just about carry off without damaging the lighting. The less industrious simply recycled some Christmas cracker hats or, in one case, wore a standard-issue hard hat. Mine was somewhere in between, a bit ecclesiastical in shape with some colouring-in to enhance its appearance.

Somehow port became the main drink of choice in the bar for a while, served neat, with large quantities of it suddenly stocked and poured whenever a round was offered. People stockpiled cheese from dinner and the pantry in order to complement it, albeit as an optional extra. As soon as a few people changed between trips, the craze seemed to fizzle out.

The return to normality meant that the main requirement in the bar was for beer or soft drinks, which were easily stocked and handed out. Spirit consumption was rare by comparison and usually considered a bit fussy compared to beer, although occasionally I did sail with heavy drinkers of vodka or gin. They usually sat behind the bar to ensure their pouring and mixing requirements troubled no-one else. The notion of sailors drinking rum belonged to a bygone era and a different kind of ship anyway, although a bottle was always visible and occasionally poured with cola.

Another obsolete view of seafarers was that we all had tattoos! Some certainly did, but I think they were in a minority. At the time tattooing lacked the mainstream appeal it has gained since, and any mystique was accompanied by a hint of danger, like smoking. On one of these trips, a crewman's new tattoo became badly infected and he had to be taken off the ship for treatment, never to return. This incident may have deterred some of his shipmates from getting "inked".

The addition of Bombay to the schedule on two trips provided some new opportunities even if I was not destined to sail further east and see any more of the "Orient" referenced in the company name. There was the chance to revisit some old haunts, and to buy a large and heavy Indian coffee table, being able to carry it home easily by sea whereas flying with it would have caused difficulties. I was also able to pay a short but nostalgic visit to *Dwarka*, which was still in service and with some personnel unchanged.

For one of the ship's electricians, universally known by his sobriquet "Aussie Bob", Bombay was a chance to immortalise, in his own way, an unfortunate incident on the ship's outward passage.

Maidan and central Bombay after heavy rain

Just after entering the Mediterranean the ship had collided with a whale, leaving it trapped across and around our bulbous bow. This shape at the waterline improves water flow around the hull and helps to increase a ship's speed and fuel efficiency. The whale was identified as a sei, one of the larger types and estimated at 50 feet long and up to 30 tons in weight. This may sound substantial but it was tiny compared to the ship, and especially at the "sharp end" at full speed. At first it was reported that the whale had broken in two, with the halves held in place by the ship's motion; this was revised when slowing down proved insufficient to dislodge it, although no-one was ever sure whether the creature had survived or not. I took some pictures from the forepeak but these only showed it to a limited extent, although its face looked calm and I think an eye was open. Eventually, after much manoeuvring, it was shaken off.

Aussie Bob designed a T shirt showing a large whale across the ship's bow, with the creature saying 'I'll never find another Ewe.' He had these embroidered in Bombay and later modelled one in the company magazine. I understand the sei is now a protected species; this cannot be solely due to freak accidents with merchant shipping.

On our return voyage to the UK there was a delay at Suez; we were just too late for the morning convoy and could not transit until the next day. Someone called the ship on the VHF and offered a day trip to Cairo for £20 each. A few officers, including myself, were cleared to go, and along with two of the wives we were collected by boat and minibus for a two-hour drive into Cairo. Once there we were taken to the Muhammad Ali Mosque, the Pyramids, a souk and for a meal at a restaurant which also featured a belly dancer. We were never going to be able to cover everything Cairo had to offer but it was a special, and unexpected, day out.

Still, three trips were enough and I decided it was time for a change.

14 Vendee

m.v. Vendee	Refrigerated Cargo Liner
Built:	1972, Sunderland
Tonnage:	6,088 (gross), 2,478 (net), 7,004 (deadweight). Subsequently extended.
Dimensions:	Length 434'0"(132.28m), beam 64'1" (19.53m), depth 38'6" (11.73m), draught 24'1"(7.34m)

Origin of name: Département of western France

On a January evening I met up with Second Mate Steve, who I had recently sailed with on *Strathduns*, and Fourth Engineer Doug, at Heathrow. We boarded an Air France Caravelle for a flight to Marseille, speculating nervously on the age of the plane once we set eyes upon it. Had we known the Caravelle's accident rate (5.5 times that of modern airliners, apparently) it would have magnified our concerns. Still, we landed without incident and were driven by the shipping agent to the port, arriving in darkness at our next ship, *Vendee*. This had once been one of the company's most wished-for ships, as under its previous name, *Zaida*, it had plied a route between Japan and New Zealand. Now, along with its sister ship, it had been renamed and chartered to the owners of the fruit and vegetable company Carmel, whose name had been applied to the funnel. The route served just two ports, carrying produce in both directions between Marseille and Ashdod, Israel. The sister ship, *Vosges*, followed the reverse route, being in Ashdod when we were in Marseille and vice versa, and the two ships tended to pass close and greet each other in mid-Mediterranean.

This Mediterranean route was a welcome break from trips to the Gulf, falling between those of *Strathduns* and *Strathewe* in the previous chapter. However its attractions soon waned through being so limited to the two cities, despite each having their interesting aspects.

The radio room featured a Marconi console, integrating all the main communications equipment at the desk within a single housing, with the exception of the large main transmitter. These consoles seem to be fondly remembered among former R/Os. It all felt familiar despite the different hardware of my previous two trips, and quite reliable too. A few faults did develop over my five months but I was able to fix them all. My record was only slightly dented on my very last day when a new fault appeared on the main receiver and I called for outside help then; I had no time to look at it before leaving and I wanted to leave things in good working order for the next R/O.

There was little time to see the city on our first arrival and we soon sailed out of the port and past the Ile d'If, where the conspicuous fortress provided the prison setting for Alexandre Dumas' novel *The Count of Monte Cristo*. I had to become familiar with several radio stations I had never had to contact before, and also to sometimes receive and interpret weather forecasts in French; for instance converting 'peu agitée' into 'slight' sea waves. A day later we reached the first of two narrow channels on the direct route towards Israel. This was the Strait of Bonifacio, a seven-mile wide stretch of water which separates Corsica and Sardinia; both coasts were visible. The passage has recognised dangers due to currents, small islands and hidden reefs, leading to some perhaps inevitable shipwrecks. In 1855 the French ship *Sémillante* was wrecked here, drowning 750 troops bound for the Crimea. A tanker grounding in 1993 led to a ban on French and

Italian ships carrying dangerous goods through the strait; a number of environmental measures have also been introduced over time. Our ship never deviated from passing through this strait, the most direct route. The navigable water for us was just over one mile wide, and with four course changes. After a tense half hour or so and several conversations with the VHF station at Bonifacio we passed into the Tyrrhenian Sea.

The second sea channel was the Strait of Messina, a mere 1.6 miles wide at its narrowest point, which separates mainland Italy from the island of Sicily. We passed the smouldering island volcano of Stromboli, and crossed over the ferry route linking the towns of Reggio Calabria and Messina on either side of the strait. Gradually the huge bulk of Mount Etna began to dominate the skyline, incongruously white for some months due to snow on its upper slopes.

Upon clearing the strait we sailed across open sea, passing to the south of Crete while following a single bearing directly towards Ashdod. Our destination was a planned modern city, founded in 1956 and a great deal of construction work was still going on. It took the name of a nearby ancient site dating back to biblical times. Among other past events, the Philistines took the Ark of the Covenant to Ashdod after capturing it from the Israelites, bringing misfortune with it (1 Samuel, Chapter 5). The uncouth reputation of the Philistines has been reassessed in recent times and Ashdod now actually hosts a Museum of Philistine Culture.

Being in Israel and with time available, we could not resist booking a trip to Jerusalem. We piled into a minibus and were taken to see the Wailing Wall, the Old City, Citadel Tower and the sights of Temple Mount (Haram esh-Sharif). There seemed to be insufficient time or information to do the city justice, but we loitered by the Dome on the Rock eavesdropping on other guided tours and trying to learn something. As night fell we were taken on to Bethlehem, which at the time did not involve crossing a border, and we visited Manger Square and the Church of the Nativity before a long drive back to Ashdod.

People seized the opportunity to buy Israel T-shirts, seeing them as a little provocation or wind-up material when worn, at least in the bar, on their next trips to the Gulf. I had already seen an officer wearing one of these ashore in Basrah, Iraq, thinking no-one would understand the writing. As soon as someone wished us all a good evening his face froze and he rushed back to the ship to change, which was probably his best decision that day.

The French fruit and vegetables were unloaded and the ship filled with Israeli avocados for the return journey. Avocado cultivation is very successful in Israel and around 70 per cent of its crop is exported.

Passing by *Vosges*, *Vendee*'s sister ship, in the Mediterranean

Despite our geographical circumstances the ship was registered as a BI vessel, with many of that line's traditions. One of these was chicken curry being the main course for Sunday lunch. This was particularly welcome as the ship's crew were Indian so we could expect some authenticity, but getting a curry to suit all tastes was very difficult. Captain

Kelso was a BI man, so when he asked me across the table 'What's the curry like, Sparks?' I replied that it was very mild.

He tasted some. 'It's very hot,' he said.

I was quite surprised but as I looked at the mute faces around the table I saw that no-one else was. He asked the steward to pass his comment back to the galley, and at the subsequent management meeting demanded it be recorded in the minutes that the curries should not be so hot.

Many officers disagreed, once out of earshot, and agreed to form a curry club and seek a crew member with the skills to produce something more authentic. The result, served in the officers' bar one evening, was sensational. Wavering officers signed up to the club and a larger order was placed for the following week. We got something the captain would have approved of. An inquisition below decks revealed that the club chef had been berated by his colleagues and strongly directed to produce a "European" version. Another chef stepped forward, who also produced a very good curry followed by a very bland one; the same conversations had taken place behind the scenes. Then we gave up. A change of captain on board also made no difference to the Sunday curries; the new one seemed interested in anything French, but little else.

Once back in Marseille there was always French food and drink, although the use of Franglais yielded some unexpected results. Two officers sat outside a bar enjoying their beers when they noticed pasties on the menu and ordered one each. They looked forward to their meaty taste of home and were bewildered when served glasses of yellow spirit: pastis. At least the main street full of bars could be counted on for the product sounding like its name: Canabière.

Cheese and wine could also be counted on, and since I had again taken charge of the bar I was also asked to organise something suitably French. I went ashore and staggered back with two holdalls crammed full of different wines and cheeses, putting out an impressive-looking spread that evening. Although most cheeses were eaten in the end, the main focus was upon the drink and I maintained a simple approach: put out the more expensive bottles first and top them up from cheap boxes later. The outcome after a few hours was carnage, with determined souls barely able to stand (if at all) yet still polishing off the last of the most basic stuff imaginable while offering slurred opinions on how good the Beaujolais was. This met all the criteria for a successful evening and once everyone could speak again afterwards I was asked to plan something similar for each visit.

Managing the films was another unofficial part of my role, and as ever there were always opportunities to swap with other ships and see something different. One day a Russian ship arrived behind us in Marseille, and two Russians came over with a film to exchange. I knew their films were not compatible with our projector but they said they had a western projector as well as the Soviet one, so I took their details and just allowed them to take a film. The following day they returned it, said how much they had enjoyed it and asked if they could borrow two. On the third day they returned the films, said they had one more night in port and asked if they could borrow our three remaining films. Soon after they had left, the engineers stepped into the bar on their break, or "smoke-o" as it was known, even to non-smokers. The deck cadets also arrived for their own break. One of them commented 'The Russian ship's sailing.'

'What?' I shouted, springing to my feet.

An engineer asked 'What's the problem?'

'I've just given them three films!'

Loud laughter filled the bar, along with comments on how much trouble I would be in. I was not about to be fooled. 'They must be having a drill. They haven't got any tugs.'

A few minutes passed. 'Here come the tugs,' said one of the engineers, and we saw them approaching the Russian ship. My head went into my hands as the banter flared up again.

'Will somebody come with me to fetch them back?' I asked. This provoked more laughter and, after some recriminations and cajoling, one of the cadets strode along the wharf with me. A junior engineer, wearing boiler suit and flip flops and carrying a beer can, shuffled along some way behind us. We reached the Russian ship where the gangway had already been raised.

'Hey!' I called up to the bridge deck.

An officer looked over. 'What do you want?' he called down.

'Give us our bloody films back!'

'We haven't got your films!'

We disagreed with each other for a while until he asked me for the names of the people who had borrowed the films. I read out the details the Russians had given me. The officer on the bridge deck had the final word: 'That is the other Russian ship around the corner!'

I walked red-faced around the ship for a day or so as the story spread.

There was seldom much interest in going ashore as tourists from *Vendee*. Perhaps people soon felt they had "seen it all" due to the repeated visits to the same two ports. Perhaps the social nature of the crowd and the lively bar kept people together on board, despite the apparently small scale of such a world.

As was often the case I had more spare time than most and spent some of it walking around Marseille, shopping, people-watching and trying to improve my French. I bought French newspapers and magazines and even some French music, and felt I was making good progress for a while. The local coast station must have disagreed, or at least thought I had not already endured enough humiliation lately. I was asked to put through someone's phone call home via the VHF on a day when we were just outside the port. He and one of the mates watched, apparently impressed, as I called the station on Channel 16 and arranged everything in French once on a working channel. Then he asked me for the phone number. I named the town, introduced the code and the number separately and gave each digit in French, feeling pleased with myself. There was a pause, and the operator came back with 'Yes, can I have that again in English please?' My colleagues fell to the floor with laughter while I stood open-mouthed, gripping the handset and wondering how it could have gone so wrong.

Seconds later my vindication arrived, but sadly it was mostly out of earshot. Before I could bring myself to speak to the radio station again, their operator came back with 'Did you say…?' He proceeded to repeat exactly the details I had given him! If only he had said something like 'Can I just check…' in the first place. My laughing audience had moved along the bridge just then and when I told them what had just happened they were a little bit sceptical, even though the phone call went straight through.

One day I managed to walk up the 489 foot hill overlooking the port and visit the basilica on the top, Notre-Dame de la Garde. This is apparently Marseille's busiest tourist attraction but I had the place to myself, a cool and calming experience. I should have gone there straight after the film debacle, and perhaps at some other times too.

On one occasion we were invited to a bigger event, an inter-ship football tournament. This was played on a cinder pitch beside a few athletics facilities, all since redeveloped, next to Olympique de Marseille's football stadium. We played two matches, unusually in front of a reasonable crowd of visitors and other teams and, bizarrely, were each expected to attempt a shot put from a throwing circle behind one of the goals. This enabled the organisers to promote it as having been a "sports" tournament, for reasons of their own, rather than just a football one. We lost both of our games and thus failed to progress further, which was probably just as well as our lack of match fitness was exposed and we all lurched painfully around the ship for some days afterwards. The most memorable moment, except for when we scored our only goal of the two games, was during the second match when I took over from one of the cadets in goal to reacquaint myself with that position and allow him to run around for a while. Due to the nature of the pitch a goalie needed long trousers, and this meant borrowing the cadet's jeans. These were really too small for me and I had to hold them up with one hand. This was bound to cause difficulty at some point, and when a long ball was played into our half for their striker to chase, I had to run out to intercept. I got the ball, but only after using both arms to balance myself; I then tried to dribble it forward, and with each step the trousers fell further and further down until my run became an ungainly waddle and I began to hear laughter. At the last moment I managed to kick the ball safely into touch before falling over, much to everyone's amusement. After the match I was the most-recognised player among the crowd and the focus of some attention!

Radio room, *Vendee*

On a later visit to Ashdod I tried to drum up interest in another trip to Jerusalem, unsuccessfully due to time and possible cost. I became determined to go, and having been before I decided I could get by without a guided tour. I went into Ashdod and caught the bus. I remember it as taking about three hours, along slow and winding roads and probably with some detours from the direct route, but I got there and walked around for an afternoon. I saw many of the same sights as before but also visited the Church of the Holy Sepulchre, believed to be built on the site of the crucifixion. I have since seen documentaries showing the place bulging with tourists, but I remember it as being quiet. As with the basilica in Marseille, I must have picked a good day. It must also have been a peaceful time to visit that part of the world; I think I wandered around both the Christian and Muslim quarters, and noted what seemed to be peaceful coexistence.

Since I had shown it was possible to travel around easily, one of the electricians and I took a bus from Ashdod to Tel Aviv where we passed a leisurely day on the beaches and in the nearby bars. After the World Trade Center this became the other place I associate with pina colada, but with a side order of falafel.

Despite these occasional breaks, there were other times when the monotony of the route took hold, and when days were simply being counted. Three or four round trips might have been deemed acceptable, but thereafter it began to feel grim, however nice the ship. People compared notes on how many circuits they had completed and how mentally "shot away" they were becoming over time. Just as on the *Dwarka* I completed seven round trips, and grew another beard. This time there was a change of routine in the end, as a summer low season for fruit took the ship out of the Mediterranean. This provided an opportunity to leave in Le Havre and I did so, penning a sketch within the invitation to the leaving "shout" for myself and an engineer, Pete, who was departing at the same time. It featured the two of us starring in *Escape from Venditz*, as the ship was becoming known:

Scene: the highest tower, containing the Commandant's beer stocks.

AUSTIN	We made it! Almost out of here now…
PETE	Let's have a beer first. (*They drink beers.*)
AUSTIN	What happens next?
PETE	(*consulting script*) We jump out of the window.
AUSTIN	Oh. Can we have another beer first? (*They drink several more beers.*)
PETE	I don't want to escape any more.
AUSTIN	It's not so bad after all. (*They drink several more beers.*)

We were adamant we would not really change our minds like that, although there were some similarities between the sketch and the evening. Next day we caught the overnight ferry to Southampton, passing some of the journey sharing drinks below decks with some of the crew after being welcomed aboard by a former shipmate. It was a close-knit world.

15 Triangles

m.v. Stratheden General Cargo Liner, identical to Strathewe

Origin of name: River in Fife

m.v. Strathesk General Cargo Liner, identical to Strathewe and Stratheden

Origin of name: River in Midlothian and East Lothian

Joining *Stratheden* was contrary to all my plans. I had a few months of leave but was asked to join the ship after only six weeks. I had made my first attempt to leave the sea, unsuccessfully, and suddenly my time for more applications had expired early. More of my former college classmates had moved to jobs ashore, with some joining Portishead Radio. GCHQ also still regularly advertised vacancies, for both technical and operational roles. It was good to know that these were available options while I investigated other industries, and I knew I would have to make some kind of change soon as the fleet continued to shrink. Of the 72 cargo ships owned by the company five years earlier, only 17 remained. Another 14 new ships had been added, making a fleet of 31 ships. The company still provided officers for a variable number of other companies' ships, but these hardly amounted to long-term career prospects.

The personnel lists circulated from head office to ships were also becoming ever smaller. Groups of officers perused them and tried to deduce by omission who had left the company and how, with references to Orwell's *1984* in which people disappeared from print in the same way. Discussions on all this inevitably affected morale.

If the situation was bad for working officers, it was even more challenging for prospective ones. Although cadets were still working their way through the system, and being sponsored by the company, few were being promoted into officers afterwards. It appeared to be worse still for radio students, who were still mostly self-funding yet vacancies were diminishing even as they trained. I realised that the rank of 2/R/O had become very rare in the company, a clear sign of the recruitment situation. I accepted an invitation to give a careers talk at my old school, but decided that the job prospects had become so poor that it was hard to recommend what I did. I talked about how I had qualified, showed them slides from my more recent trips and answered a few travel questions.

Also, it was an identical ship to *Strathewe* and following the same UK-Gulf route. I could accept that the route was always the most likely one, but I was hardly at my most motivated at the time. I found that some others on board were similarly downbeat and I remember the atmosphere on board, especially during the early months, encompassing Hull, Glasgow, Liverpool, Tilbury and the Gulf ports, as being quite subdued. Several other officers clearly did not want to be there at the time. Most officers still had to collaborate over work but as the R/O was a one-person department this felt quite a lonely trip.

There was a strange day in Tilbury when Mr Merry paid an unexpected visit. I had not seen him for a long time and he was surprisingly polite and almost pleasant, which I was unsure how to respond to. He had lost his assistant to redundancy by then and perhaps like many of us he was in the process of adjusting to a new world. Or maybe he had just won the football pools. Whatever was going on, I never met him again. He actually had no complaints about the radio room, and I wondered if my five years with the company had given me some of the status I had lacked at our earlier meetings.

In contrast to the drinking culture which formed part of life on many ships, this one featured a craze for dieting and healthy eating. The catalyst for this was a large industrial balance scale, situated in a small chamber on one of the upper decks; no-one knew why it was there and I don't recall seeing one on *Stratheden*'s sister ships, but people began to weigh themselves regularly and enthusiastically. A chart was produced and put up in the bar, making everyone's weight and weekly change very public. Food and drink consumption fell, along with reductions in attendance in the bar and dining saloon. It was all good for me in some ways, and I did lose a significant amount of weight, but "good" does not always equate with exciting or memorable.

There was a morsel of entertainment as we anchored off Port Said waiting for a Suez Canal convoy. We were visited by the "Gillygilly Man", an Egyptian magician who regaled us in the bar with a range of conjuring tricks. These were accompanied by his trademark 'gillygilly' patter and the frequent appearance of chickens, which should not have been surprising as his large and baggy suit constantly clucked and moved of its own accord. He would probably have been unsuccessful on a UK TV talent show, but in the circumstances he brought smiles to jaded faces and we made his visit worthwhile for him.

Once in the Gulf there was an important development as the ship was moved onto the triangular run featuring East Africa and the USA, that which I had partially experienced on *Strathdirk*. It remained on this route long enough for me to complete over five months on board, which this time included the US East and Gulf coasts before leaving in Barcelona as the ship returned towards the Gulf. I took five months' leave, became more motivated and refreshed, and only tried a little to find something new before flying to Dubai to rejoin the same ship for another four months. By then some personnel had changed and others mellowed, and the atmosphere on board seemed much better. The scales had been forgotten too, which may not have been a coincidence. After this trip I was assigned to another sister ship, *Strathesk*, which had also begun to serve the same route.

Some things were the same on any trip to the Gulf. One of these was gadget shopping in Dubai; I bought a huge ghetto blaster there, which accompanied me on each subsequent trip, thanks to the indulgent airline policies towards in-flight hand baggage at the time. Other regular activities included music shopping in Abu Dhabi and leisure at the British Club in Bahrain. I also got to see more of Kuwait, thanks to a friendly agent showing me around; this included visiting the newly-built Kuwait Towers, surrounded by sand, sheds and building materials. A picture I took at the time forms quite a contrast to the development within and around the towers today. The Strait of Hormuz became less visually interesting as shipping lanes were introduced, a one-way system for the high number of ships passing through. The lanes kept us more distant from the Omani hills and islands we had once sailed close to, especially on the way in. The Royal Navy were seconded to enforce the new routes, calling ships which deviated to remind them of the correct course to follow.

Dar es Salaam was welcome for sightseeing, especially as we actually berthed alongside the dock on these voyages, eliminating the previous issues with boat services. There seemed to be many shortages around the city, with basic food items absent from the shops despite the food stalls on the beach being well-stocked. Expats appeared on board asking if they might buy any spare supplies.

Six of us decided to check out an expensive-looking restaurant facing the harbour. It looked the part, outside and in, with nicely-laid tables, pleasant décor and large, leather-bound menus. We were its only customers, although six uniformed waiters milled around the empty spaces. We ordered local beers and studied the menus. We tried to order starters, and everything we chose was met with a shake of the waiter's head. 'All is off,' he said. Undeterred, we started to order main courses instead. It took a while to realise that none of these were available either, until the waiter filled another pause with 'All is off.'

'What *have* you got then?' someone asked.

'Calamari.'

We all looked at each other. 'Okay, squid and chips six times, please.'

The waiter departed and we waited. We ordered more drinks. The waiters continued to circulate around the still almost-empty room, or huddle near the pass. 'Is the food coming soon?' we asked.

'Very soon,' we were told.

Doubts were creeping in. 'Maybe they have had to go out and buy it somewhere.'

This may have been the case as we waited for over an hour before our main courses arrived. The food was actually good, and we ate quietly for a while. After the six empty plates had been cleared we were offered a dessert menu. When we tried to order from it, we were again told that 'All is off.' Why had they brought us the menu? We would never know, so we asked for the bill. Fifteen minutes passed while the waiters argued among themselves back at the counter before admitting they had lost our bill, the only one in the restaurant. We had seen enough and, like the menu, we were off. We pooled together what we felt was a fair price for the meal, based on the menu prices we had seen. We piled this up on the table and walked out. The waiters followed us outside and down the road, demanding more money. They had not even counted the money on the table, and when we stopped and asked them how much the meal should have cost they simply looked at each other, having no apparent idea. We continued to walk and the waiters returned to the restaurant, perhaps concerned that someone might steal in and raid their pantry. I later wondered if someone else may have had a similar experience there and been inspired to write of a gourmet night in a Torquay hotel.

In Mombasa it became customary for a group of us to hire a Mini Moke for a week or so and use it to take us to and from all the city's attractions; mission, shops, restaurants, night clubs, beaches and hotel swimming pools. On one occasion we took the Moke to a small safari park outside Mombasa. The vehicle was impractical for some of the terrain, being low and open, and we became covered in dust and sand, choking on it at times; I could barely muster more than a croak for a few days afterwards. Despite this we had a good day out, covering as much ground as possible, seeing a few animals and watching a tribal dancing display. On our way back, the officer driving took a corner too quickly and crashed the Moke. I saw it coming and called out, reaching for the low door at the same time, but we hit the bank and were all thrown forward and back. Once we had recovered we found we had crashed into soft earth and thick vegetation and that the damage was only cosmetic. We carefully returned to the ship where we managed to repair and clean it well enough to return it without having to confess the incident.

Strathesk went into dry dock in Mombasa; this meant repeating my experience on *Somerset* of having to venture beneath the ship and make checks. Once this scary scramble around on the dock floor was over I had plenty of leisure time, largely passed relaxing at the nearby yacht club which allowed us to use their facilities while watching the boats and ships pass in and out of the port.

Both ships produced football teams for games at the missions in the East African ports. There was little interest on *Stratheden*'s first voyage there but by the second we had a team, albeit an unsuccessful one. We lost 5-0 to a local team in Mombasa who arrived performing ball tricks worthy of the Harlem Globetrotters, while most of our team lurched slowly from the minibus clutching beer cans and cigarettes before finding themselves chasing shadows for 90 minutes. I was in goal and made a few saves to keep the score down, particularly with a flying leap near the end which the team remembered and celebrated long after choosing to forget what had passed before.

Strathesk in dry dock, Mombasa

By contrast *Strathesk* raised a very good team which strolled to an easy win in Mombasa and patiently secured a more hard-fought one in Dar. I was in goal again for these games. Despite everything it was still my preferred position and one which made sense to people; after all, the adages were that goalies were mad, and sparkies were mad, so who could compete with me for that place? We had a steward named Terry who acted as player-coach, and we took to the field filled with his motivational talk, ready to play against a South Korean ship. The pitch sloped steeply from one end to the other, and we soon faced an onslaught from opponents who were playing downhill. An early move ended with a shot from the edge of the box, and I dived to my left in order to save it. At that moment Terry stepped into the ball's path and deflected it into the opposite side of the net as I fell helplessly. Afterwards people blamed him for allegedly scoring an own goal, although the shot was really on target and the moment just an unfortunate one. The more he tried to assert all this in the weeks that followed, the more people repeated the fiction, while smiling behind their drinks at his discomfort. I had little to do for the next hour as our team attacked and did everything but score. Then a Korean breakaway put their striker though on goal against me. Everyone stood and watched as he ran up the slope, while I waited on the edge of the penalty area with my arms outstretched. Eventually he began to falter and attempted a shot; I blocked it, collected the ball and cleared it downfield. All this proved decisive; we could have been two goals down but within seconds we finally equalised. Shortly afterwards we went 2-1 up, and as our opponents' heads dropped we dominated the later stages to win 4-1.

By this trip I was trying to take my fitness a bit more seriously, if only to become slightly more mobile and minimise the aches and pains which followed the games. My job was one of the least active on board, and we had nothing which passed for a gym so I devised ways to improvise. I managed to train a little by walking the decks and then sprinting up and down all the steps on board, five decks from my cabin deck down to the laundry deck and the same back, over and over while hoping no-one stopped me to ask anything important. Swimming was also helpful, when the pool had been filled between ports.

One northbound trip made a stop at Assab, then under Ethiopian rule but within the territory of Eritrea which became an independent country in 1993. I was told there was little to see ashore but I decided to take a look. My resolve lasted until I reached the dock gates, patrolled by heavily-armed guards. After a glance down at my camera, my experience in Khorramshahr came to mind and I retreated. Decades later I heard the explorer Levison Wood describing how while walking the Nile he carried cigarettes, even as a non-smoker himself, to hand out at times like this, and it may well have been good advice for me too. Instead, as the ship loaded coffee from more scenic regions, I looked out from the bridge upon low-rise buildings and a refinery.

Each transatlantic voyage brought the prospect of highly changeable weather. On two of these trips the conditions were good, but the third brought even more stormy weather than my crossing on *Strathdirk*. This necessitated making the ship "heave to"; simply maintaining our position and ensuring we faced the right direction, during the worst weather rather than attempting to drive through the heavy seas. For day after day the ship rolled by 40 degrees or more, to port and then to starboard, motions we could quantify from a gauge on the bridge. It was reported that the company's flagship had measured a 43.5 degree roll during a recent storm and there were frequent checks to see if we had beaten it. Some rolls were clearly over 40 degrees but no-one could watch the gauge constantly so the flagship's record probably just about remained intact. It was something of a multi-sensory spectacle as in addition to its huge rolling the ship also pitched up and down, crashing through the troughs between the waves, shaking violently and releasing a deep, tortured mechanical noise which drowned out the constant roar from the sea. There were moments when people's faces briefly showed concern, especially after an unusual roll or lurch, but these were rare; we had all encountered similar conditions before. As on a previous crossing I spent whole working days sitting on the radio room deck, adding barely-legible scribbles to the radio log and trying to stop too many books and objects from sliding around. I would rise to my knees to tune the transmitter or receiver and sit down again to send, receive or merely wait.

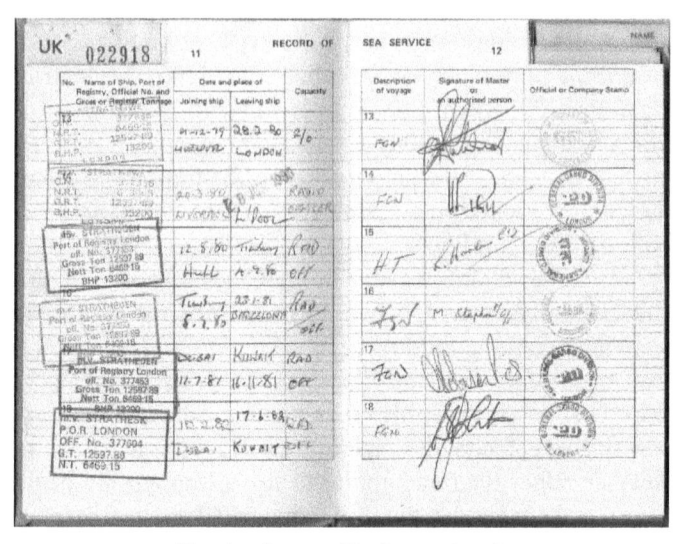

Entries in my discharge book

Stratheden's first arrival in New York coincided with surprisingly mild December weather. We had no guide this time but I felt comfortable finding my way into Manhattan and navigating the streets and subways. I bought a ticket to an ice hockey game at Madison Square Garden, a few days in advance. I also had some paperwork to clear before planning too much more time ashore; monthly account abstracts to complete and send in, and the inevitable Admiralty corrections.

One morning I started work on these and tuned into a local radio station. I was mainly focused on the paperwork but after a while it occurred to me that they had only been playing Beatles songs. I didn't mind this but as the sequence continued I began to try other stations, only to find they were playing the same. Just then a steward brought my morning coffee, along with 'Have you heard about John Lennon?' He had obviously been up and about for longer than I had, and heard all the details of the shocking overnight event.

We talked about this for a while and after he left, the music paused and the DJ spoke solemnly, something like this: 'That was a tribute to John Lennon, who died last night. Now we are returning to our normal programme.' And the next record played? Queen's *Another One Bites the Dust*! Surely this was American humour?

Later that day a few of us went ashore and, despite having no plan, somehow found ourselves outside the Dakota Building. We were shocked by the crowds of people outside, wondering what they could have been thinking, before we stopped and asked ourselves the same thing. We walked on into and around Central Park until deciding to head downtown in search of a restaurant for dinner. In addition to all the photography shops the Times Square area also had several record and tape shops, and the music from their open doors filled the streets with songs from John and Yoko's *Double Fantasy* album while people queued for their copies.

I enjoyed the hockey game, and my subsequent visits to New York took in other seasonal sporting events: two baseball games and a day at the US Open Tennis Championship at Flushing Meadows. There were also more Broadway shows, including *Woman of the Year*, another show scored by Kander and Ebb, this one starring Lauren Bacall. I looked around lots of shops, from the famous department stores to the more independent locations such as those in Greenwich Village, exploring everywhere I could. I was an unashamed tourist, and despite the stories some people told of the city's mean streets I never felt unsafe. This even applied when I went to an event in Harlem one evening, a location far more notorious then than it is now; I simply researched my route and walked purposefully from the subway. On my final visit the ship moored in Brooklyn rather than Newark, making access to Manhattan easier and also showing me some new neighbourhoods. I made a final visit to the World Trade Center and was able to photograph the ship, albeit at a distance, from the observation deck.

Another regular port for unloading was Savannah, Georgia. We found this an attractive city with many historical buildings and squares, saved from destruction during the American Civil War by its prompt surrender to Sherman's Union Army forces in 1864 after its Confederate defenders had fled. It boasted lively riverfront venues and a restaurant called The Pirates' House, within what is claimed to be Georgia's oldest building. This was particularly popular for its Sunday buffet lunch with live jazz.

The port is located along the city's eponymous river and we had to approach by passing under the Talmadge Memorial Bridge. On one occasion we must have unloaded more cargo than usual since it was found that while the bridge clearance was 132 feet, our highest point had risen to 135 feet. A brave crewman was despatched up the radar gantry and then beyond, up a narrow, exposed additional mast ladder clutching a shifting spanner to loosen the fittings of a VHF aerial and allow it to hang downwards. There was no suggestion of a safety harness being used, and I couldn't even bring myself to watch. In theory this situation with the ship's height cannot happen today as the bridge was replaced with a new one in 1991, with a clearance of 185 feet. However, after further expansion within the port, it was suggested in 2018 that an even bigger bridge may be needed to accommodate the next generation of container ships.

Sailing around Florida brought on some wistful regret that its ports were not on our route, and we could only watch the planes flying into Miami and imagine lying on the beaches. Being in this area always initiated some talk of the Bermuda Triangle. The term was coined after a group of US Navy planes disappeared during a training flight out of Fort Lauderdale in December 1945. Other disappearances and accidents were subsequently swept into a vague area which began to be publicised as a triangle. Sometimes people laughed at the notion as we sailed uneventfully through the corner of the area, especially during daylight hours. At other times they became thoughtful, staring into the distance during dark nights at sea when stories of lost ships and the paranormal began to be told. There had been some high-profile ship losses at the time, particularly the sudden disappearances of large bulk ore carriers, which served as reminders of our vulnerability should some catastrophic failure happen. Nights like this often led to the playing of Gordon Lightfoot's *The Wreck of the Edmund Fitzgerald*, his song of a bulk tanker carrying iron ore which was lost with all hands during a storm on Lake Superior in November 1975.

Visits to the next three ports were made exceptional thanks to meeting some wonderful and hospitable people.

Earlier along the route several of us found ourselves chatting with some officers from a US Merchant Marine ship. One of the electricians, Alan, introduced me to his counterpart, Harry; I think I spoke with him for a minute or two and continued to circulate, but later it became evident that Alan had spoken with him for much longer. Harry had provided his home details even though he did not expect to be there himself, and suggested his wife would like to meet us. After we arrived in New Orleans, Alan called her from a phone box; she was expecting the call and arranged to drive into town and find us. Settling on a meeting place was difficult as we only knew the Bourbon Street area, and this was only thanks to our visits to some of its lively jazz bars. The street may have been memorable but how we got there from our dock on the Mississippi, or back afterwards, was not. Eventually it was decided that she would arrive at a junction on the dual carriageway Canal Street, a busy but unmissable downtown route, with her headlights on. We saw the car at red traffic lights from the other side of the road and ran across the traffic lanes and tram tracks, dived into the back seats and introduced ourselves. Fortunately it was the right car.

She drove us across the Twin Span Bridge over Lake Pontchartrain to the neighbouring city of Slidell, where we also met Ursula and Harry's daughter and her boyfriend. We all went for a pizza and were then taken to the family home, set within bayou country. We stayed in this atmospheric location overnight, mostly sitting overlooking the watery darkness and chatting over drinks.

Ursula told us her interesting back story. She was brought up in Dresden, and while growing up she had visited a fortune teller who told her she would escape from fire and cross a wide expanse of water. As a teenager she was in the centre of Dresden when the huge bombing raid began in February 1945; she described hearing the sirens and seeing the planes approaching, and a man with a large torch signalling upwards as if helping them to locate their target area. This element of the tale particularly intrigued me; who could he have been, and where from? She ran away from the centre for as long as she could, and escaped the firestorm. Her move to America followed some time later.

The following day we brought our overnight hosts onto the ship and entertained them with drinks and food all day. Other officers came and spoke with them in the bar as they formed the centre of the day's social life. They accompanied us to a football match we had scheduled to play that evening; predictably after more than a day of unconventional preparation it did not go well and when they left they were probably unimpressed with our performance.

Street caricature, New Orleans

My first impressions of Houston were not good; *Stratheden*'s first visit there meant enduring Christmas all but lost within a huge port surrounded by oil facilities. The festivities aboard were austere too, as people continued to watch their weight. By the second trip we were in a more accessible location and discovered the very good mission (or, rather grandly, International Seafarers' Center) nearby and progressed to seeing some of the city. By the time of my visit on *Strathesk* I was thinking of a place Houston was particularly well-known for, and I asked a couple working at the mission how I could get to the Space Center. They told me it was halfway to Galveston, which sounded a long way, but they then added, looking at each other to confirm, 'We haven't been there for a long time ourselves, so we should go again. We can take you this weekend!' This led to myself and Les, the Fourth Engineer, accompanying them on an excellent day out.

Houston was also the scene of my final football match for *Strathesk*, and indeed for a ship's team. It took place under floodlights on a warm, humid evening while untold numbers of mosquitoes feasted greedily upon us. Our other adversaries were a Norwegian ship's team which seemed technically far superior to ours and soon took control. I was in goal again and made a string of saves, although we finally went a goal down after half an hour when a rebound from one of my saves was tucked away. Our opponents pushed for a second goal and we began to fear the worst; then one of our deck cadets found he could run at a gap in the Norwegian defence and he scored two almost identical goals to put us ahead at half time. We faced more pressure in the second half until I kicked a long clearance upfield. This had led to a goal against the Koreans back in Dar-es-Salaam, and now it provided another. The cadet ran onto it with only the goalkeeper to beat and completed his hat trick; three goals from as many shots, and probably our only attempts on target. After more determined defending we saw out the rest of the game, which ended after a huge scramble in our goalmouth; eventually I managed to dive full length through a crowd of players to smother the ball and preserve the 3-1 scoreline. This was our greatest win and we celebrated it accordingly, even if it was against the run of play.

Despite its gritty reputation Baltimore had, and has, much to offer. Stays in port there brought about visits to its smartly regenerated waterfront area and to the historical Fort McHenry, famous for its part in the Battle of Baltimore in the conflict known as the War of 1812. The survival of the fort's flag during a British bombardment led to Francis Scott Key's composition of a poem, *The Battle of Fort M'Henry*, which evolved into *The Star-Spangled Banner*, the US national anthem. I also got to see another baseball game, and a pre-Broadway production of Shakespeare's *Othello* starring James Earl Jones, the voice of Darth Vader which also happened to suit this more traditional role.

One day Les and I sat at a waterfront bar. Next to me, someone near my own age also sipped a beer while trying to entertain his toddler daughter. We got talking and soon found we were discussing music and that we had many shared tastes. He introduced himself as Rafael, a reporter with the *Baltimore Sun* newspaper, and it transpired that the drink was an interlude after covering The Jam's press conference prior to a show that evening. He and a photographer were going to cover the show and he invited us along. Les was working but I was free, so that evening Rafael and the photographer arrived on board for drinks. We then drove down to the outskirts of Washington DC for the show at the University of Maryland, in a typical college hall which represented a much smaller venue than the band were accustomed to playing back home.

Rafael had been unimpressed with Paul Weller at the press conference but once the show started he warmed to The Jam while gathering opinions from the crowd we mingled with. One teenager shouted something about the band being part of the 'British revolution', an unfamiliar phrase just then but it was one of the times when British acts were succeeding in America. People looked to me for a British comment and I made them laugh when I impulsively said something like 'It's nothing like the French revolution!' Rafael later sent me a cutting of his review, which named me and the ship and also paraphrased this exchange. In the written version I had delivered a stern-sounding lecture in an upper-crust accent, a description I found funny. A great night out, in unexpected circumstances, taking in a band described at the time as the biggest since The Beatles and who I never expected to see. I was just in time, as the band's breakup was announced a few months later. Rafael went on to become a published author and a writer for TV, most notably on the US crime series *The Wire*.

Once the final general cargo was on board, the hatches were closed and containers loaded on and around them. We would typically load 30 to 40 lashed onto the deck and either singly secured or stacked two or three high. This was just a miniscule slice of the container trade, whose purpose-built ships competed with and gradually superseded general cargo vessels and which could carry thousands of the equivalent units, or TEUs.

After leaving Baltimore on *Strathesk* I had to send an original urgency message, prefixed by the "XXX" signal after some discussion with the Captain whose specific authority was required. We sailed at night into heavy seas and in the morning a block of six containers was missing. It transpired that there were originally only four, containing cigarettes, and that at the last minute two heavier containers carrying furniture had arrived and been secured on top. They were assumed to be intact, locked together and afloat, presenting a hazard to shipping. Following the same format as when other items (or people) had been lost over board from ships, I had to provide the obvious details and urge nearby shipping to 'keep sharp lookout' and to report any sightings.

This can hardly have been a new hazard even then, but it has become more significant on seas dominated by large container ships. The World Shipping Council estimates that on average 1,382 containers were lost each year between 2008 and 2019. The latter year far exceeded this, mainly due to the Japanese ship *One Apus* losing 1,816 containers overboard in a Pacific gale. Another thousand or so became dislodged into an unruly pile which had to be carefully offloaded and sorted according to integrity or damage.

As *Strathesk* crossed the Atlantic, football became a dominant topic once again, and in addition to the usual supporters of the most high-profile teams teasing each other, a craze for betting on games seemed to appear from nowhere. The betting was a new development but one which seemed to captivate people during a long passage back towards the Gulf, even taking their minds off the Falklands conflict at times. While I watched and listened to football I was uninterested in betting, yet was forced by major peer pressure one day into accepting a bet of £1 on a cup match. I was winning until the final few minutes, but lost and paid up, witnessed and cheered on by a surprising gathering of interested people given the small sum involved. Instead of that being the end, I found myself under even more pressure to accept a £5 bet on the next one. This saved me from any further scrutiny until the game was played, and this time I won to come out ahead at the end of the season.

Sailing back towards the Gulf usually led to speculation on returning home, and my receiving company messages beginning with 'herewith officer reliefs' were eagerly awaited. These led to my leaving the triangular route once in Barcelona and twice in Kuwait. My final seaborne visit to the Gulf thus ended in the middle of yet another tour of its ports, staying over in a company house in Kuwait with stewards in residence to provide meals and soft drinks. The place also had a new-fangled video player on which I first saw the BBC's *Dwarka* documentary. Significant events elsewhere in the world would determine my next, and final, trip.

16 Falklands

m.v. Strathesk   Details in Chapter 15
m.v. Strathewe Details in Chapter 13

There was uproar on *Strathesk* when Argentina invaded the Falkland Islands. Although it was reported that many people in the UK did not even know where they were, seafarers were first-hand experts on geography and besides felt mortally offended for their country's prestige despite its years of hard times. For a while I was producing extra-long and multiple news sheets detailing the latest developments, in Parliament and as the task force assembled and sailed to the South Atlantic. During the ten weeks or so from invasion to conclusion there were cheers at early successes, times of despair over losses, and frustrations over the duration of the ground campaign, the latter mainly because we did not yet know about the challenges involved, such as how to move troops and supplies without the helicopters lost on the destroyed container ship *Atlantic Conveyor*. There was a near-unanimous will to sail there ourselves if such a thing were to become possible. Finally there was a huge celebration on board to mark the surrender. My leaving "shout" followed almost immediately afterwards, serving up an unusual quantity of soft drinks to a still-recovering crowd.

Meanwhile merchant ships were being requisitioned by the Ministry of Defence (MoD) to take supplies to the Falklands, both to support the task force and to deliver the materials needed to rebuild. This initiative was called STUFT, or Ships Taken up From Trade, and *Strathewe* was added to this, being in the right place when needed. Soon after I went on leave, *Strathewe* sailed from Southampton carrying general cargo and, on deck thanks to the ship's heavy lifting capacity, two ramped landing craft belonging to the army.

They were back in the UK within two months, having unloaded quickly at Port Stanley. The requisition remained in place for a second South Atlantic voyage and I joined the ship in Teesport, near Middlesbrough. The cargo was mainly building materials and once loaded we were sailing direct to the South Atlantic. There was one last-minute drama as the Captain was abruptly replaced; I didn't see what happened as I had already turned in, but complaints were made over his late-night conduct in the bar and the company acted unusually quickly. The hastily-summoned replacement was none other than Captain Holmes. My last four years had featured no terrible captains and I had begun to hope they had all been despatched ashore. I tried to hope for the best with the reappearance of Holmes, and to tell myself that long ago he might not have been all bad and that I had encountered worse afterwards. At first he was indeed quite businesslike but, just as seven years earlier, this would change. There was more than one way to sail into a conflict zone.

Despite the undeclared war having ended three months before, travel to the Falklands area was still classed as dangerous, and the sheer quantity of MoD paperwork and messages underlined the voyage's military connection. Wives arrived on board initially but were banned from the voyage on safety grounds, leaving during a short pause in the Thames estuary. However we did carry passengers: undertakers to prepare the bodies of British servicemen killed in action, along with a team of army sappers to help with exhumations. Inevitably our cargo included a consignment of coffins. None of them returned with us. While we were still in the Falklands a ship arrived in Southampton bearing the first 64 bodies; 63 servicemen and a Chinese civilian employed as a laundryman on *HMS Coventry*, one of the warships lost during the conflict.

These amounted to around a quarter of the conflict's British dead. Some servicemen were buried in the Falklands and the recovery of the remainder continued beyond our stay, a long process for the teams we had transported there.

The facilities on board had been downgraded from the previous trip. Satellite communications had been provided then, presumably to facilitate radio silence in what had been a war zone in the recent past, but for my trip the box and aerial had been removed. It still left me with the equipment I had always used, but put me at a disadvantage in the South Atlantic compared to other requisitioned ships. Once anchored off Stanley I had the impression I was the only operator still using Morse, with all the issues of matching transmission to the varying propagation conditions and trying to make myself heard from the other end of the world. I sometimes spent hours attempting what ships with satellite dishes could clear in a few minutes.

As if to compensate for the removal of important equipment, a video player arrived. Any excitement soon faded as it was found to be a large U-matic box, an old (even then) Sony format used in educational and professional facilities but not something people could bring their own videotapes on board for. It was a bizarre thing for the company to have spent money on, if they even had rather than finding it in a cupboard; it was like providing a computer with no software. Just as it was consigned to a corner of the radio room, a single compatible videotape arrived. It was of that year's FA Cup Final replay, in which Tottenham Hotspur had beaten Queens Park Rangers 1-0 a few months earlier. This interested people for all of seven minutes, after which the only goal had been scored and attention drifted away. Fortunately we also carried the usual stock of conventional movies.

We sailed south in pleasant weather, optimistic that this would be another short trip based on the evidence of the last one. We would have a quick opportunity to see the

Falklands, take a look around Stanley and then depart. Even the undertakers were cheerful, sharing some of their professional anecdotes, told with what can only be described as "graveyard humour", and joining in with occasional drinking games. It was refreshing to see this outwardly sombre profession's more human side, which would have to be locked away again upon arrival.

Expectations became more serious with stories of the aftermath of the conflict, and of streets and open spaces filled with rubble and military hardware. There were numerous tales of injuries from booby-trapped items waiting for the unwary to find them, typically consisting of concealed grenades with pins already removed. These were supposedly hidden within potential military souvenirs or everyday items such as food containers. There was also some growing realisation of the scale of the Argentinian minefields as an additional hazard around Stanley and elsewhere.

Another concern was that Chinook helicopters, which had been instrumental in unloading some of the early cargoes, had all been grounded. This followed a crash at an air display in Mannheim, Germany, in which a Chinook crashed while carrying parachutists who were about to attempt a world record for forming a circle in descent. Instead a transmission failure following a change in maintenance procedures caused the front and rear rotors to mesh together, the resulting crash killing all 46 on board.

As I finished an evening watch off the Brazilian coast, some officers were talking about lights in the sky behind the ship, which they thought may have been UFO activity. There was nothing to see outside by then, but the following evening I stepped outside and saw, low on the aft horizon, some bright coloured lights similar to those described. Their being so low made me think they were in the same position as those reported 24 hours earlier and I called a Brazilian station to enquire. They told me that some daily testing of weather rockets had been taking place. I asked if I had missed a warning message, but they said they had not issued one. At least the mystery was solved.

The seas became heavy as if heralding our arrival, and we were pleased to sail into Blanco Bay, relatively sheltered water outside Port Stanley, and drop anchor. Several other ships were anchored nearby: more requisitioned cargo ships, and vessels from the Royal Fleet Auxiliary which supports the Royal Navy. Also present was *Norland*, a well-known P & O ferry which had carried the Second Battalion of the Parachute Regiment from Portsmouth to San Carlos Water. It was later used to carry prisoners of war back to Argentina, and then sailed between Ascension and the Falklands until being released from service in January 1983. Stanley and its shallow inner harbour were visible through a narrow strait between two headlands. The twin mountain peaks of Two Sisters were visible, themselves a reminder of the recent land battles; when these disappeared from view, we knew bad weather was approaching.

We waited to unload cargo. The Mate assured everyone that he had successfully harried the authorities last time and that his contacts would deal with us quickly. This line soon lost credibility and by the time we received our first attention a few days later, people were already becoming tetchy. All unloading was to be done using the ship's cranes, lowering cargo onto Mexeflotes. These were powered metal rafts which could also be linked during military operations to form jetties or pontoon bridges. Each flat raft was furnished only with a motor and one forklift truck, and was staffed by a few army personnel who shivered in the driving wind; we felt really sorry for them. It was clear there were only a limited number of rafts, arriving singly if at all, and that unloading would be a slow process. Evidently the cargo we carried this time was of low importance.

Mexeflote arriving to unload cargo

A boat service was set up and it became possible to visit Stanley. The gangway was lowered, usually down to the water but it depended on conditions. In choppy weather a jacob's ladder (a rope ladder with wooden slats) was fitted down the side of the ship and it was necessary to step from the gangway across to the ladder, climb down the lower slats while suspended above the water and drop into the boat. The reverse was followed when returning, a safer option than manoeuvring through 90 degrees to somehow gain a foothold directly onto the gangway but an adventure at times. There was actually one occasion when I had to leap through the air from the pitching boat to grab the ladder.

Everyone on board was issued with camouflage jackets and matching trousers, ensuring we would blend in ashore. We had no alternatives to our uniform shoes and wore them however rugged the ground, meaning we all had footwear which looked like that of old cartoon tramps by the time we sailed home. The jackets also became de facto uniform items on board in place of our midnight blue ones.

Despite everyone knowing that Stanley would be a small place, there were still exclamations of 'Is that it?' We went into the only shop, saw the house with 'Snack Bar' hand-painted outside, and drank in the Globe, the only pub in town and itself a symbol of the British nature of the islands. We also noted how British the island people sounded, despite being so far from the UK, and tried to pin down which regional accent most closely matched the dialect. We followed the waterfront until the settlement ended, and found a monument to the Battle of the Falklands. This was not the recent conflict but the 1914 naval battle just outside Stanley in which the Royal Navy defeated a German cruiser squadron, sinking four warships including the large armoured cruisers *Scharnhorst* and *Gneisenau*. Making our way back, we saw the Governor's House, which had been a much-publicised location during both occupation and liberation, beyond which stood Christ Church Cathedral and its whalebone arch. Passing the Globe again we found the graveyard, facing the waterfront with a sign reading 'Cemetario Militar' lying flattened at the entrance. Once inside we saw numerous plots partially filled with subsiding earth, and toppling wooden crosses on which were written 'Unknown Argentine soldier.'

The streets seemed to have been largely cleaned up, but there were other signs of recent history. Some houses still bore visible damage, and alongside in the inner harbour was the naval landing ship *Sir Tristram*, one of the vessels attacked in Fitzroy Cove, East Falkland, as British forces closed in on Stanley. It was bombed by Argentinian planes along with *Sir Galahad*, the latter being destroyed with the loss of 48 lives. Two lives were lost on *Sir Tristram* and despite suffering bomb damage it was subsequently towed to Stanley where, even with its visibly distorted superstructure, it was used as troop accommodation and for the lifting power of its forward cranes.

Just beyond *Sir Tristram* was Whalebone Cove, where the remains of an old three-masted ship rested. This was *Lady Elizabeth*, which pulled into Stanley for repairs in 1912 after bad weather while carrying lumber from Vancouver to Mozambique via Cape Horn. After running aground in the harbour it was written off and served as a coal hulk until breaking its moorings in 1936 and running aground again, where it has remained since. A row of grounded Argentinian Pucara planes, twin propeller-driven fighter bombers, could be seen just beyond, at the perimeter of the airfield.

Lady Elizabeth, Port Stanley

There was another reminder of the territory's maritime history. *SS Great Britain* had suffered a similar fate to *Lady Elizabeth*, rotting away for decades in nearby shallow water before being rescued and returned to Bristol in 1970. Its mizzen (aft) mast had collapsed during the salvage operation and this remained on display by the water in Stanley.

Some people said that a single walk around town was enough for them, although in practice there were other such tours, either on the scheduled boat service or using one of the ship's lifeboats on days when the deck officers were not busy with cargo. Inevitably there were more visits to the pub, which was popular with all the services and others such as ourselves, and frequently filled with uniforms, camouflage jackets and smoke. We became stamp collectors, buying significant quantities of first day covers from the shop, franked in Stanley, South Georgia and other territories. Some interest in coins followed, and we bought silver liberation crowns from the post office, official fundraisers for rebuilding which were considered collectible souvenirs.

Gradually the unloading days became more frequent, requiring more attention from the deck officers. I was asked if I would perform bridge watches in addition to handling a surprising number of MoD and company messages. The ship was technically in port, which would normally have negated the need for either activity, but the situation was an unusual one. I did not mind doing the watches and passed long hours on the bridge each day, looking out for unexpected events as I paced the wide space or occupied the high pilot's chair. Sometimes Hercules transport planes arrived over the bay at the end of their long, slow flights from Ascension Island, scaring onlookers by making steep dives towards the airfield before levelling off and landing. Performing these watches filled much of my time during the ship's first stay in Stanley. At other times, particularly at night when conditions were most favourable, I continued to handle messages and glare at the space once occupied by the satellite equipment.

There were some attempts by the Argentinian Air Force to fly towards the exclusion zone and test the air defences on the islands. When this happened we received alerts, alarms were sounded and everyone had to wait outside on the boat deck in their life jackets until an all-clear was received. RAF Phantom fighters arrived in stages as a deterrent after flights from Ascension, assisted by multiple in-flight refuellings from tanker aircraft which also had to refuel each other in a cascading pattern before returning to their base in stages. The leading Phantom flew towards the airfield, dipped its left wing and climbed rapidly, rolling to the right over and over. The succeeding planes in the group also climbed over the bay with flypasts and loops, providing the town and ships with a memorable aerobatic display.

A month passed with slow progress out on deck; although the floats were turning up on most days they were small and lightly-manned, and once loaded there were long intervals until they became available again. Chinook helicopters began to appear in the skies again, but they came nowhere near us. Frustration set in as people realised how open-ended the stay in Stanley appeared, just when they expected to be already heading home. People began having to contact their families, warning of changed plans; tempers became shorter and the use of bad language increased from what could already be described as "masculine" and "military" levels.

A football match was arranged with another ship, for a day when no cargo work was expected. We were told that the pitch had been swept for mines and that 16 games had been played on it since the conflict ended. A Mexeflote unexpectedly appeared and the game was cancelled. The army swept the pitch again and found an unexploded mine.

Then more ports were added; we would unload some cargo in San Carlos and Goose Green before returning to Stanley to finish. It would be almost a grand tour of headline locations, an even longer trip but with some added interest. However, just as in the past, the Captain was becoming louder and more aggressive. His phone conversations could be heard from two levels away, preceded by an even louder answering of 'Master!' His rare appearances on the bridge carried an air of menace and the blunt rebuffing of any attempts at conversation. When I returned some message confirmations to his cabin he chose the moment to sound off about the R/O's role generally, telling me for no particular reason that 'It's not a difficult job!' As on my first trip, he was directing comments at me which he would not have dared make anywhere else on board. I let it pass and backed out of his office, but wondered afterwards if my tolerating this encouraged him towards his next, more extreme, actions. A flash point arrived soon afterwards when I presented him with various weekly and monthly documents to be signed off; once these were laid out on his desk, he saw my overtime sheet.

R/Os were not known for performing much overtime, and I was no exception. Although weekend work in port was a recognised necessity, with its own special form, it was four years before I claimed any at all and I had only submitted forms on rare occasions since. My claim for bridge and communications work in Stanley was a significantly larger one but should not have been a surprise to anyone. The subject had been touched on when I was asked to do bridge watches, and the total was comparable to all the other claims being approved on board.

'I'm not signing that. You're not on,' the Captain roared. I asked him why not.

'You're just not on,' he repeated.

'You know I've done the work. What exactly don't you agree with on there?' I asked. He repeated himself again and we went around in circles.

Finally I tried a different tack. 'Well, I don't see how you can expect me to do more bridge watches.'

Without another word he reached for the log book and wrote my name into it. It was almost as if he had it ready on his desk for just this moment, either for me or anyone else who might have crossed his path first. If so I was the lucky winner, and I think I was more disgusted than shocked at the sudden escalation. 'You can't really be serious,' I said. He ignored me and slowly added, in writing, that I had disobeyed a direct order from the Master. As he did this I just shook my head repeatedly, saying he was making a fool of himself.

Once the incident was in writing, there was no going back. Being written into the log was unlikely to be career threatening in itself, but it was still an attack upon my character and reputation which could not be erased. I had the opportunity to dictate my response to the charge and I began by pointing out that he had not given an order in the first place. I then spent the next half hour describing exactly what had happened, ensuring he wrote down every word, even though he looked up at intervals to say 'Haven't you said enough now?' Once we were done I reminded him that good will was at an end, and left him staring down at all his handwriting in the log book. If he had planned the episode for some reason, perhaps it had not gone entirely as expected.

I went straight down to the bar to report what had happened. 'The Old Man's shitting in his own nest,' said someone I had known for several years, and I listened to numerous other supportive comments, including the familiar observation that my reporting directly to the Captain may have convinced him that he could misuse his power where I was concerned, without having to justify himself. Another attempt to explain the situation was, and I'm leaving out the expletives used to describe the Captain, that people like him set out to bully others but could not cope when someone stood firm or pushed back. I tried to look at how I projected myself too; perhaps, for example, I could have rationed my time more and made it seem more valuable. No doubt other possible psychological evaluations could be made towards both persons involved, but I'll leave it there. It was also unfortunate that the overtime from a long month with five weekends went onto one form, and the reaction may have been different had we arrived in Stanley in the middle of a month. Or maybe not.

I reverted to simply covering my own duties. When the Mate heard what had happened he recognised that my stepping away from the bridge would stretch his deck resources and tried to persuade me to change my mind. It was too late for that, barring some kind of massive climbdown from the top, which was just not going to happen. I felt that the Captain going straight for what I saw as the "nuclear option" left no room for compromise. He could hardly tear up the log book.

I sent a long message to the company to report what had happened. When I received no reply I sent something similar to the Radio Officers' trade union, a separate entity from the main officers' union and quite vociferous on some issues. They simply said to wait and see what else happened, with a view to following up when the ship returned to the UK. Until then I was on my own.

I learned that the Captain had been elsewhere and called the company to ask for me to be replaced. Had anyone asked me I would have said that I was happy to go, but the company refused his request. It was probably too difficult to arrange for someone to fly out on the slow and uncomfortable Hercules military planes which served the islands, or to persuade anyone to do so just to sail home again.

We sailed around the north coast of East Falkland and into San Carlos Water. This had been notorious as 'Bomb Alley' a few months before as Argentinian fighters persistently attacked ships moored there while British soldiers disembarked and materials were unloaded. We anchored close to the tiny settlement of San Carlos itself, and the small military cemetery surrounded by a white picket fence could be seen on the nearby hillside. We felt particularly vulnerable there, knowing we were within more accessible range for any possible Argentinian attack, and when yet another alert forced us outside we scanned the skies anxiously.

After completing we sailed on down Falkland Sound, the water which divides the two main islands. We made a short stop at Fox Bay on West Falkland, unloading a few crates of cargo into a boat in the dark. Then we moved on again, around the south of East Falkland and into Choiseul Sound, anchoring close to Goose Green. This had become famous due to the battle to liberate it from Argentinian occupation in late May 1982, releasing its population of 114 from captivity in the settlement's community centre. Over 1,000 Argentinian soldiers were captured and the airfield taken out of service.

Goose Green; *Strathewe* just visible at far left

We were the largest ship ever to visit Goose Green, and inevitably we anchored in the sound and established another boat service. A group of us went ashore, finding the small settlement apparently deserted. 'They're not still in there, are they?' someone asked as we reached the community centre. We peered through the windows into the empty space beyond.

As at Stanley, most military hardware had been cleared away although an arms dump, with all items clearly labelled in Spanish, remained behind barbed wire. Beside this lay some napalm tanks, made for fitting to Argentinian Pucara aircraft and looking alarmingly large. We approached the grass runway and saw someone for the first time; a soldier walking towards Goose Green from Darwin Hill. We called across and asked if the area had been swept for mines. He replied that it had, after which we walked the grass runway and climbed over the abandoned Pucara planes, looking for souvenirs and photographing each other in the cockpits. We later learned that the airfield had not been swept at all. Several minefields were subsequently identified near the runway and around the wider area.

Goose Green airfield

An obsession had grown on board for collecting brass artillery shell cases, fuelled by all the anecdotes of items lying around waiting to be taken as souvenirs. In practice there was little of anything left, although the warnings of possible booby traps continued to circulate. Sometimes groups of military officers and other ranks visited the ship in Stanley after being invited over drinks, usually in the Globe. Some brought shell cases as offerings which were soon snapped up. Time was running out for those of us yet to secure one, and as we walked from the airfield towards our boat I decided to knock on the door of one of the houses. A couple came to the door and I explained who we were and asked if there was anywhere we might find shell cases. They called into the front room and their two sons appeared, who were quietly sent to fetch something. The boys returned and handed me a shell case.

After thanking them I invited them to visit the ship. The parents expected to be busy but we arranged for their sons to take the next day's boat. I met them, showed them around and organised places for them in the saloon for lunch. I was one of the few people on board able to make time to host such a visit.

We returned to Stanley and spent another two weeks anchored in the outer bay. It was almost summer in the southern hemisphere but the weather was getting worse. Heavy snow fell at times, and one day 'cruise to the sun with P & O', a reference to the passenger division's advertising slogan, had been written into the white stuff on the bridge deck. There were sudden high winds and choppy seas, even in the supposedly sheltered anchorage.

Remembrance Sunday arrived, the first since the conflict. Three of us went ashore by boat in our uniforms plus camouflage jackets adorned with our striped epaulettes, and joined a full congregation for the moving service in the cathedral. This was followed by a wreath laying ceremony at the cemetery's Cross of Sacrifice, a focus of Remembrance ceremonies there since 1926. The graves had been smartened up, with the previously-unfinished burial plots now capped by piles of stones and the marker crosses neatly arranged. A walk beyond the town towards Sapper Hill gave us a view from an elevated position but also some warnings. Field guns surrounded by earth and debris still sat by the roadside, and some large areas were cordoned off with barbed wire, displaying signs warning of mines. Some 19,000 were cleared from around Stanley in a project in 2009-10, and after clearing some 30,000 mines in total it was announced in November 2020 that the entire islands were completely free of mines after 38 years.

I decided to try to visit the airfield. Air Force visitors to the ship told me I just needed to thumb a lift on the road towards it, and indeed the first Land Rover stopped for me. It was the station commander, of all people; he dropped me at the security gate and said someone would show me around. Once he had gone inside the base, the guards told me he had just instructed them to drive me back into town!

I could understand the need for some security but was less sure about the dishonesty. I met our original visitors again; they drove me to the airfield, signed me in and showed me around, even close to the Phantoms where I was able to take photographs.

Roadside warning just outside Stanley

One night the ship dragged its anchor in bad weather and drifted onto nearby rocks. It was just as well that a deck officer was keeping watch rather than a volunteer. An all-night drama followed, with repeated engine boosts and assistance from two tugs, to return the ship to its anchorage location and begin to assess the damage.

The Captain and I were speaking only when we had to; we mostly just left stuff on our respective desks for each other. The only exceptions were when I presented myself on the bridge with an offer to assist in any way during the grounding, which he actually said was very good of me. The second was when, just as we thought we might be almost ready to leave, we received word from MoD expressing concern over our patched-up hull repairs. We were to remain in Stanley for an extra three weeks and then be escorted by a naval vessel as far as Ascension. He looked up from his desk. 'F***ing hell,' he said, and I think I managed one syllable of agreement and a nod. And that counted as a civil exchange, with more words than usual.

It was devastating news for the ship's company; there was a palpable undercurrent of anger, and even the most normal conversations became peppered with swear words. One person actually became known as 'F***ing Jimmy', and there was an instance in the bar when I heard exactly why. He spent two minutes describing a helicopter arriving over the deck, during which time I counted 38 "F words" and several other expletives. The fact that this delivery surprised or offended no-one probably says it all.

Some lobbying took place, along with reassurances over the quality of repairs to the hull, and we were eventually cleared to leave without an escort. A group of army officers were sent on board to return to the UK as passengers. I got one of them to sign something certifying that my shell case was explosive free, a UK customs requirement. Another saw how I often played winning games of Scrabble and challenged me to what became an epic and closely-fought series throughout the return trip; I sealed overall victory as we arrived in the Channel. Some cargo was loaded for taking back to the UK. The anchor was raised and the horn sounded as a salute to the other ships in the bay. Horns sounded back, and the VHF filled with comments on how lucky we were. Smiles actually broke out for a while, until we began to roll in heavy seas which battered us for a few days.

More bad news arrived: the ship was being sold, along with its sister ships. This was a shock as our ship still seemed so new, with only four and a half years in service. The remaining opportunities for seafarers in the company had been cut again. The fleet of 31 ships from two years earlier had already diminished to 11; four from the 1975 list and seven "newer" ones. The SD-14 ships, also only a few years old, had already been sold, as had one of the Polish ships. Now the remaining five of these were going; despite the company's continued seconding of staff to foreign owners, everyone's futures had just become even more uncertain.

The mood on board continued to deteriorate, despite the prospect of getting home for Christmas after all. It was a long way back in bad weather after a stressful few weeks, and conflicts seemed to arise out of nothing, fortunately soon forgotten afterwards. My issues with the Captain were in a different league though. It occurred to me that I had been on two ships with a terrible atmosphere on board, and that he was what they had in common. He began to bark insults during moments when our paths happened to cross. It was reminiscent of the later stages of our first trip together all that time ago, only without actual sentences. My tolerance now simply extended to a 'Whatever' as I turned my back on him. In a small act of retribution I turned off the communal aerial whenever his beloved stock market update programmes were starting, and made sure I had something to transmit in Morse at the same time for good measure. It sounds petty and may well have made no difference to him, but it made me feel better at the time.

If anyone seemed to remain calm it was the small contingent of crew from the Isle of Barra. They maintained an amiable bearing in their soft voices while others were losing their heads, and they were a pleasure to chat with. When I placed their phone calls home, their whispered Gaelic was so faint I could barely hear them from the next seat, yet they seemed to converse easily over long distances unlike most people who tried to shout down the receiver. Decades later I was reminded of the Barra crews by the BBC Alba programme *Sgeul Seolaidh*, in which some shared their memories. I may have even recognised one of them.

After 19 days at sea we finally arrived in Hull, and people gathered around the TV for a while to scrutinise the newly-launched Channel 4. A Navy captain arrived on board to present the ship with an Admiralty plaque commemorating its two South Atlantic voyages. We gathered around in the officers' bar and watched the presentation; even in the official picture Captain Holmes' expression looked like that of someone about to start a fight. A group of us were unknowingly photographed watching the event and looking rather sullen. I don't recall what happened to the plaque; there was little point putting it up.

Three days in port followed before paying off. I received a predictably bad report from the Captain, with my communications marked as 'adequate' and everything else unsatisfactory. I pronounced this ridiculous and typed my own long letter to the company describing his conduct and deficiencies. Our main Personnel contact, Peter Burns, arrived on board and had clearly heard about the dispute. He seemed very sympathetic, and even more so when I described my report and handed him my letter. A meeting in London was arranged to try to resolve matters.

Captain Holmes left early, unnoticed during perhaps his only-ever quiet activity on board and definitely unmissed. I was delighted to find that his replacement was Alan, the Mate from my earlier time on *Strathewe*, who had secured his well-deserved promotion at last.

The ship was being stripped of any loose items not included in its forthcoming sale. I sent back the almost-unused video player, but while numerous deck and engine items were sent back to various company departments I was asked to leave a surprising amount of equipment and spare parts on board. I only took one souvenir. The company's Polish cargo ships had pewter tankards on hooks above the officers' bar, inscribed for each role and dated 1978. They were rarely used, but people often commented on the

285

prospect of sailing on a ship's final voyage and of being able to take away "their" mug afterwards. This had once been assumed to be an event in the distant future. Now the moment had arrived, and, like most of my colleagues, I left with mine.

17 Sequels and Endings

The meeting in London was a farce. The Personnel Manager sat with a company surveyor, arguably Mr Merry's spiritual cousin, both stony-faced and determined to stand by their captain. The man from my union sat with me, mostly silent as I defended myself. "Defended" was the operative word as there was no attempt to conduct the meeting in a constructive way or work towards any mutually acceptable outcome. They produced the Captain's report on me, and I referred them to my letter. I was told that I should have done everything possible to assist during the difficult voyage; I replied that I had done so and been treated badly for it. Apparently I should have been 'professional'; I asked if that applied to a captain too, and pointed out that I had carried out far more work without expecting additional payment, and continued to perform my own role after the dispute without claiming for more overtime. There had been no point even thinking about any such payment as I knew it would not be signed off, but I had still set out to do my own job well. The union man simply interrupted occasionally with 'Can't we just sort this out?' I don't think he ever received any meaningful reply, and the meeting broke up with nothing resolved.

Outside, the union man said there was nothing more he could do. I was disappointed with this and have never joined another trade union. Subsequently, and without explanation, the company paid about eighty per cent of my overtime claim. I decided not to ask them how it was calculated.

I heard of more redundancies, but nothing dropped through my letter box. Part of me wondered if the company had a more subtle revenge planned; that it would turn me into one of the officers I had seen over the years who had remained at sea for too long. Perhaps albatrosses had been unknowingly harmed during one of my voyages and I would go on to become the company's latest Ancient Mariner, doomed to wander its remaining ships? Surely not; they lived in the present and had moved on from even the recent past already. Perhaps this had always been the company's approach, developed subconsciously over time; to "forgive and forget", and not to dwell upon whatever had happened. If so, I was just as likely to be offered another ship as any difficult captain or other officer.

I was still employed and with plenty of accrued leave, but forgetting what had happened was difficult for me and I could not bring myself to imagine going away again on whatever ships the company still owned, or crewed. The growth of satellite communications and of easily board-swappable solid state circuitry told me the role as I knew it was becoming obsolete anyway. The call of the sea, or whatever it had ever been, had now left me. It was time to look for new career opportunities again, and this time something looked genuinely promising.

I decided to call Personnel. It felt like a hopeful request which could be easily rebuffed, but which might just ease my way towards an important life change. I rehearsed what to say, yet sat staring at the phone for an hour, occasionally reaching for the handset and then withdrawing. Eventually I spoke with Peter Burns and, taking a deep breath, asked if the company was still seeking any volunteers for redundancy. I was unsure if they had requested volunteers at all or if it had just been hearsay, but it seemed worth asking the question. He did not rule it out, and promised to get back to me.

He did, and soon afterwards I received an illustration of my redundancy settlement, should I choose to volunteer. It was still optional, with a way back, but the offer was too good to refuse. It would support me while I took a chance on something new. My seagoing career had lasted for longer than most, but it was time to move on.

*

Tekoa was sold to Austasia Line, Singapore, in July 1980 and renamed *Mahsuri*. It was sold to shipbreakers at Kaohsiung, Taiwan, in January 1984.

Somerset was sold to Damarika Shipping Corporation, Greece, in November 1979 and renamed *Aegean Sky*. It was sold to shipbreakers at Chittagong, Bangladesh, in November 1984.

Dwarka was sold to shipbreakers at Gadani Beach, Pakistan in May 1982.

Strathdirk was sold to Empresa Navigacion Mambisa, Cuba, in December 1981 and renamed *Batolome Maso*. It changed hands again in 1988, 1994, 1996 and 1997 before being sold to breakers at Aliaga, Turkey, in May 2002.

Strathduns was sold to Biman Shipping Company, Panama, in November 1981 and renamed *Ruby Islands*. It changed hands again in 1987, 1990, 1998 and 2000 before being sold to breakers at Chittagong, Bangladesh, in March 2001.

Vendee was sold to Witchen, Hong Kong in April 1984 but continued to be managed by P & O. It was sold again in June 1986 to Ofer Brothers, Israel, and renamed *Avocado Carmel*. I wonder how they dreamed up that name? In 1996 it was sold to Ithaca Maritime Corporation, Nassau, and renamed *Carmel Topaz*, and finally sold to breakers at Alang, India, in May 2004.

Strathewe was sold to Sealift Company, Greece, in January 1983 and renamed *Lindelbels*. It was sold again in 1988 to Islamic Republic of Iran Shipping Lines, Iran, and renamed *Iran Mahallati*. It was sold to breakers at Alang, India, in September 2009. It was the only one of my ships to gain even a passing mention in P & O's official book marking the company's 150th anniversary in 1987.

Stratheden was sold to Fairtrans Company, Greece, in April 1983 and renamed *Merapi*. It was sold again in 1986 to Waterpulse Shipping, Cyprus, and again in 1988 to Islamic Republic of Iran Shipping Lines, Iran, and renamed

Iran Kolahdooz. In December 2008 it was renamed *Despina* and finally sold to breakers at Alang, India, in September 2010.

Strathesk was sold to Bulktrans Company, Greece, in November 1982 and renamed *Altenbels*. It was sold again in 1986 to Wateroath Navigation, Cyprus, and again in 1993 to Islamic Republic of Iran Shipping Lines, Iran, renamed *Iran Bagheri*. In December 2008 it was renamed *Danoosh*. On 22nd April 2009 it was involved in a collision with a small Indonesian container ship near Singapore and intentionally grounded in shallow water to allow repairs to take place. Press images show it lying low in the water and listing slightly to starboard. It was sold to breakers at Alang, India, in May 2010.

I imagine long papers could be written on exactly how a multitude of international companies were able to run some of these ships, presumably profitably, for so much longer than P & O had the skills or will to. I understand about variations in cost overheads between different countries, but when a company disposes of an asset after four years or so, and that asset goes on to be usable for up to another 27 years, I wonder if that can be the whole story. How much more might be down to some companies' outlook, and whether too many "easy" decisions have been taken over time? This can be applied not only to ships, but to whole companies and industries, and from there to how such decisions might affect the long-term interests of countries.

*

I didn't look back on the sea for a long time, other than retaining some good memories and, like most people, some regrets too. I undertook numerous technical, managerial and arts courses, finding I had somehow become a much better student who submitted homework on time and consistently passed exams. My practical abilities seemed to have improved too.

Many years later I worked on an IT project at Lloyd's Register of Shipping, which has since been renamed without the final two words. While at their building in Fenchurch Street I passed some of my breaks in their library, reading about maritime history in general and eventually becoming curious over what happened to the ships I had sailed on. I have had to update this knowledge since, but all their stories are now fixed in the past.

P & O, meanwhile, continued to change, making substantial investments in, among other things, passenger ships, container shipping and property, the latter including stakes in the new ports required to service the larger ships. Sales of each of these businesses have since dispersed the company's assets and legacy.

In 2000, P & O formed a new company, P & O Princess Cruises Ltd, which was floated on the London Stock Exchange. In 2003 it was merged with Carnival Corporation and the former UK-based business became Carnival plc, a separate business entity from the larger multinational corporation.

The company's container business went through a number of changes. In 1986 P & O took full control of Overseas Containers Ltd (OCL), previously a consortium of themselves and three other companies. The name changed to P & O Containers Ltd, and in 1996 this was merged with the Dutch shipping line Royal Nedlloyd, who themselves had once operated a similar cargo fleet to P & O, to form P & O Nedlloyd, or "PONL". In 2004 Nedlloyd became the majority shareholder and listed the company on the Dutch stock exchange. It had a 6% share of the global container market, and the P & O part of the name remained in place. In August 2005 the combined company was bought by A P Moller-Maersk, P & O and Nedlloyd's Danish erstwhile cargo-shipping competitor and mainly trading, with a 12% container market share, as Maersk Line. This development brought me into working contact with P & O again and so I saw a little of how the company, or at least part of it, came to an end.

Merging the two companies was a massive undertaking and I was hired to project manage the IT aspects of the UK integration. This became a wide-ranging programme. It was actually seen as beneficial that I had once worked for P & O, since the connection, however tenuous by then, potentially made some changes easier to accept within PONL. In practice my old career was more or less irrelevant, barely mentioned again after initial introductions.

Maersk in the UK saw the takeover in terms of their having vanquished their main rival, which was perceived as P & O; Nedlloyd was seldom mentioned. P & O staff described the deal as acceptance of a good offer at a time when freight rates were falling. This was the same P & O which sold half its bulk tankers in 2000 in order to cash in while freight rates were high; perhaps selling was still the answer to every question. Maersk, still a family-controlled company, took a more long-term view.

There were some cultural differences between the respective companies. Maersk maintained an impressive modern office network and a business run by highly-motivated and focused staff who arrived early and worked for as long as necessary. The dress code was strictly business smart; the British staff blamed the conservatism of the Danes for this yet seemed to embrace it themselves, many male staff even retaining their double-cuff shirts, ties and suit jackets along with their denims on the Jeans for Genes charity days. P & O also had good people, many of whom were to buy new clothes and transition into Maersk, but at the outset even if the zombie apocalypse had been taking place right outside the main doors it might not have been enough to persuade anyone to remain in their dim and dated offices for a minute longer than necessary.

Maersk's London office was on the 31st floor of One Canada Square, the main and original tower in the Canary Wharf complex. This felt a little daunting in the post-9/11 world, especially as planes approaching or leaving London City Airport seemed to use it to line up their route before passing close by. They maintain more distance now. Helicopters would fly past the windows, and sometimes below them. New arrivals commented constantly on the planes and the height, while everyone who had passed through that stage took little notice. Another heart-stopping moment sometimes occurred when the whole tower shuddered for a few seconds, prompting people to look up and around, especially as the air conditioning paused at the same time leaving a sudden silence. The overall cause seemed to be something involving electrical generators. As if to reassure everyone, not least the relevant authorities, there was an evacuation drill for the entire tower. Each floor had a designated stairway to spread the numbers evenly, but we still had to ease into crowded spaces beside people who had joined from upper floors, and make room for others arriving lower down. It took us over half an hour of slow shuffling to reach ground level, and much longer for those from the floors above, whereupon we were crossed off lists and able to ride back up in the lifts.

The company provided free lunches in a canteen with a stunning view west along the Thames towards the City and beyond. Employee welfare was one consideration, and another was that this limited people's need to descend into the shopping malls and open spaces far below during a working day. Lunch together was also good for teamwork, as was the whole London-based business being on a single large floor.

Each day we would hit the ground running, the tone set by the IT Director who arrived at staggeringly early hours in the morning, citing his earlier military training and routine. Others arrived early to initiate discussions centred on his office, which tended to mean that anyone arriving after, say, 8 am had already missed some or all of the day's crucial moments.

The UK activities involved 23 sites in total, as some were closed, new locations commissioned and the remainder refurbished and upgraded. The IT project's scope included new hardware and software for users, expanded helpdesk and support functions, new networks in 13 sites and new WAN (Wide Area Network) data links. Some old, or "legacy" software systems from PONL were still needed in the larger company, and these had to be modified for use on the new network and then migrated over from their old one. IT projects sometimes attract adverse headlines but each of these activities could only begin after considerable debate, design and approval, and engaging good suppliers and service providers. Most issues arise when corners are cut or vested interests override what is required, but Maersk allowed all the time and space needed to make good decisions and to bring them to life.

Staged user moves took place to make space for refurbishment and installation works, which included new structured cabling for data and voice networks. Weekends were filled with some what became a total of 2,000 user moves, as some people's workstations moved on several occasions through whichever spare spaces became available. They must have been disorientated sometimes, especially on Monday mornings. The main IT tasks had to be coordinated with all the new building or refurbishment works. This often meant my standing in for the IT Director and representing the project at senior country-level meetings, presenting my plans and reports and advising on requirements for prospective new locations. Sometimes the property people would forget themselves and excitedly announce that they had sealed the deal on a new office and would move staff in within a week. I then had to remind them of the likely timescales for the WAN, cabling and other installations and thus restore some realism, while still trying to sound positive and reassuring. I could then add the new site to my burgeoning plans.

Decommissioning tasks also had to take place before and during the above, with redundant equipment audited and removed into storage, a central data centre closed down, old network links terminated and surplus offices wound down, or "sunsetted". Large quantities of old PCs were donated to charities after being cleaned and having their software and local data removed.

It was a busy time but there was quite a lot of fun too, thanks in part to the new bars and restaurants nearby, and winter also saw us all floundering on Canary Wharf's temporary ice rink.

Ultimately the merged UK head office took full residence in the refurbished Beagle House, PONL's former UK headquarters at Aldgate East, London. It had become almost unrecognisable from its old incarnation and was renamed, with great originality, Maersk House. I could almost see across to the long-closed and redeveloped Beaufort House of my past P & O days. The Canary Wharf office was closed down. An additional challenge was presented as the company decided to move a key worldwide function from Singapore to London, and a floor was prepared at Maersk House to accommodate them. Some new IT was then extended to even more teams, for example the previously separate road-based logistics arm, and to a separately-branded container business. Just as I thought I had everything covered, there were always new sites and requirements to discover.

After an intensive year the project was declared complete. I attended a ceremony at the National Maritime

Museum, Greenwich, to mark the securing and transfer of company archives as well as the 50th anniversary of the first containerised shipment. However businesses seldom stand still and nine months later I was invited back to Maersk to work on the company's approach to IT provision in the UK in response to new global guidelines. These had been issued from Copenhagen, largely based upon a consultancy report recommending that each country streamline, modernise and make more use of outsourcing, and that this could save £50 million globally. No evidence was provided to support this figure. There was little recognition of how much the UK had already achieved during the merger, and I was asked to produce a detailed report and supporting presentations showing how far the UK already met, and even exceeded, expectations. There were also some areas in which it was possible to devise and document more new strategies, and I incorporated these too. It was hoped that we would save jobs as well as preventing wasteful repetitions of work we had already completed. This was arguably successful in the shorter term, but ultimately the continued movement of highly-mobile tasks and teams between locations, and the evolution of technology, did lead to the scaling down of Maersk UK, and a likely reduction of operations in other countries too. Ultimately Maersk London moved to smaller premises and Maersk House was demolished in 2015 to make way for a new, larger office building which was named One Brabham.

The remainder of the quoted P & O company, with its ports, ferries and other vessels, was sold to Dubai-based DP World in 2006 in a deal valued at £3.3bn. There were complexities at the time, and further developments since, but essentially the story of P & O as an independent entity ended at that time. The name continues to be valuable as a link to the past and the prestige associated with it. The web site for Dubai-owned P & O Ports claims a 200 year old history for the company, and, along with the ferry business, displays the famous P & O quartered flag. The company also maintains the P & O Heritage web site. Meanwhile Carnival also still uses the P & O name, differentiated with a new font and logo, in its UK and Australia businesses.

I had a subsequent maritime project, managing a winning bid for IT support and upgrades within a large passenger shipping company, and then delivering the changes and resources required. This led me to more new ports, ships and challenges before a successful service handover. Further details will deviate too far from my aims in this book.

*

Muller House, the home of my old college in Bristol, was redeveloped into apartments, quite desirable-looking ones with large windows and high ceilings within the listed building. The radar scanners were removed; I thought this a pity as they were part of the building's heritage, giving it a "steampunk" look which might have provided added interest for passers-by and prospective flat owners. The Unity Street site also became apartments.

The larger college complex across the road from Muller House was filmed for a time as a hospital in the early days of the BBC TV series *Casualty*. Its stone buildings still form a backdrop to the Gloucestershire county cricket ground, as well as being the Ashley Down Centre within the multi-site City of Bristol College. There is now an official pedestrian crossing in place.

North Bristol Baths and the adjacent pub, The Bristol Flyer (another haunt from my college days) also doubled as TV filming locations. The pub was one of several in London, Bristol and Brighton which served as the Trotters' local, the Nag's Head, in *Only Fools and Horses*, while the baths became a police station in the same comedy and in *The Young Ones*. The swimming baths closed in 2005, and after more than a decade of planning wrangles the building was "developed" as a mixed-use space.

For some time I visited the Brunel and Poly sites when in the area, as well as looking in on Mrs B. The political fire remained alight. On my later visits I thought her too frail to walk around the house unnecessarily so I made and served the tea. As soon as I sat down with my cup, she began to tackle the issues of the day. 'Right, Austin, what do you think about….?'

*

In 1988 a treaty amendment was announced in order to phase out the use of Morse code on ships from 1992. It would be superseded by the satellite-based Global Maritime Distress and Safety System (GMDSS). An art was being replaced by a cold and impersonal science, one which would become mandatory for all ships of 300 gross tons or more from 1st February 1999. Stations began to close their telegraphy operations as the use of Morse code for distress and other messages declined. In January 1997 the French Navy retired its Morse operations, broadcasting a well-publicised final message: 'This is our last cry before our eternal silence.' The US Coastguard's stations had already closed in similar fashion, ending with Samuel Morse's 1844 test message: 'What God hath wrought.' Some commercial stations in the US continued to use Morse until a final message was transmitted from KFS, a station near San Francisco, on 13th July 1999. Most UK coast stations sent out coordinated goodbyes on 31st December 1997, some quoting Samuel Morse or otherwise expressing the poignant nature of the moment. By contrast, Cullercoats Radio (GCC) transmitted a valedictory rhyme:

A fond farewell from Geordy land
Sent with a sad and shaking hand
For many years with signs we spoke
And now it all goes up in smoke
So thanks and all the very best
As GCC is laid to rest.

Portishead Radio gradually scaled down its operations and sent a final message on 30th April 2000, conveying thanks and good wishes to all and also paying tribute to Marconi for initiating the radio era.

The 500 kHz distress frequency became unmonitored. Some radio stations around the world have since become museums, preserving both the equipment and the memory of how ship-to-shore communications took place. Sadly nothing remains of Portishead's facilities, as the site was demolished and replaced by a new housing development.

In 2001 the Marconi Centre was opened on the cliff top at Poldhu, Cornwall, close to the site of Marconi's experiments and famous transmissions there 100 years earlier. The building doubles as a museum and as the home of Poldhu Amateur Radio Club. The adjacent former hotel, built in 1899 to accommodate Marconi staff, is now a care home.

Poldhu: the Marconi Centre (right) and former hotel

It is also possible to see Marconi's Lizard Wireless Station near Housel Bay, a short drive away; one of the two huts hosts a restored radio station managed by the National Trust, while the other is now a holiday cottage.

The 2000s brought legislation and company regulations banning the consumption of alcohol across many countries' shipping lines. Whether any ship is genuinely safer under today's directives might be questioned; it must have been easy to assume that they would be, yet perhaps there were times in the past when people were more careful because they knew within themselves that they really needed to be.

Suicide kills the highest number of seafarers. Many concerns have been expressed on this subject, and the depression, isolation and poor mental health which might drive it. I read one report which acknowledged that in the past seafarers may have sometimes been deterred from suicide and mitigated any mental health issues by consuming alcohol, but perhaps inevitably it then concluded that such behaviour led to alcoholism. This was certainly true of a small minority in my experience, but simply polarising between prohibition and alcoholism hardly makes a proportionate or nuanced argument. Most of us managed to strike a balance somewhere along the scale other than at the end, perhaps varying from ship to ship, before ultimately leaving the sea with no such damaging or long-term effects. No-one has easy answers to the range of problems faced by seafarers but the downgrading of a social hub and outlet on board can hardly be beneficial on its own.

Ships and people continue to have accidents despite numerous changes in safety regulations and the stakes being higher with modern large vessels and increasingly-valuable cargoes. This was particularly highlighted by the grounding of the Evergreen container ship *Ever Given* in the Suez Canal in March 2021, trapping hundreds of other ships and affecting global supply chains. The incident itself was not an isolated one. That August the bulk carrier *Panamax Ostria* ran aground in the Gulf of Suez after transiting the canal. In October 2021 the container vessel *Zim Kingston* lost over a hundred containers off Vancouver Island during a storm and subsequently most of its crew had to be evacuated by the Canadian Coast Guard during a serious fire among the remaining boxes on board.

In February 2022 a Maersk container ship, *Maersk Mumbai*, ran aground in the North Sea near Bremerhaven. In the same month the large car-carrying vessel *Felicity Ace* caught fire near the Azores, sinking some two weeks later with the loss of 4,000 vehicles. In March 2022 another Evergreen vessel, *Ever Forward*, was grounded for over a month after sailing from Baltimore with 4,964 containers. Investigations revealed that the pilot was distracted by personal phone calls, while possible management issues on the bridge also contributed to the incident. It is estimated that around 50 major ships and numerous smaller vessels are lost, grounded or otherwise badly damaged every year, most of which are unreported by mainstream media. Incidents affecting smaller vessels around the world seem to be recorded at a rate of approximately one per day. Super-sized vessels enable goods to be transported at lower costs per unit while increasing the challenges around ship stability, especially in unexpected conditions. Hazardous substances carried as cargo can be difficult to identify, store and manage yet are routinely transported within larger consignments. It has been estimated that a fire involving containerised cargo occurs on average every two weeks (Gard, 2020).

Public awareness of shipping and associated issues remains low in Britain despite its history as a maritime nation. Yet despite the shrinking fleets referenced in this book, some 50,000 merchant ships still serve the world's needs, employing some 1.89 million seafarers (BIMCO/International Chamber of Shipping, 2021). Many ships are registered to countries with relatively low regulatory requirements, leading to numerous safety and welfare issues, and concerns over accountability when nations are not obliged to record the true ownership of vessels registered there. Suggested reforms often fail to secure full international agreement.

All these issues only receive any degree of prominence when they lead to major incidents, or during other exceptional times; for example during the Covid-19 pandemic when isolation requirements forced seafarers and, seemingly more importantly passengers, to remain quarantined on ships. The sketchy nature of people's shipping knowledge was also illustrated by public reactions to Dubai-owned P & O Ferries dismissing 800 employees to replace them with agency staff in March 2022. The ensuing dispute led many to express concern over their bookings with Carnival-owned P & O Cruises, or to boycott the completely-separate company and seek other cruise options.

Other misconceptions of life at sea are cultivated by modern drama and reality TV. An episode of the TV series *Billions* featured someone explaining that a ship without power had to drop anchor and transmit a distress signal (series 5, episode 9). This was despite the ship in question crossing the Atlantic Ocean at the time, in waters too deep for anchoring. The docu-reality series *Deadliest Catch* showed one of the long-established Bering Sea crab fishing boats, *Time Bandit*, suffering from navigation equipment failure after losing its satellite signal. No charts or other items were produced, nor a course plotted from the last-known position, and after some expressions of concern for the boat's safety it was apparently sailed in the direction of a single star until it was able to follow another boat into port (series 18, episode 12). Despite this curious moment I continue to avidly follow the latter programme.

Having rediscovered the sea in some slightly unexpected ways through my later work, I have since maintained more interest in it although I am happy to simply travel as a passenger. I have also reconnected a little with Morse code, occasionally transcribing from online stations and archive coast station tapes. It is like a language skill which is never completely lost, and there is some pleasure in training my mind in this way again. My knowledge of the Q codes is quite patchy now though; after all, there were many which I never even needed to use. More significantly I'm pleased to count myself among a finite number of people (whatever that number is) to have performed a unique role while it existed, and to have benefitted from the travel and life experiences it afforded.

Some former R/Os, radio amateurs and enthusiasts speculate on whether their skills will be needed again in the future, should, for example, Earth's satellite network fail. This is not an unthinkable scenario due to the possibility of solar flares ("space weather"), war or cybercrime, and while not to be relished there is always a place for realistic outlooks. Perhaps there is a case for retaining some old technologies and skills as contingencies, should the newer ones fail us. The US Air Force apparently believes so as it was reported (in 2015) to be continuing to train ten people per year in Morse; the US Navy also apparently trains some recruits. Newer may be faster, more scalable and many other things too, but the resilience born of simplicity can be highly beneficial too. Simple things are particularly valuable when they are all we have, as was the case at the dawn of the radio age.

Milton Keynes UK
Ingram Content Group UK Ltd.
UKHW010201230823
427286UK00001B/15

9 781803 697888